The Worst Tax?
A History of the Property Tax in America

STUDIES IN GOVERNMENT
AND PUBLIC POLICY

The Worst Tax?
A History of the Property Tax in America

Glenn W. Fisher

University Press of Kansas

*To our grandsons Mark, Michael, Brandon, and Justin:
may they live in a world in which the dream of political equality
and fair taxation remains alive.*

Published by the University Press of Kansas (Lawrence, Kansas 66049), which was
organized by the Kansas Board of Regents and is operated and funded by Emporia
State University, Fort Hays State University, Kansas State University, Pittsburg State
University, the University of Kansas, and Wichita State University

Library of Congress Cataloging-in-Publication Data

Fisher, Glenn W.
    The worst tax? : a history of the property tax in America / Glenn
W. Fisher.
      p. cm. — (Studies in government and public policy)
    Includes bibliographical references and index.
    ISBN 0-7006-0753-6 (alk. paper)
    1. Property tax—United States—History. I. Title. II. Series.
HJ4120.F57   1996
336.22'0973—dc20   95-40704

British Library Cataloguing in Publication Data is available.

Printed in the United States of America

10 9 8 7 6 5 4 3 2 1

The paper used in this publication meets the minimum requirements of the American
National Standard for Permanence of Paper for Printed Library Materials
Z39.48-1984.

CONTENTS

FIGURES AND TABLES

ACKNOWLEDGMENTS

There is a certain sameness in the acknowledgment section of scholarly books. The author acknowledges indebtedness to others and accepts final responsibility for the result. This situation is not due to a lack of originality, but reflects the nature of the scholarly process. An author owes a great debt to many people, known and unknown, but cannot escape the responsibility for selecting and applying the insights that others have provided.

This is especially true of this book. Tax history, per se, is not a well-developed field of study, but taxation is so important and its effects so far-reaching that insights come from many disciplines. Taxation, an economic process, is one of the determinants of government structure and function, and it has widespread social effects. Levying and collecting taxes is a intricate process in which political, legal, accounting, and administrative aspects are interwoven.

The tax historian must extract from the accumulated knowledge in all of these fields and report those facts and conclusions that tell a story that is important and accurate. I have chosen to emphasize the relationships between the political and administrative aspects of the property tax and to report how these interactions have affected the evolution of the property tax and the structure and function of the governments financed by this tax. This choice and the resulting conclusions are entirely my own, but obviously I owe a great debt to many persons in many fields of study. Many of these are acknowledged in the endnotes and bibliography, but even the rather lengthy bibliography does not list all of the scholars, living and dead, whose work provided information or influenced my thinking. A special thanks to Robert A. Becker, whose book on the property tax in the Colonial and Revolutionary period provided a historic and intellectual starting point.

Work on this book began almost ten years ago while I was on a sabbatical leave. Wichita State University not only provided that leave but provided a stimulating environment to study taxation from both an academic and an applied standpoint for almost twenty-five years. The director of the Center for Urban Studies, Joe Pisciotte, and other members of the staff provided valuable support. I owe specific thanks to many student assistants who worked on some aspect of the book. Among them are: Rebecca Allen-Bouska, Susan Penner, Bradley J. Mears, Alison Brown, Elizabeth Owens, Timothy Johnson, Mary Knopick, Kathie Sparks, Cynthia Crawley, and Colin McKenney. Thanks are due to a number of librarians at Wichita State University, the Kansas Historical Society, and the Kansas State Library.

A number of people read various parts of the manuscript and all provided valuable suggestions. Among those were Ed Flentje, Fred Stocker, Ramon Powers, John Wong, Joan Youngman, Ann Lousin, John Born, William Unrau, Phillip Thomas, Lynne Schall, Susan Penner, Pete Davis, Lynne Holt, and Ed Hays. Two anonymous referees helped shape the book into its final form.

I owe a special thank-you to my wife Marvel, who provided unfailing support and encouragement.

INTRODUCTION

A modern American counterpart of the Boston Tea Party occurred in California in 1978. As one of the principal organizers of the California Tax Revolt put it: "California voters were 'Mad as Hell.' "[1] Many of them had cause. Rapidly escalating real estate prices, aggressive reappraisal, and high government spending had resulted in rapidly rising property tax bills. Taxpayers on fixed incomes who wanted to retain their homes gained nothing from the rising real estate prices but higher tax bills. One homeowner described her reaction to a 250 percent property tax increase, "I forgot all about where I was and what I was doing and fixed, like tunnel vision, on the bill. . . . Inside, I got hysterical. . . . I was filled with fear and also anger, and it was such a mix of emotions that I just stood there, and I think I vibrated for about ten minutes."[2]

The organizers of the drive to put the Proposition 13 property tax limit on the ballot in California submitted 1,263,698 signatures to the California Secretary of State. They had another 300,000 that could not be processed in time.[3] Almost all were obtained by volunteer solicitors—not by the professional firms that normally gather signatures for California referenda.

The proposed limitation was denounced by most of those who made a careful study of its provisions and it was opposed by big business, most labor organizations, and most political leaders. Nevertheless, 64.8 percent of the voters approved the measure, cutting property taxes by more than $6 billion. School systems, city governments, counties, and park districts lost one-fourth to one-half of their budgets. Shock waves reverberated through the American political establishment as political leaders scrambled to head off similar referenda.

Ironically, the passage of Proposition 13 provided far less relief than the proponents expected. Much of the immediate relief went to businesses, although most business organizations had opposed the proposition. After the surpluses in state and local treasuries were used up and some obvious slack taken out of the system,

California's local governments imposed a variety of fees and charges. The legislature acted to centralize finance and weaken local governments in ways that may make government even less responsive in the long run.

Whatever the effect in California, Proposition 13 was an important chapter in the modern history of taxation. It became the model for tax limitation proposals in a number of states. Not all were successful, and some that were had relatively little effect, but political rhetoric was immensely influenced. In Washington, D.C., and in the state capitals the words "tax revolt" entered every discussion of tax or expenditure policy.

Many observers attribute this modern day tax revolt to the unresponsiveness of politicians. The literature describing the tax revolt in California is replete with examples of disappointed protestors who felt that the officials to whom they appealed, "Don't get it." It is clear that California officials greatly underestimated the anger over property taxes, but it oversimplifies the case to assume that government officials are not aware that taxes are unpopular. Many such officials have been the object of mass demonstrations, letter writing or calling campaigns, and most have survived political elections in which taxes were a major issue.

Missing from the accounts of unresponsive politicians is a full account of the complexity of the system. For every individual and interest group demanding lower taxes there are an equal number demanding additional expenditures. Every politician knows the hard arithmetic of public budgets. To respond to the tax protester is to be unresponsive to those who demand that existing programs be maintained and new ones added. Politicians also know that any tinkering with the tax system to grant relief to a particular taxpayer or group will have widespread and sometimes unanticipated consequences. Particular industries or governmental units will be affected in different ways and new demands for tax relief will arise.

To maintain a constitutional system of government, it is necessary to balance these competing demands. Every government requires revenue and every democratic government requires support by a large bloc of its constituency. If revenue or support is insufficient, the constitutional order and the tax system will evolve until revenue and support reach an equilibrium that is sustainable, at least briefly.

This book is the story of the property tax as it evolved in the United States. The tax was brought from England to the colonies as specific levies on specific kinds of property. Inevitably, the list of taxable items and the schedule of rates favored the politically powerful. During the American Revolution and in the early years of nationhood, taxation was made more palatable to an equality-minded citizenry by broadening the base and equalizing the tax rates. In many states the schedule of specific tax rates was gradually replaced by a constitutionally mandated general property tax—levied on all property at an equal proportion of value.

Implementing the constitutional ideal of equal taxation of all property proved to be difficult. Perhaps it could have been achieved by a professional, centralized administrative organization, but that was in conflict with the Jeffersonian/Jacksonian concept of democracy that prized local administration by elected officials. Not surprisingly, the uniformity provisions in constitutions and statutes were modified and local deviations from statutory provisions became common practice. Because there was no reasonable alternative source of local revenue and because the portion of the tax falling on real estate was easier to administer than the portion falling on tangible or intangible personal property, the tax became, in many states, a local tax falling largely on real estate.

To comprehend this evolutionary process, it is essential to understand the technical aspects of writing and administering property tax statutes. These are similar in all states, but their details differ. To elucidate the process, a portion of this book is devoted to a case study of the property tax in Kansas. Kansas is an appropriate case study because it has been a heavy user of property taxation and it entered the Union near the middle of the constitutional uniformity period. Often developments in Kansas were representative of earlier developments in the older states to the east, but on occasion Kansas was in the forefront.

The final chapters will summarize the lessons that can be learned from the history of the property tax and survey the current status of property taxation in the United States. The most important lesson from the past is that the current tax revolt, like earlier ones, will have consequences not foreseen by those who revolted.

1
The General Property Tax

A century ago, noted tax economist E. R. A. Seligman, speaking of the uniform tax on all property mandated in many state constitutions, said:

> Practically, the general property tax as actually administered is beyond all doubt one of the worst taxes known in the civilized world. Because of its attempt to tax intangible as well as tangible things, it sins against the cardinal rules of uniformity, of equality and of universality of taxation. It puts a premium on dishonesty and debauches the public conscience; . . . the general property tax is so flagrantly inequitable that its retention can be explained only through ignorance or inertia.[1]

Today the general property tax is history, but the property taxes that evolved from it are scarcely more popular.

Proposition 13 in California and its imitations in other states are the latest in a long series of tax revolts or tax reform movements. Paradoxically, the property tax still provides more than three-fourths of the tax revenue of local governments in the United States. As shown in the following tabulation, it provided an astonishing 97.5 percent of the direct tax revenue of school districts in fiscal year 1991. It was least important as a revenue source for municipalities but, even so, accounted for over one-half of the tax revenues received. The tabulation shows the property tax as a percentage of the tax revenue of other types of local government:

Cities	52.1%
Counties	74.0
School districts	97.5
Townships	92.8
Special districts	69.5
All local governments	75.3

The key to the continuing importance of the property tax is not, as Seligman thought, ignorance or inertia. Rather, it is the symbiotic relationship between the tax and the fragmented system of small overlapping local governments in the United States. In the century since Seligman wrote, state governments have turned to other forms of revenue, particularly sales and income taxes. Nonproperty taxes are used at the local level, but the property tax remains the financial backbone of local government. This form of taxation has survived because it is important to local government autonomy and, ironically, because the uniformity ideal has often been sacrificed to political expediency.

The symbiotic relationship between taxation and government structure is of interest today because of the renewed, worldwide interest in the formation and modifications of political systems. The most dramatic example is in Eastern Europe where the former communist states are struggling to create new constitutional orders. Other examples are in developing nations where the lack of a competent, stable government is the biggest impediment to development. Western Europe is struggling to establish economic and political union amid mounting demands for ethnic and regional autonomy. In the United States, citizens are cynical about government at all levels. State and local governments seem to be incapable of solving problems that are national or worldwide in scope, while the federal government has run up massive deficits and has frustrated state and local officials by imposing ill-considered regulations and expensive mandates.

Among the most difficult issues to be resolved when new constitutional order is created or modified are those pertaining to the "scale" of government and those revolving around finance. Should the sovereign powers of government be lodged in a single national government or should sovereignty be divided between a federal government and one or more levels of regional governments? Whatever the answer, the system of finance must be appropriate. No unit or level of government can long maintain independence of action unless it has the power to extract the economic resources needed to carry on its functions.

The founders of the American republic dealt with this question by creating a federalism in which a general or federal government shared sovereignty with the constituent states. The federal government was to deal primarily with foreign affairs, maintain a system of currency, a patent office, and a postal system. Much of the ordinary business of government was left to the states. Both the federal government and the states were given the power to raise revenue.

The constitutional language set the stage for a continuing evolution of the relationship between the federal and the state governments. Ideology, military involvements, court decisions, and administrative reality all played a role. This book focuses on those events surrounding the struggle over the tax powers. An especially important development was the rise of the general property tax. This tax is, arguably, uniquely American. It developed from European roots, but took on a different character in America where it was seen as a uniform, universal tax on all kinds of property. This promise of equality was appealing in a nation breaking away from the class-dominated European social order. The tax proved to be capable of providing revenue to finance a decentralized system of government in nineteenth century America. Unfortunately, achieving uniform taxation required a degree of centralization and professionalization of administration that conflicted with deeply held political values. In the face of these conflicting values, the tax evolved into a less universal, less uniform tax, which is the major source of revenue for American local governments.

The history of the property tax illustrates that public policy, and even the structure of government itself, can be transformed by legal and administrative details that seem of little importance to those who write constitutions and statutes. This aspect of public policy has often been neglected by scholars who lack knowledge of these matters or who fear that readers may find such detail uninteresting.

FINANCING A CONSTITUTIONAL ORDER

An essential part of the constitutional order or regime[2] is a system or procedure for extracting economic resources. Without economic resources governments cannot maintain order, carry on wars, or provide the services that citizens of a modern nation expect.

A system for extracting resources is subject to many limitations. No regime can exist long without a degree of support from citizens or subjects who perceive that the benefits received are great enough to justify the loss of resources imposed. The benefits are much broader than the value of governmental goods and services normally discussed in public finance textbooks. A leading political scientist points out that citizens value the existence of an established regime because it provides predictable limits or boundaries for political behavior.[3] David Easton has said:

> The alternative would be for the rules and aims of political interaction in a system to be largely random and indeterminate. In that event, members of the system would have to argue about day-to-day actions and decisions at the same time as they questioned the fundamental assumptions about the way in which these daily differences should be settled.[4]

Rules of taxation or other methods of extracting economic resources are part of the constitutional order or regime. Taxpayers support rules that will minimize the extraction from them, but they also value rules that are predictable, fair, and consistent with the broader constitutional order. In David Easton's terms, members of a system may support the system of decision-making even though a particular decision has gone against them. At times, such support may drop dangerously low and threaten the constitutional order. Therefore, methods of extracting resources must produce the necessary resources without unduly diminishing support for the order.

The problem of developing an extractive system is complicated not only because of its effect upon the constitutional order, but also because it interacts in complex ways with the economic system. Taxes affect economic behavior, such as consumption and investment. This modification of behavior may have major impacts on the total economic output of a nation as well as on the relative share going to various individuals, industries, or regions.

Historically, methods of extracting resources have varied with the stage of political development and the nature of the economic system. The earliest method was simply to seize the economic resources needed. Today, this method is not commonly used except against conquered peoples. Confiscation places the burden entirely on those who happen to own the resource that the government needs and is an example of a random and indeterminate interaction of the type mentioned by Easton in the preceding quotation. Members of a system are far more comfortable if the government buys what it needs in the open market with money obtained by a systematic method of taxation.

Governments may resort to borrowing as a way of obtaining money to buy resources. Like any other creditor, governments borrow by promising to pay interest on the sum until some future time when the principal will be returned. The attempt to establish new governments, at both the federal and state level, was accompanied by a combination of borrowing and money creation. Government suppliers, including those in military service, were compensated with some kind of paper promising to pay or ordering the treasurer to pay a sum of money. These warrants or orders were sometimes interest bearing and they often circulated as money. The extent to which they were discounted depended upon the prospects for eventual payment at face value and the availability of specie or other kinds of "hard" money. This meant that banking and currency policy was closely bound to the question of taxation. In fact, histories of the development of American financial policy devote far more time to these questions than to tax policy.

As economic and political systems become more stable and better developed, taxation becomes the principal method of extracting economic resources. Today, elaborate systems of taxation are created in an effort to extract money while minimizing adverse effects on the economy and maximizing support for the constitutional order. The tax system and the accompanying expenditure policy must convince a sizeable percentage of the population that the economic and political benefits received justify the taxes levied. In other words, they must believe direct benefits from government expenditure and indirect benefits from the maintenance of a constitutional order are equal to or greater than the taxes paid plus costs incurred in complying with the tax laws.

Support for a constitutional order is strengthened by a tax system that is perceived as fair—not only in the way the burdens are distributed, but also in the way the tax is administered. This fact was recognized by Adam Smith in 1776. He devoted three of four tax maxims to administrative concerns. Maxim II states that taxes should be certain with the amount, time, and place of payment plain to every person. Maxim III states that tax payments should be convenient and Maxim IV declares that taxes should be economical to collect and pay, and that taxpayers should not be tempted to evade or be subjected to frequent visits and odious examinations from tax gatherers.[5]

In a federal nation the extractive system has to meet an additional requirement if the concept of shared sovereignty is to be meaningful. Both the federal and the state governments must have independent access to adequate economic resources. The failure to provide the Continental Congress with the power to raise taxes was one of the principal reasons for the failure of the constitutional order established under the Articles of Confederation. The United States Constitution remedied that defect, but placed limitations on the exercise of tax power by both the federal and state governments.

Specific limitations on state tax power include the prohibition on import or export duties and the requirement that Congress consent to tonnage taxes. Many important limitations on state tax powers arise from constitutional provisions not dealing specifically with taxes. For example, treaties are part of the supreme law and can override state tax laws. States cannot impair contracts and cannot discriminate against citizens of other states. The commerce clause prohibits states from imposing taxes that burden interstate commerce. Due process of law and equal protection of the law provisions of the Fourteenth Amendment sometimes limit state and local action in the tax field. Judicial constructions such as the federal instrumentalities doctrine, which prevents states from taxing federal agencies and federally chartered institutions (e.g., national banks) without congressional consent, have constrained state taxation. Local governments are not mentioned in the U.S. Constitution, but as creations of state governments, they are subject to all federal constitutional limitations on states as well as to any limitations placed on their tax power by the state government.

ADMINISTRATIVE THEORY AND POLITICAL REALITY

One approach to maintaining support for a tax system in a modern state is to provide that taxes be levied by a representative legislative body and administered by an impartial administrative organization, following clearly established rules of procedure. Legislation should be explicitly written, there should be a hierarchically organized bureaucracy with defined lines of authority, administrative regulations should be clear and known to interested parties, and there should be fair and adequate appeal procedures.

This approach is generally advocated in schools of public administration, but was not the system used to implement the property tax in the United States. The task of administering the property tax laws was left to part-time elected local officials who were sworn to support the law, but had no administrative superiors to interpret the law or to coordinate their work. The severe legal penalties for administrators and taxpayers who violated the law were rarely imposed. Indeed, administrators were given inherent incentives to violate the law in ways that would insure re-election.

One of the purposes of this book is to inquire why the property tax was successful in fulfilling the basic purpose of a resource extraction system, even though it fell short of the ideal of equality that inspired its adoption. An important part of the answer is suggested by the phrase "Equality or Democracy?" Equality is an important component of the democratic dream. Uniform taxation of all property seems to exemplify equality in taxation and uniformity clauses in statutes and constitutions were accepted with little debate. It turned out that implementing a tax that fell equally on all wealth required measures that were contrary to other widely accepted values. These values, symbolized in American history by Andrew Jackson, had wide appeal. Jacksonian values never disappeared and are periodically restated and reemphasized by political candidates and political movements. The Jacksonian doctrine emphasizes that all men, not just the educated elite, can hold government office and that there should be many elected officials and frequent elections. The Jacksonian doctrine, like the tenets of Thomas Jefferson, emphasized the importance of local government and were opposed to Alexander Hamilton's concept of centralized, expertly administered government.

The administrative history of the general property tax is a history of a struggle between Jacksonian and Hamiltonian concepts. The equality articulated by Jackson was an equality of process, not of result. Jacksonians believed that all were capable of participating in government administration and the right to do so was high on their list of priorities. If given the choice, most Jacksonians probably would have chosen imperfect local administration of the property tax over a centralized, elite administration that resulted in greater equality of tax burden.

Leonard White, one of the important figures in the development of the discipline of public administration, pointed out that from the inception of American public life until the opening of the twentieth century, conditions were unfavorable to the development of powerful administrative agencies. He stated that "[a] combination of a relatively undeveloped economic structure, a dominating individualism born of the frontier, and a philosophy of democracy epitomized in Andrew Jackson conspired to hold the American administrative structure to a model characteristic of a rural rather than an urban community, of an individualistic rather than a cooperative society, of a democratic rather than a bureaucratic state."[6] The history of the property tax not only illustrates his point, but also reveals that local government was distrusted less than state government. There was a symbiotic relationship between the structure of American local government and the property tax that helped both to survive, in spite of criticism from those who preferred efficiency and tidy administrative arrangements in government structure and taxation.

DEVELOPMENT OF THE GENERAL PROPERTY TAX

When the colonial legislatures won the right to levy their own taxes, they turned to those fiscal instruments that were familiar in England. Among these were taxes on property. Such taxes were levies against specific items of property enumerated in the legislation at specific rates per item, per acre, or per head. This form of taxation was the source of a great deal of conflict within the legislative body as various individuals and interests attempted to secure more favorable treatment. In a few cases, conflicts went beyond the legislative bodies and organized resistance to paying taxes occurred.

During the American Revolution, concern about the loyalty of those who might be alienated by higher taxes led to movement toward uniform, ad valorem (according to value) taxation. In the nineteenth century most of the constitutions of the newly forming frontier states contained provisions mandating uniform ad valorem taxation of property as the major source of both state and local government revenue.

The concept of equality, embodied in the phrase "uniform taxation of property," was a symbol that contributed to support for the constitutional order that slowly and painfully developed in the new land. The concept also had a real impact on the politics and administration of the tax. Reformers and those who felt disadvantaged often rallied around the uniformity flag and sometimes won victories on the judicial, legislative, or administrative battlefield. By the end of the nineteenth century, however, many believed that the battle had been lost. Criticism of the tax from government officials, reformers, and ordinary taxpayers was intense. Many still urged reform of the tax while others counseled for abandonment. Administrative reforms were attempted and, one by one, states gave up the pretense that they were taxing all property uniformly.

THE THEORY OF THE GENERAL PROPERTY TAX

The first National Conference on Taxation, organized by the National Tax Association in 1907, was devoted largely to denouncing the property tax as "unsound in theory and practice," but it is impossible to cite a document that spells out the theory being denounced. The general property tax did have five distinctive characteristics that together could be called a theory.

Uniformity. Probably the most fundamental characteristic of the general property tax is uniformity. All property in a taxing district must be valued and taxed alike.

Ad valorem. Taxation is on the basis of value. The practice of establishing specific tax rates for specific kinds or classes of property cannot produce uniformity. Value is the only way of differentiating among different items in a class and the only common denominator for equalizing taxes on different classes of property. It is impossible, for example, to conceptualize the meaning of equal taxation of a merchant's stock in Boston and the land of a farmer on the Western frontier, unless money or value is used as a common denominator.

Universality. The general property tax is applied to all property—real and personal, tangible and intangible. The only commonly recognized exemptions were property used for religious, charitable, educational, and governmental purposes and, sometimes, a very small exemption for widows, orphans, or others in financial distress.

In rem. The general property tax is levied in rem, that is against the thing, not in personam, or against the person who owns the property. Although early tax writers and tax administrators did not always recognize the importance of this concept, it is an important part of the whole history of general property taxation. It turned out that the in rem character of the tax was one of the most important aspects of its suitability as a source of local revenue, especially in the case of real estate. It means that the tax can be administered without knowing the name of the owner and that the tax becomes an automatic lien on the property—an extremely valuable characteristic for a tax administered by nonprofessional local administrators.

Tax Day. The property tax is levied on property at the place and at the value it has on a specific day of the year. Loss of value or changes in location are not recognized for tax purposes until the tax day of the following year. Early exceptions were made to this rule in the case of property that was subject to manipulation for tax avoidance purposes or where obvious inequities would result. For example, many states taxed merchants' and manufacturers' inventories on the basis of average values rather than at their value on tax day.

These five characteristics describe a tax system which, for a time, was perceived as ideal. The early history of the property tax in the United States is the history of evolution toward the ideal.

2
Revolution and Reform

Although taxes are commonly cited as one of the proximate causes of the American Revolution, the statesmen and political philosophers who wrote and spoke about the colonies' grievances spent little time discussing the principles of taxation. The dispute with England was less concerned with the form or the magnitude of the taxes, than over the right to levy them. These disputes were intimately tied to beliefs about representation, sovereignty, and the relationship between local and central governments.

In colonial times, British taxes were small, temporary imposts, which had far less impact on the average American than did the taxes levied by the colonial legislatures. The colonial levies were important because their levy and collection were part of the process of creating a constitutional order. Independence could not be attained or maintained unless the new governments could extract the economic resources necessary to fight a war and establish a new order. Extracting economic resources in thinly populated, economically underdeveloped areas was no easy task. The problem was compounded by the lack of an adequate central monetary system and the desire to maintain support for the political system.

The taxes existing in each colony at the beginning of the revolution were the result of many years of development, but all had their origin in the British tax system. It is appropriate, therefore, to begin the study by briefly reviewing British taxation.[1]

Professor Cannan, in his classic study of British taxation, claims that the concept of taxation according to ability or substance, as a principle for apportioning taxes, was widely accepted as early as the fourteenth or fifteenth century. At that time, ability and substance meant much the same thing. "A man who has a large income without having a large capital is a product of modern civilization."[2] He points out, however, that the concept of taxing things, rather than people, had not taken possession of the ordinary mind, even in the sixteenth century. The tax contribution required of each person was apportioned as the assessors thought fit or according to some common agreement. Over time, valuation lists became accepted as guides to the relative ability or substance of ratepayers (local taxpayers). In agricultural areas, ability to pay taxes was indicated by such things as the number and quality of acres cultivated, or the number of sheep and cattle pastured. In a town, the size and the quality of one's house reflected one's substance. Cannan believed that when this became the settled custom, it was natural that the tax would come to be regarded as a tax on acres and houses.[3]

The concept of taxation according to ability naturally spread to the American colonies. Robert A. Becker begins his comprehensive study of colonial and state taxation during the Revolutionary War period by stating, "Men should be taxed in proportion to their ability to pay: by 1763 this had become so self-evident a truth in New England that few public men dared deny it."[4] It is also a self-evident truth that the practical difficulties of measuring ability to pay are reenforced by the natural tendency of those in power to favor their own self-interest.

Five types of taxes were in common use in the colonies:

1. Poll (capitation or head) taxes were flat-rate taxes usually levied on all adult males and sometimes on slaves of either gender.
2. Property taxes were usually specific taxes, levied at fixed rates on items enumerated in the statute, but some kinds of properties were taxed according to value.
3. Faculty taxes were levied on the "faculty" or earning capacity of persons following certain trades or having certain skills. Unlike income taxes, they were not levied on income actually earned, but on estimated ability to earn.
4. Imposts were levied on goods imported or exported from the colony.
5. Excises were levied on enumerated items of consumption goods, especially liquor.

The dividing line between types of taxes was not always distinct. For example, poll taxes levied against slaves were, in effect, property taxes. Faculty taxes sometimes resembled property taxes and sometimes a modern income tax.

TAXATION IN THE NEW ENGLAND COLONIES

One hundred thirty years before the Declaration of Independence a Massachusetts statute outlined the broad features of the tax system that was to be maintained in that colony and, to a considerable extent in all of New England throughout the colonial period.[5] The system was a combination of poll, property, and faculty taxes. Each male sixteen years of age and older was required to pay an annual poll tax of 20*d.*; all owners of estates, whether land or goods, were to pay one penny for each 20*s.* of value, and every laborer, artificer, or handicraftsman was to pay 3*s.* 4*d.* annually in addition to his poll tax. All others—butchers, bakers, cooks, victuallers, and the like were to pay, "according to their returns and incomings."

During the early period, merchants and others whose estates were "not so obvious to view," were to be rated by the "will and doome of the assessors."[6]

Each town was required to elect a town commissioner to join with the selectmen in assessing incomes and estates and in making a list of males subject to the poll tax. On the second Wednesday of the month following assessment, all the commissioners of the county were to meet in the shire town to act as the board of equalization. This did not provide equalization among shires and in 1668 a state board of equalization was created to revise assessments "so that there may be a just and equal proportion between county and county, towne and towne, merchant and husbandmen."[7]

The specification of rates in the statutes was probably not common practice in the later colonial years. More commonly, taxpayers submitted lists of their taxable property, which could be altered by the assessors or selectmen when they found evidence of fraud or concealment. From these lists the total taxable wealth of the town was computed and the property tax was apportioned to each town. Local officials used the lists to collect the colonial tax plus any additional local tax that had been added to it.

In theory, the property tax enabled collection from each taxpayer in proportion to his ability to pay, but Becker finds it did nothing of the kind. Only two New England states reassessed annually. Elsewhere the lists of property, often called general estimates, might be as much as five years old. In addition, the assemblies relied upon the taxpayers themselves to make the estimates of value or allowed them to be made by assessors using crude methods of valuation. In Rhode Island, for example, assessors tried to determine value of real estate by estimating what it would have rented for fifteen to twenty years earlier.

Connecticut and Massachusetts left less to the assessor's discretion and fixed the value of real property by law according to the quality of land, its location, use, and productivity. The Massachusetts law of 1771, requiring a new general estimate, was typical. Assessors were to rate agricultural property according to its average yearly rent, but this value was to be determined by use and productivity. Assessors were to report the number of acres of pasture and the number of cows it would support. Orchards were to be rated according to the number of barrels of cider that could be made in a year. The annual yield of corn or other grain was to be reported for plowland as was the number of tons of hay produced on a salt marsh.

Legislators made special efforts to tax merchants, moneylenders, artisans, lawyers, and others who did not live off the land. Massachusetts taxed ships of more than ten tons burden, whether at home or abroad, and taxed merchants stock-in-trade, paid for or not, and money at interest. By 1770, all the New England colonies had adopted a faculty tax. Connecticut assessors estimated the annual "gains and returns" of craftsmen and tavern keepers. The Massachusetts faculty tax was the most extensive. Levies were made against the "incomes and profits which any person or persons . . . do or shall receive from any trade, faculty, business or employment whatsoever, and all profits which shall or may arise by money or commissions of profit, in their improvement."[8]

Exemptions or reduced rates were sometimes granted to encourage economic development. Connecticut encouraged manufacturers by exempting locally produced goods when taxing merchants stock-in-trade and encouraged local merchants by placing special taxes on goods brought into the colony by nonresidents. Connecticut encouraged opening new lands by exempting newly cleared acreage from taxes for four years. To encourage fishing, fishing vessels were exempt from the property tax and fishermen were exempt from the poll tax.

TAXATION IN THE MIDDLE COLONIES

Although there was much controversy over taxation in New England, there was a certain unity in the systems of the various colonies. All New England colonies regularly used the property tax as a source of income and all accepted, at least nominally, the idea that taxation should be related to ability to pay, somehow measured by property and faculty. In the middle colonies, there was far less agreement. Becker concludes that the only unifying principle in the tax systems of the middle colonies was that wealthy landowners weres protected whenever politically possible.[9]

New Jersey's property tax was the major source of revenue for the colony. Each county had a quota to raise, but the legislature supplied the assessors with detailed instructions as to the values to be assigned to each type of taxable property. Homes, all kinds of commercial mills, stills, breweries, boats, male slaves, or servants over sixteen years of age, livestock, all profitable tracts of improved land held by patent, deed, or survey were taxable. New Jersey taxed a few occupations in a drastically reduced version of New England's faculty tax.

New Jersey taxed the capital value of land rather than following the English precedent of taxing its annual value, but assessment was poorly done. At one point the governor complained that the capital values assigned did not exceed one year's rent or income. Because only improved tracts of land were taxable, landowners found that they could sever unimproved areas of land from the part containing the improvements and avoid taxation.

During the decade before independence, Pennsylvania taxed the clear yearly value of real estate and personal property at 18 pence on the pound. Unlike New York and New Jersey, Pennsylvania taxed unimproved land if it had been surveyed, but encountered problems with resourceful citizens and local officials who found loopholes in the law. For example, the tax act of 1764 allowed landowners a reasonable quantity of tax-free timberland for repairs and fuel. This timber allowance was widely abused and great inequalities resulted. The 1774 legislature responded by limiting fuel and timber allowances to thirty acres out of each hundred. Pennsylvania also supplied the assessors with lists of minimum and maximum values for land.

Becker summarizes the situation in the middle colonies, as the colonial period drew to a close, by suggesting that all the colonies had tax systems riddled through with loopholes, fraud, and special interest provisions. The wealthy landowners who controlled the writing of laws made sure that taxes fell gently on the great wilderness tracts. The exception was Pennsylvania, where a strong antiproprietary party saw advantage in taxing, or at least appearing to want to tax, the large tracts of wilderness land held by the Penn family under a proprietary grant.

The attempt of the landed wealthy to minimize their own taxes had significance, not only for the internal distribution of taxes, but also for relations with Britain. Controlling the power to tax not only meant keeping power out of the hands of other classes in the colony, but also out of the hands of Parliament. The New York assembly's strong stand against the Townsend taxes and the Stamp Act sprang in part from the suspicions that such taxes were but a step toward a parliamentary land tax.

TAXATION IN THE SOUTHERN COLONIES

The politics of southern taxation, like those of other sections, were complex. As usual there were a variety of interests. The interests of settlers in the piedmont and mountain regions were often different from those in the lowlands. Large planters and small farmers had different interests, but sometimes they united against commercial interests. Some planters also purchased and sold crops of others and thus shared the interests of the merchants. The result was that by 1763 each colony relied on a different mix of taxes to meet the expenses of government and the extraordinary expenses of war. Again, however, there was one common factor. In all the colonies those men of landed and established wealth, who normally dominated the southern legislatures, erected a tax system that favored their interests.

In North Carolina virtually no taxes were levied on landed and commercial wealth except for the poll tax on slaves. Penalties on the poor for nonpayment of poll taxes were severe. Personal property could be auctioned off and, if this failed to raise enough money, the delinquent could be jailed for a month and then sold as an indentured servant. The laws provided that paupers might be excused from taxes under certain circumstances, but sheriffs often violated these provisions and attempted to collect from those unable to pay. The North Carolina tax system was also the most corrupt. Fraud and theft by sheriffs were common. In 1767 the colonial governor estimated that only about one-half of the taxes collected ever found its way to the colonial treasury.

The oppressive administration of tax laws in North Carolina led to disturbances, and in 1764 Governor Arthur Dobbs issued a proclamation forbidding the taking of illegal fees. This allayed the discontent, but it arose again, and in 1768 protestors organized what they called "The Regulation."[10]

There was a clear connection between the unfair tax system and the rise of the

Regulator Movement. A resident of Mecklenburg asked, "Is it just that a man worth £10,000 pays no more than a poor back settler that has nothing but the labour of his hands to depend upon for his daily support?" Petitioners from Orange and Rowan counties in 1768 complained:

> A few shillings in taxes might seem trifling to gentlemen roiling in affluence, but to Poor People who must have their Bed and Bed-clothes, yea their Wives Petticoats taken and sold to Defray [taxes] how Tremenjouse judge must be the consequences: an only Horse, to raise Bread by an Only Cow, to give Milk to an helpless Family by which in a Greate Measure are Otherwise Supported, seized and sold.[11]

Petitioners from Anson County demanded a complete revolution in the revenue system. They wanted the right to pay taxes in farm commodities, they wanted a new paper money emission funded by a loan office, and they wanted the poll tax replaced by an income tax so that each individual might pay in proportion to the profits arising from his estate.

South Carolina differed from other southern colonies in two ways: the wealthy planters dominated the legislature more completely than in any other colony and the colony had the South's only major commercial port city. In 1765 all members of the assembly owned at least £2,000 in property and malapportionment almost completely excluded westerners. South Carolina's tax system was less regressive than that of North Carolina, but it served the interests of the dominant class by imposing land taxes on an acreage basis, rather than on an ad valorem basis. Demands for reform came from Charleston and from the back country of South Carolina, where land was worth far less than in the plantation country.

The South Carolina Regulators called for court reform, for accurate surveys of parish lines, for public schools, for effective antivagrancy laws, for public roads and for bounties on upcountry hemp, flax, and flour. They wanted land of less value to be taxed at a lower rate than valuable land near a market.

Virginia, like South Carolina, was dominated by a wealthy, landowning class led by families such as the Lees, the Burwells, and the Randolphs. Tobacco export taxes supplemented by quitrents and poll taxes paid the ordinary costs of running the government. When the frontier war with the French began in 1754, in Virginia the House of Burgesses imposed an acreage land tax. This tax fell much more heavily on western farmers with less valuable land than it did on the wealthy planters with easy access to the sea, but the rates were relatively low.

Disputes over taxation in Virginia brought into prominence a group of fiery young leaders who were willing to speak up against the aristocracy. Patrick Henry first gained prominence as a young lawyer in a tax case. In 1758 a poor tobacco harvest drove up the price of tobacco and the burgesses passed the Two Penny Act, which, among other things, permitted the counties and vestries of Virginia to pay their Anglican ministers at the rate of two pence for each pound of tobacco owed.

Because the bad tobacco crop had driven up the price of tobacco, ministers paid in cash received less than if paid in tobacco. The ministers appealed to the Privy Council in London that invalidated the Act of the Burgesses. Several ministers sued county collectors for additional pay. Patrick Henry, an unknown country lawyer, defended the tax collectors of Hanover. With the easy task of defending lower taxes at the expense of an unpopular Anglican clergy, Henry made an inspiring speech and got the collectors off with a fine of only one penny. The speech attacked not only the clergy but also the king. It came very close to treason, but launched Henry's political career and taught him and others that being a taxpayer's friend can be a good route to political prominence.

IMPORTANCE OF THE COLONIAL EXPERIENCE

The colonial period was a long one; conditions in the colonies varied, and communication was poor. As a result, there was considerable variation in the tax systems of the colonies, but the highlights of colonial history that have been reviewed illustrate some important points. The struggle for power to levy taxes, given to or assumed by the colonial assemblies, was an important step in the journey toward nationhood. The colonies had the machinery for levying and collecting taxes and this made a war for independence thinkable. At the same time, it is clear that the journey to nationhood would be a long one. Although the colonists might unite against English taxation, it was by no means clear they would pay the much higher taxes that would be necessary to fight a war against a great imperial power. As Becker reported, "the tax laws overburdened the politically impotent and favored the politically powerful, especially the landed classes."[12] Obviously, this could be a problem for those who would make a revolution based on the concepts of equality.

FINANCING A REVOLUTION

The trouble between the American colonies and the British government began in 1764. The Seven Years War, known in the New World as the French and Indian War, had just ended and the British were masters in the North American continent. The British government, reasonably enough, decided the American colonies should pay part of the cost of maintaining a small military force for their defense. The question was whether the colonial share should be levied by the colonial legislative bodies or by the British Parliament. Previously, requisitions had been sent to the colonies to pay troops and the colonies had been ordered to cooperate with British forces. The war had shown how inefficient and unfair this system was and the lack of cooperation had impaired military operations.

The halfhearted cooperation of some of the colonies led to proposals for levying a parliamentary tax on the colonies. The first move was to enact a new Sugar

Act lowering duties in the hope of reducing smuggling and increasing revenue.[13] Estimated revenues from this act were less than the colonial share of military costs. Sir George Grenville, Chancellor of the Exchequer, proposed a stamp tax on the colonies, but the collection of the tax was to be deferred for one year to give the colonists an opportunity to suggest a plan more to their liking.

The proposal raised a storm of protest in the colonies. Historians are not in complete agreement, but it appears that the principal objection was to the parliamentary imposition of an internal tax. Benjamin Franklin testified before Parliament that an external tax was a duty laid on imported commodities that was added to the cost and became part of the price. Customers had the privilege of refusing to pay the price and thereby avoid the tax. An internal tax, on the other hand, was forced upon people without their consent, unless it is levied by their own representatives.[14] George Grenville asserted that he could not understand the difference and William Blackstone could find no distinction between internal and external taxes in statute or common law. Blackstone also denied that the right of imposing taxes arose from representation. Regardless of the legal theories, the argument that internal taxes could not be levied without representation was widely held. Apparently, Americans had made an operational distinction between internal and external taxes and elevated it to a constitutional principle.[15]

Agents of the colonies, among them Benjamin Franklin, pleaded for the old method of raising revenue. Grenville countered by asking if the colonies would agree on the quotas each should raise and whether it was certain that all would be paid. In view of past experience, the agents could offer no such guarantee and Parliament passed the Stamp Act of 1765 with a heavy majority. It required the use of stamps on all legal and commercial papers, pamphlets, newspapers, almanacs, cards, and dice. There was to be a stamp distributor for each colony. The estimated yield from the Sugar Act and the Stamp Act was less than half the cost of garrisoning troops in the colonies.

The series of blunders and misunderstandings that escalated tensions between the colonists and Britain need not be recounted here, but tempers were brought to a boiling point by the "Boston Tea Party" and the retaliatory measures against the Massachusetts colony by the British government. These resulted in the assembly of the First Continental Congress, held in Philadelphia in September 1774 in order to redress the colonial grievances. Most of the colonies sympathized with the Massachusetts colony and saw that colony's cause as their own, but there was considerable disagreement about the ways and means of securing redress. In the end, the Congress adopted a declaration of rights and grievances, proclaimed a boycott of British goods, and agreed to reassemble the following May.

Before that date, the first bloodshed had occurred at Lexington and Concord. In June the Congress received news of the bloody battle at Bunker Hill. The Congress then put aside the instructions to find a way to restore harmony and, assuming most of the powers of a government, began to organize an army. The effort was hampered by reluctance of the independent minded colonists to create a strong and efficient government. Benjamin Franklin's proposal for a confederation was not given serious attention.

The Continental Congress never assumed the power of taxation but it borrowed heavily. A total of $242,552,380 of paper money to be redeemed by the states was issued. Depreciation set in immediately and prices reached unheard of levels. Speculation and counterfeiting demoralized the financial structure. The states refused to pay cash requisitions and requisitions on the states for corn, beef, pork, and other supplies proved unsatisfactory. Direct loans and gifts from foreign nations improved the situation somewhat, but much of the burden of financing the war fell directly on the states.[16]

The colonies all had well-established tax systems, but raising tax rates to the levels that would have been required to pay the states' own war expenditure, not to mention paying the requisitions of the Continental Congress, would have been completely unacceptable. The new states responded by raising taxes as well as by using a variety of credit devices to postpone payment. Several states modified their tax system in ways that would have important implications for the future of taxation in the United States.

WARTIME TAXATION IN NEW ENGLAND

The structure of New England taxation was changed very little by the Revolutionary War, but the politics of taxation were altered considerably. The heavier taxation brought on by the war drove many New Englanders, especially those of the interior farming towns, to the brink of ruin while others profited. The wealthy and those profiting from the war wanted strict enforcement, collection in specie, and high poll taxes. The poor, particularly western farmers, demanded reduction or elimination of the poll tax and tax relief, such as the acceptance of farm commodities for payment. Revolutionary leaders, such as Samuel Adams, John Adams, and John Hancock, quickly made it plain that whatever their views of Parliament's taxation, they had no intention of reforming the colonial revenue system of Massachusetts.

The revolutionary governments were concerned about the level of taxation. The high English taxes had been cited as a prime cause of the Revolution and leaders of the Revolution were afraid heavier American taxes might bring another revolt against the revolutionary government. Such fears were not unfounded. Loyalties were still untested and violent protests against taxes were possible. Developments in Massachusetts and New Hampshire illustrate the tensions.

The legislature of Massachusetts turned first to a nontax method of extracting resources: the issuance of paper money. By 1777 it was clear that the war would be long and expensive, and the Massachusetts General Court (legislature) began to formulate a more conservative economic policy. It declared the first paper emission no longer legal tender and announced that the notes would not be accepted for taxes after December of that year. At the same time the General Court began to levy massive taxes to reduce the amount of paper money in circulation. Eventually, Massachusetts imposed heavier taxes than any rebelling colony and collected many of them in specie rather than in quartermaster's certificates, soldiers' pay certificates, or commodities, as was done in several states.

Demands for reform of the 1777 program were important in the attempts to draft a new state constitution. Many began to see the connection between taxes and property qualifications for voting. Both issues were major concerns in the Massachusetts constitutional convention of 1780. Men like John Adams, who were leaders in the fight against tax reform, were also strong advocates of property qualifications for voting. Adams warned that property qualifications were necessary to keep power from the hands of men who pay less regard to the rights of property because they have nothing to lose.

The conservative viewpoint prevailed and the new constitution provided that members of the house of representatives have a freehold estate of £100 or other taxable property worth £1200, and members of the senate a freehold estate of at least £300. The existing tax system, including poll taxes, was incorporated into the constitution itself. The percentage of taxes obtained from poll taxation actually increased and was proportionally greater in less prosperous rural areas. The shift to greater use of poll taxes resulted, in part, from poor administration of the property tax. Assessors greatly undervalued property, especially the more valuable property.

Massachusetts' success in curbing inflation and currency depreciation through heavy taxation made it more difficult to pay taxes, especially in the remote towns where very little money was in circulation. The resulting unrest led Governor John Hancock to request tax reform in 1781. The General Court offered piecemeal adjustments, including excise taxes on rum, wine, brandy, tea, and coaches, and some increase in imposts. Conditions grew worse in western towns and sporadic violence occurred. In 1782 it was reported that the "middling people" were becoming more distressed than the poor. Warnings were generally ignored and conditions grew worse laying the foundations for Shays's Rebellion of 1786.[17]

Developments in New Hampshire parallel those of Massachusetts in some ways. Many New Hampshire men opposed independence and Tory supporters warned, accurately, that independence would bring at least a tenfold increase in taxes. To avoid testing the uncertain unity by imposing heavy taxes, New Hampshire leaders first issued paper money and planned to spread the taxes to fund the Revolution over a long period of time. By 1777 the legislature began to tax heavily under laws almost identical to the colonial laws. There was a slight reduction of poll taxes in 1780 and the government responded to back country demands by permitting the taxation of land owned by nonresident proprietors and the sale of land for nonpayment. Then discrimination against nonresidents became so blatant that the legislature tried, not always successfully, to restrict local authority.

There were instances of refusal to pay taxes. Some towns tried to avoid taxation by not electing assessors or collectors. In 1781 the legislature countered by making the property of each individual in a delinquent town liable for the whole amount of the town taxes. Many towns claimed that there was not enough money in the town to pay even one-quarter of the taxes demanded and when taxes were paid they disappeared to the east without a trace of visible benefit or accounting. In 1781, forty-three western towns met in convention and resolved to secede from New Hampshire and join the embryonic state of Vermont.

TAXATION IN THE MIDDLE STATES

In the middle states, the power of the groups that had dominated taxation in the colonial period was reduced and significant tax reform occurred. To many of the conservative leaders, the result seemed to be democracy run wild, rather than fulfillment of the democratic dream.

The revolutionary government of New York probably faced greater problems than that of any other state. Support for royal government was strong. More than one-half of the Americans who fought for the king were from New York. Most of the residents of southern New York, the Mohawk Valley, the Lake Champlain frontiers, and the tenant farmers in the Hudson Valley were Tory sympathizers.

By the time New York began to levy general war taxes, New York City and most of the lower counties had fallen to the British. Tax reform began with the tax law of 1778 which provided for ad valorem taxation on both improved and unimproved land. Value was to be estimated by elected assessors. Taxes on Tories and on neutrals who refused to swear allegiance to the rebel government were doubled. There was also an excess profits war tax. Anyone suspected of having earned £1,000 or more by "trade merchandise, traffic or manufactore," from September 1775 on, had to report earnings, swear a special oath, and pay a special tax of 5 percent.

The wealthy leaders saw the excess profits tax and the land taxes as indications of dangerous "leveling" tendencies. Robert Livingston condemned the excess profits taxes as an unprecedented violation of individual rights. Chief Justice John Jay argued that the laws violated the state constitution. The council of revision rejected excess profits tax, but the assembly overrode the council's veto. The following year, the assembly granted assessors virtually unlimited power to rate (tax) war profiteers. This time the council vetoed the law and the assembly agreed that it was too vague, but within a year the assembly applied the same provisions to all New Yorkers not in occupied territory.

Later in 1779 the assembly again altered the tax system by reimposing the old system of quotas for each county. Assessors were to distribute taxes within their counties with estates, ability to pay, and other circumstances collectively considered. This law gave virtually unlimited power to popularly elected assessors to rate not only property, but also income. The result was a chorus of complaints from the landed gentry. Robert Livingston's mother begged God to deliver her from the persecutions of the lower class and the assessors they had elected.

As taxes continued to rise, other New Yorkers were convinced that reform had not gone far enough. Newspaper essays, political speeches, and the actions of the legislature suggest that many believed the American Revolution was a rich man's war, fought and paid for by the poor and "middling sort." The old rivalry between upstate New York and New York City continued. The delegates from the occupied counties continued to vote in the assembly and they, with their lands safe from taxation behind British lines, voted for high taxes and rigid collections. Even with reform, taxes were heavy, collections were poor, and protests frequent. Alexander Hamilton, receiver of taxes, and his supporters wanted assessors and collectors appointed rather than elected. Robert Morris pointed out that collectors would be more effective if far removed from popular influence. Hamilton's supporters also wanted to replace the ad valorem taxes with acreage and poll taxes. Wealth, Hamilton noted, could not be accurately measured, and therefore the only practical basis for tax assessments was land and numbers. Despite Hamilton's efforts and cautious support from Governor Clinton, much of the revenue due remained uncollected. Hamilton's conviction that the national government must have the power to directly levy taxes was strengthened.

Demand for tax reform was strong in New Jersey and several petitions asked that money at interest be taxed. In 1776 an issue of paper money was authorized. Taxation to support the issue and tax reforms, such as the taxation of unimproved land, mortgages, notes, and bonds, were to begin in 1787. Proponents of intangible taxation argued that property of whatever kind ought to bear its proportional part of taxes and those whose wealth was in money rather than land should be taxed. Opponents saw taxation of intangibles as a dangerous manifestation of the leveling spirit. An anonymous writer, "T. W.," writing in the *New Jersey Gazette*, argued that nothing should be taxed unless it was visible, and that the public did not have the right to meddle with paper debts, bonds, and mortgages. He conceded that the tax would be popular, but that that alone was a poor excuse for dangerous experiments. He said that if it were adopted, "beggars would smack their lips," and it would please those among us "who behold their superiors in life with an envious eye, and right or wrong would gladly drag them down to a level with themselves."[18]

The outcome of this dispute was affected by the adoption of the New Jersey constitution. The House of Representatives, where 75 percent of the members had been wealthy men, was radically altered in composition. Two-thirds of the new members were farmers. The new members soon made their influence felt and a new tax law was passed in 1778. The assembly abandoned the county quota system (although it was soon restored) and imposed property taxes directly on individuals. Estates were taxed at the rate of two shillings in the pound of presumed annual value. Developed land, houses, mills, and other improvements were assessed at 5 percent of the real and salable value thereof. The assessors' powers were circumscribed by the insertion of minimum and maximum values for several kinds of taxable property and by imposing fixed taxes on other kinds of property, such as livestock. Unimproved land was to be rated at one-thirtieth of its market value, bringing wilderness land under taxation for the first time. Some luxuries, such as carriages and coaches, were brought under taxation, and all mortgages, bonds, bills, and notes at interest were to be assessed at one-thirtieth of the principal thereof.

In 1779 a faculty tax was imposed and assessors were told to examine the circumstances and ability of each person together with annual profits, emoluments, and advantages stemming from business, occupation, trade, or profession. They were also granted power to increase assessments when strict conformity with the letter of the law would not yield equitable assessments.

By 1780 the New Jersey reform movement had spent itself. In December 1779 the legislators withdrew the extraordinary powers granted to assessors, and by 1781 the money-at-interest provisions had disappeared. New luxury taxes, however, were imposed on gold and silver plate, clocks, and watches.

Compared to many other states, New Jersey's taxes worked well. When New York and Pennsylvania were struggling to collect one-third of their taxes, New Jersey collected almost 90 percent of the taxes levied and ended the war with a smoothly functioning system that, although it did not tax intangibles, was closer to the ability-to-pay standard than it had been before the war for independence.

WARTIME TAXATION IN THE SOUTH

At the beginning of the war the southern colonies had tax laws that were, on the whole, more regressive than those of the colonies to the north. The New England colonies imposed high poll taxes but taxed land on an ad valorem basis. The middle colonies protected wealthy landholders, but they did not levy general poll taxes. The southern colonies, by contrast, levied poll taxes and their relatively light land taxes were equal per acre, therefore, favoring the owners of the great plantations and other holders of valuable land.

In several of the southern colonies there had been protests against the tax system. These had been largely unsuccessful, but memories of protests were not dead and the revolution provided an opportunity to bring about reforms.

The most sweeping of these reforms occurred in North Carolina, the colony that imposed the most regressive taxes. Many of the colony's revolutionary leaders opposed revising the colonial constitution in any significant way. However, the people of the state gradually became aware that a revolution could not only secure independence from Great Britain, but that it could also be used to change the government of North Carolina. The result was the constitutional convention of 1776 that sharply curtailed the power of the eastern counties and gave more representation to the interior counties.

The first legislature under the new constitution met in 1777 and substituted an ad valorem property tax for the poll tax. The tax was one halfpenny for each pound value of all the lands, lots, houses, slaves, money, money at interest, stock-in-trade, horses, and cattle in the state. The only remnant of the poll tax was on freemen with an estate of less than £100 assessed value. A law adopted in November 1777 of that year stated that men ought to be taxed in proportion to the ability of each individual to pay.

In the end, North Carolina ended the war with a much reformed tax policy, but the assembly's willingness to respond to popular pressure also resulted in inadequate funding of debts. Tax suspensions and poor collection tended to affirm the conservative leaders' view that democracy had been carried too far.

Virginia, like most of the colonies, first responded to the war by issuing paper money and postponing the taxes to support it, but clamor for tax reform began almost immediately. As usual, this alarmed the wealthy and conservative men who dominated the government. Landon Carter wrote a worried letter to George Washington stating that some people were defining "independency" as "independent of rich men." He reported that some irresponsible men were seeking election to the legislature by denouncing taxes and asserting that they had been passed largely to serve the needs of the rich. Carter added that the worst of it was that the appeal seemed to work and that such men were getting elected.

The war years did see a reduction in rich men's influence in the Virginia House of Burgesses, but it was not the sweeping or dramatic shift in power that occurred in some states. Petitions to the legislature conceded the need for new taxes, but demanded reform. In 1778, after a long and heated debate, the Virginia assembly passed a tax law that considerably altered the way taxes were levied. Equal acreage taxes were eliminated and the assembly substituted an annual tax of 10s. for each £100 of value of all land, plate, slaves, horses, mules, all salaries, and the net income of all offices of profit. Continental military officers were exempted. The law tripled the taxes of anyone who refused to swear allegiance to the revolutionary government and abolished all quitrents except those paid to Washington's friend, Lord Fairfax. The poll tax was set at five shillings and taxes on money, interest payments, spirits and exported tobacco were imposed.

Assessors were to rate property at the amount they believed it would sell for in money, taking account of the situation of land and other circumstances. Administrative problems soon developed. It was reported that the assessed value of similar slaves might be as low as £70 and as high as £1950. Some assessors based their assessments on what the property would sell for in specie, others on what it would sell for in paper currency. Some attempted to reduce taxes paid by their county by estimating what land would sell for if all the land in the county were offered for sale at the same time. These evasions cut deeply into the expected revenue and by the end of 1778 the assembly reluctantly raised taxes across the board.

Because of the failure of the assessment process, the Virginia legislators began looking for an alternative. Proposals were made to divide land into several classes depending on quality and location. In 1779 the assembly adopted a plan suggested by Thomas Jefferson to divide land into six classes. In November 1781, the class system was abandoned and valuation was turned back to the discretion of local officials. About a year later, the valuation process changed again and land was divided into four classes based on location, with a fixed value for each class.

As in so many other states, in Virginia the problem of uncollected taxes was serious. By 1780 about half of the counties were delinquent in tax payment and about half of those had paid nothing into the treasury. The legislature responded by postponing the collection of levies from time to time, but by 1783 the question of collection policy had become a major political issue. The issue in Virginia is of unusual importance because of the identity of the men involved in the dispute over the proper policy. On one side were James Madison, John Tyler, Joseph Jones, and usually George Mason, who considered it imperative that the Confederation Congress be supported and that public debts be honored. On the other side was Patrick Henry whose faction supported tax suspensions and other relief measures to help small farmers and backcountry men. The debate was not simple and even conservative men were concerned with those who suffered because of the war. George Mason sometimes supported suspension of tax payments and Thomas Jefferson pointed out that taxes could not be higher than what a man could spare. The debate also involved currency and state debt. At one point the state allowed military supply certificates to be used to pay taxes, but this seriously undercut the state's financial position. For a time in 1781 the state refused to accept such certificates, which led Patrick Henry to ask whether it was just for a state to insist on prompt payment of debts from its citizens to whom the state itself owed large sums that it could not pay?

Virginia's inability or unwillingness to pay congressional requisitions helped convince Madison that Congress must have the power to coerce the states into paying. Governor Benjamin Harrison feared that such powers of taxation and coercion would destroy Virginia's power to shape its own policy. These debates were to continue through to the ratification of the U.S. Constitution by Virginia in 1788.

QUESTIONS FOR THE FUTURE

The early American colonist came from a highly ordered, hierarchical society in which every man and woman found his or her ordered, often inherited, place. Transplanting members of this society to the open wilderness did not automatically destroy the ideas on which the society was founded. In fact, a leading student of American civilization reports that these ideas mightily flourished.[19] Certainly, many of the leaders who supported the Declaration of Independence and the War for Independence did not favor universal suffrage or radical changes in the tax system. Probably they saw little, if any, connection between such ideas and the rhetoric of the Declaration of Independence.

On the other hand, the idea of equality had been let loose in a vast underdeveloped region and, as the attempt to build a nation continued, its application to such mundane matters as taxation became a matter of much debate and some violence. Dissatisfaction with the existing tax system had been expressed in many of the colonies and the war presented opportunity to renew previous demands. In several of the colonies the chances for success were improved by new constitutions that resulted in more representative legislatures. These new legislatures modified the tax laws to reduce favoritism to the rich and moved toward taxation according to ability to pay. Often this meant eliminating or reducing the poll tax and substituting ad valorem property taxation for taxation levied at specific rates on specified items of property.

Men like Alexander Hamilton and James Madison, who were involved in the attempt to raise revenue to carry on the war, saw the need for a central government with the power to tax and the capability of establishing an efficient, professional tax administration. Others saw these ideas as inconsistent with the concept of freedom and equality for which they had fought.

The issue was compromised at the Philadelphia constitutional convention and out of that compromise grew a new form of government—federalism. The Constitution of the United States gave limited tax power to the federal government, but it would have to prove that it had the political support and the administrative capacity to exercise that power. In light of the apparently limitless tax power of the federal government today, it may come as a surprise that the issue was ever in doubt.

3
Federal Finance, 1775–1836

The Declaration of Independence, proclaimed on July 4, 1776, declared the thirteen British colonies to be independent states but did not establish a constitutional order for carrying on a war or governing a new nation. However, in response to the obvious need for a united effort in the war with Great Britain, the Continental Congress appropriated to itself some of the elements of sovereignty. These were limited because of a deep-seated fear of efficient government and, in some quarters, hesitancy that almost amounted to repugnance toward any effective union.[1]

Nevertheless, the Continental Congress approved a draft of the Articles of Confederation on November 17, 1777, and sent it to the states for ratification. Several states ratified quickly, but the articles did not become legally binding until Maryland ratified them on March 1, 1781.

The Articles of Confederation provided for a perpetual union among the states, but each state remained sovereign and independent and retained all rights not expressly ceded to the general government. There was a single agency of central government, the Congress, entrusted with the management of foreign affairs, of war, and of the postal service. The states were to appoint two to seven delegates, but each state had only one vote.

FINANCE UNDER THE ARTICLES OF CONFEDERATION

The Articles of Confederation stated that the treasury was to be supplied by the several states in proportion to the value of the land and improvements in each state, but explicitly stated that taxes should be laid and levied by the authority and direction of the legislature of each state.

These provisions denied the Continental Congress one of the essential elements of sovereignty, the power to tax. This was to prove a serious handicap in the effort to carry on the war with Britain. Militia were paid by the states and did part of the fighting. States made little contribution to financing the continental army under the command of General George Washington. As a result, the Continental Congress was able to finance the war only through issues of paper money and loans made by Great Britain's enemies.[2]

Like the states, Congress extracted economic resources by the simple expedient of printing paper. The infamous "continental" was legal tender money, but Congress also issued a variety of certificates of indebtedness. This led to inflation and to speculation in the various kinds of paper. The phrase, "not worth a continental," became a permanent part of the language and one member of Congress reported in May 1779 that prices in Philadelphia had doubled in three weeks.[3]

Superintendent of Finance Robert Morris made a number of suggestions to state governments and took a number of initiatives to encourage states to expand their fiscal capacity and to collect the taxes levied. As part of his effort, he appointed Alexander Hamilton as receiver of taxes for New York. Hamilton proposed a complete revision of New York's tax system, but the mostly loyalist New York legislature was not anxious to place more taxes on its citizenry for the benefit of Congress and showed little enthusiasm for his plan.

Morris was a nationalist who believed in a strong national government with many additional powers. A number of the actions he took were directed as much at strengthening national governments as in making the requisition system work. For example, in 1781 Congress, at Morris' insistence, refused to accept either supplies or state currencies in payment of requisitions and states were not permitted credit for funds used for direct payment of their troops. Instead, the states were asked to pay $8 million in specie or in the closest equivalent, which was financier's notes. These notes were guaranteed by Morris in his private capacity as well as in his public role as financier, or head of the Department of Finance.[4] With actions like this making the requisition system even more unworkable, the nationalists in Congress attempted to provide independent taxing authority for the central government. The first step was the attempt to secure an impost of 5 percent on all imported goods. In 1781, even before the last state had ratified the Articles of Confederation, Congress adopted a proposed amendment that would have authorized this impost. To become effective this amendment had to be ratified by all the states.

The nationalists were well aware that a large debt could be an important factor in nation-building. They knew that the funded debt and the national bank had helped stabilize the regime in Great Britain after the revolution of 1689 by attracting the support of moneyed groups. Alexander Hamilton wrote that a national debt could be powerful cement to the union and Morris wrote to Benjamin Franklin that it was his expectation that the clamors of the public creditors would induce the states to adopt the tax amendment. To help the process along, Morris discontinued interest payments on loan certificates and proposed to make future payments contingent on enactment of direct federal taxation. The small corps of tax receivers appointed by Morris were utilized as lobbyists for this measure.[5]

These arguments and maneuvers almost succeeded. All states except Rhode Island ratified the tax amendment by the end of 1781. In that state the radical "country party" was in power and was firmly committed to limiting central authority. Opponents of the amendment in Rhode Island argued that the states would have no control over the income it would produce and that collection of the tax would be a precedent for the central government to act directly on individuals rather than dealing with the states. Rhode Islanders recognized the issue was a question of whether there would be a confederation or a national government.

In an attempt to secure ratification of the amendment, the Continental Congress authorized a delegation to travel to Rhode Island. But, just as the delegation was setting out on the journey, word was received that Virginia had rescinded its approval. With two states opposed, the proposal was dead.

The attempts to amend the Articles of Confederation did not end with Cornwallis' surrender at Yorktown in October 1781 nor with the signing of the Treaty of Paris that recognized American independence in 1783. Early in 1783, Morris attempted to get Congress to approve another revenue measure. Hamilton aided the effort by working to get congressional proceedings open to the public so that creditors could better exert pressure on the members of Congress and Morris threatened to resign if a revenue measure was not passed.

Morris' threat to resign was important because of his financial skill and his willingness to use his own fortune to help finance the war, but even more significant were the rumors of serious discontent in the Continental Army. The officers demanded their back pay and sent a three-man delegation to present a strong statement threatening "fatal consequences" if their grievances were not resolved. Mention was made of how Cromwell's Roundheads had turned against Parliament when it tried to dismiss them without back pay.

In March 1783, news of the so-called "Newburgh conspiracy" reached Washington. Two letters had been circulated through winter camp. One called a meeting of officers and the other urged soldiers to refuse disbandment until they had been paid. Washington headed off trouble by calling his own meeting and asking for moderation in demands. At this meeting the officers approved resolutions reaffirming their loyalty but reminding Congress of their claims.

Two days before news of this meeting reached Philadelphia, Morris introduced a committee report recommending a new revenue measure, and by April officers were granted five years' full pay in lieu of pensions at half pay for life. The officers' pay bill added substantially to the growing debt and Congress adopted another revenue amendment for submission to the states. The new measure included a 5 percent tariff with additional duties on salt, wines, rum, brandy, sugar, and tea. The states were also to pledge payments of $1.5 million per year for twenty-five years. The proceeds of the impost were to be applied only to payment of interest and principal, and it was to lapse at the end of the term. The states would appoint their own revenue collectors, but Congress would be empowered to appoint and to remove them if necessary.

Under strong pressure from creditors and the army, all but three members of Congress voted for the measure. Two who opposed such centralization were from Rhode Island. The other was Alexander Hamilton, who objected to the twenty-five year limit and to giving the states power to appoint collectors. Hamilton, however, urged the New York state legislature to ratify the measure.

By 1786 eight states had adopted the impost, but only three had agreed to accept their full share of the $1.5 million supplementary funding. Other states, including Rhode Island, had adopted the amendment, but there were technical flaws in their action. In New York, a bitter fight continued. Delegates from New York City and large upstate landlords supported the amendment while backcountry farmers opposed it. The legislature finally agreed to the impost if the state was permitted to collect it, but Congress found this unacceptable. In the regular session of 1787, the New York legislature held to its position and two days later Hamilton moved to appoint delegates to a convention to amend the Articles of Confederation. Both houses of the New York legislature quickly approved.

The decision of New York and other states to send delegates to the Convention of 1787 may well have been influenced by news of Shays's Rebellion. This uprising in western and central Massachusetts was a manifestation of widespread discontent in New England. The economy was depressed. Small property holders were losing property through foreclosure for debts or taxes and many faced imprisonment. Town meetings and conventions petitioned for lighter taxes, abolition of certain courts, and revision of state constitutions. Reform was rejected by the legislatures of Massachusetts and other states, and malcontents, most of whom were barred from voting because they did not own property, attempted to intimidate or close courts. In January 1787, insurgents massed in Springfield and attempted to secure supplies from the confederate arsenal. The insurgents were repulsed on January 25 and early in February most of the remaining insurgents were captured. Daniel Shays and about a dozen others were condemned to death but were later pardoned.

The armed rebellion failed, but it had political repercussions. The Massachusetts governor was defeated at the next election and a number of the reforms demanded by the insurrectionists were enacted. These events led some conservatives to despair of republican institutions, but others saw it as a reason for a stronger national government capable of suppressing such uprisings or of fostering better economic conditions in order to prevent them.[6]

THE CONSTITUTION OF THE UNITED STATES

The Convention of 1787, called to revise the Articles of Confederation, immediately addressed the writing of a new constitution. Much debate centered around two proposals known as the New Jersey plan and the Virginia plan. The New Jersey plan, which stayed closest to the spirit of the Articles of Confederation, provided that the national government's tax powers would be limited to requisitions, import duties, and a stamp tax on documents. The plan also provided stronger powers of compliance against states that did not pay their requisitions. The Virginia plan, authored largely by James Madison, provided a strong national government with veto power over state actions.[7]

The result of the debates, embodied in the proposed constitution, was closer to the Virginia plan than to the New Jersey plan. The proposal provided for a federal government with power to act directly on the people. It was not a league or confederation of governments, but there were limits on the taxing powers of both state and national governments.

Article I, Section 8, dealing with the powers of Congress, begins with the following provision:

> The Congress shall have Power To lay and collect Taxes, Duties, Imposts and Excises, to pay the Debts and provide for the common Defense and general Welfare of the United States; but all Duties, Imposts and Excises shall be uniform throughout the United States.

Section 9 of Article I contains a number of limitations applying to both state and national governments. Included are the following:

> No Capitation, or other direct, Tax shall be laid, unless in Proportion to the Census or Enumeration herein before directed to be taken.
>
> No Tax or Duty shall be laid on Articles exported from any State.
>
> No Preference shall be given by any Regulation of Commerce or Revenue to the Ports of one State over those of another: nor shall Vessels bound to, or from, one State, be obliged to enter, clear, or pay Duties in another.

Article I, Section 10, prohibits the states from raising revenue by imposing import or export duties or tonnage taxes.

The provision that direct taxes must be apportioned among the states by population is reinforced in Article I, Section 2, dealing with the House of Representatives. This section provides that representatives and direct taxes shall be apportioned according to population, excluding Indians not taxed, and counting slaves as three-fifths of a person.

It is important to note that these provisions did not establish separation of sources, or exclusive jurisdictions over revenue sources. In defending the constitution in *The Federalist*, Alexander Hamilton wrote:

> I mean the power of imposing taxes on all articles other than exports and imports. This, I contend, is manifestly a concurrent and coequal authority in the United States and in the individual States. There is plainly no expression in the granting clause which makes that power *exclusive* in the Union.[8]

The writing of the Constitution was the work of the top cadre of a relatively small group of national leaders and well-known state leaders.[9] Many were wealthy. A number were remarkably well educated and thoughtful about political subjects. Those who wrote the Constitution were concerned about the breakdown of established social order since the beginning of the revolution and the increasing role of the uneducated, the newly rich, and the fiscally irresponsible in state government.

Ratification of the Constitution by the state conventions involved a different kind of people and a different process. The anti-federalists who opposed the ratification of the proposed constitution were appalled by what they saw as the surrender of the principles for which they had fought during the Revolution. One wrote that the new constitution did not leave the states as much power as Lord North had offered to guarantee the colonies. The anti-federalists were especially shocked by the taxation clause in Article I, Section 8, which they saw as giving Congress the unlimited rights to lay and collect all kinds of taxes. They saw themselves as defending the idea of local control against an overly ambitious central government, just as they had defended it against Great Britain.[10]

The anti-federalists were unable to prevent the adoption of the Constitution, but they did use their strength in an attempt to dilute the power of the national government. Several of the states proposed a limit on the national government's ability to tax. In the first Congress, a proposal to limit the national government to requisitions and indirect taxes was defeated 39 to 9. James Madison, who served as the floor manager for the Bill of Rights, ignored proposals to include tax limits in the first ten amendments to the Constitution.[11] Clearly, those on both sides of the issue recognized the close connection between the structure of government and taxation.[12]

EARLY YEARS OF TAXATION UNDER THE CONSTITUTION

A new phase in the struggle began in the first session of Congress. James Madison made economic policy the first order of business. On April 8, 1789, three weeks before the nation had its first president, he spoke in the House of Representatives to call for an economy that was balanced, equitable, and independent of other nations. To promote these ends and to raise badly needed revenue, he proposed an elaborate system of tariffs on imports. Legislators sprang to the defense of their local interests and industries whether they be rum, beer, molasses, sugar, or coffee, but Congress quickly approved a tariff bill.[13] It was sent to the Senate, amended, re-amended by a conference committee, and signed by the president on July 4, 1789. This act, the first revenue law passed by the new government, included a long list of items subject to specific import duties and listed five classes of goods subject to ad valorem tariff rates. It provided favorable treatment of commodities imported in vessels built or owned by United States citizens and the refund of tariffs on goods later exported.[14]

Alexander Hamilton was appointed the first Secretary of the Treasury in September 1789. His administration of the customs service was a model of administrative efficiency well blended with political sensitivity. Many state customs collectors were given jobs in the federal service, but Hamilton was careful to limit his collectors' discretion in the valuation of goods. He quickly removed the occasional delinquent or dilatory collector and insisted upon strict fairness in dealing with shipowners or importers. He commended collectors who did good work and sought to improve the pay scale. The administrative organization and practices that Hamilton established were to remain essentially unchanged until the end of James Madison's term as president in 1817.[15]

The tariff bill was accepted with little complaint. It had been widely expected that tariffs would be the main source of revenue for the national government. The federal tariffs were external taxes replacing the tariffs that the states had been levying. For many taxpayers, the federal tariff simply meant that the money was being sent to a different collector.[16]

When Hamilton assumed office, the credit and money system of the new country was in chaos. The states had paid only a small portion of the requisitions. Congress had been forced to borrow and to issue paper money to finance its wartime activities. One estimate places the specie value of domestic loans obtained by Congress during the war at $11,585,000 and the value of foreign loans at $7,830,000.[17] However, the amount of paper money was far larger. By 1779, four years before the end of the war, approximately $140,000,000 in face value had been issued. At that time it had a specie value of about $37,000,000.[18]

The federalists, who controlled the U.S. Congress, were anxious to improve the credit and stabilize the monetary system. Hamilton prepared a broad report on the economy, pointing out the need to honor debts, to expand currency and credit, and to strengthen the Union by giving businessmen, as well as educated and professional people, a vested interest in the political and financial affairs of the new government. Hamilton argued that a failure to pay the debt would be a rejection of public morality and an invitation to anarchy or despotism. He proposed that the federal government assume the debts of the Confederation and state debt incurred to finance the Revolution.[19]

The most provocative aspect of Hamilton's proposal was not that the debt be assumed, but that it be assumed at face value. Because most of the credit instruments involved had been sold to speculators, often at prices far below par, the proposal opened old wounds and fed the apprehensions of those who feared a moneyed elite. Sectional interests were also involved. Some southern states had paid most of their debts; they complained that Hamilton's proposals favored the East.

Within Congress, Madison led a small but determined group that supported a proposal to distinguish between original holders of certificates of indebtedness, characterized by Madison as widows, veterans, and patriots who should receive payment at par, and speculators who should receive only market value of the securities. Outside Congress, the strong feeling against merchants, rich men, and speculators contributed to support for the Madison proposal. Many newspapers denounced the speculators as being sympathetic to the loyalist cause and willing to exploit public distress.[20]

Hamilton's ability as a practical politician was demonstrated when he and a group of his supporters made a deal with Jefferson and his supporters exchanging support for debt assumption in return for support for locating the nation's capital on the banks of the Potomac. In August 1790, Hamilton's funding proposal was adopted by a narrow margin in Congress. The capital would move from New York to Philadelphia for ten years, then to a permanent location on the banks of the Potomac.[21]

Hamilton's plan for building a strong central government included an immediate and generous use of national revenue powers, both to build support from those who benefited from the expenditure, and to build a corps of public officials and employees who would have a vested interest in the national government. The first use of these powers was the levy in March 1791 of an excise tax on spirits that gave way to a permanent law in 1792. The argument over these bills was bitter, both within and without Congress. Opponents argued that an excise tax would be unpopular and was dangerous to the liberties of the people. Josiah Parker of Virginia predicted that the excise would "convulse the Government; it will let loose a swarm of harpies, who, under the denomination of revenue officers, will range through the country prying into every man's house and affairs, and like a Macedonian phalanx bear down upon all before them." Jefferson and Madison, having agreed to the assumption of debts, felt they could not oppose any reasonable scheme for raising money, but kept as low a profile as possible.

THE WHISKEY REBELLION

The difficulties posed by the levy and collection of a uniform tax upon a large, economically underdeveloped nation are illustrated by the opposition to the excise tax that came to a head in western Pennsylvania.[22] That region was an isolated, economically struggling area. The area was heavily dependent on agriculture, but the mountains made it unfeasible to ship grain to the east. Spanish control of the Mississippi made it impossible to ship grain by water. Cash was in short supply and much of the land was owned by speculators who lived in the east. Indian raids were worrisome and the settlers were disgruntled that the government gave little help with the "Indian problem" and had failed to dislodge the Spanish from their control over the mouth of the Mississippi. Many farmers operated stills in which they converted their grain into whiskey, which was consumed widely, and also served as a medium of exchange and a source of cash. Small farmers bartered whiskey to merchants who bore the cost of transporting it over the mountains by horseback. The land tax was viewed as a more equitable method of taxation in western Pennsylvania. An ad valorem property tax would have forced the eastern speculators to sell western land at reasonable prices and would have laid more of the burden on the east where superior improvements and proximity to markets made land more valuable. That the greater political power of the east prevented the use of a land tax was seen by westerners as another example of eastern discrimination.

Several features of the federal excise tax made it especially obnoxious to the westerners. The rate was high, equivalent to about one-third the price of whiskey at the point of distilling. The tax had to be paid in cash and applied to whiskey consumed by the producer as well as to that which entered trade. The westerners also resented the inquisitions, the searches and seizures, and the registration and marking of stills that administration of the tax produced. They also resented what they considered to be high salaries paid to the unpopular excisemen. Additional irritation was caused because those charged with violating the law were required to appear in Philadelphia for trial. This meant many weeks absence from their home and the payment of attorney and witness fees by farmers who had little cash. Total costs of such a trip were said to be equal to the value of the average farm.

The administrative features of the excise tax were seen as confirmation of the argument that this tax was essentially a tax on one group (farmers) for the benefit of a small group of well-to-do easterners who held the securities that were to be redeemed. Veterans who had been forced to sell scrip received as pay for wartime service for a few cents on the dollar were especially irate at being taxed so that speculators could redeem the scrip at face value.

Political opposition to the excise tax was expressed as early as 1791 in the form of petitions and resolutions of protest. The most important of these were drawn up at protest meetings at Brownsville, Washington (Pennsylvania), and Pittsburgh, but there were others drawn up at militia musters. In September of 1791 a collector in Washington County was tarred and feathered. The deputy marshall sent to serve warrants against those responsible was so intimidated that he utilized a simpleminded cattle drover to deliver the warrants. The uncomprehending messenger was whipped, tarred, feathered, and robbed. Other incidents of direct action involved threats against those allowing their houses to be used as revenue offices.

In August 1792 a second meeting attended by several prominent men was held in Pittsburgh. Albert Gallatin, later to be Jefferson's Secretary of the Treasury, was elected secretary of the meeting. Committees of Correspondence were appointed, a remonstrance to Congress was drawn up, and a resolution against excise officers was passed. The resolution urged that all dealings with excise officers cease and that they be treated with the contempt that they deserve. The meeting received much attention in the east. George Washington issued a statement, also bearing the signature of Thomas Jefferson, warning malcontents to desist from all unlawful combinations and proceedings having as their object the obstruction of the law.

By 1793 the disturbances had quieted somewhat. Processes were served against several who had failed to register their stills and they appeared at Philadelphia for trial. Hamilton stated that obedience to the law was gaining ground, but in 1794 the pace of violence was again stepped up. Hamilton blamed the setback in obedience to the law on the rising influence of the Democratic Societies. These clubs, the forerunners of the Republican party of Thomas Jefferson, opposed the elitist and centralist tendencies of the federalists. Specifically, they opposed Hamilton's financial policies and the doctrine that government administration was the business only of government officials.

In the west, there was a lack of consensus among those who opposed to the excise tax. Many of the larger still owners, seeing the advantage of a stable government and the protection to property that it would provide, became reconciled to registering their stills and paying the tax, but this led the more radical opponents to step up their attacks on revenue officers and the distillers who had paid the tax.

In April 1794, Hamilton recommended a bill reducing the tax rates and modifying the requirement that those charged under the law must make the 300-mile trip to Philadelphia. The bill passed Congress and was signed by President Washington on June 5; but one week before this law was to take effect, writs were entered in the federal court in Philadelphia against unregistered distillers around Pittsburgh. In July, after the new law had taken effect, processes were served requiring them to appear in Philadelphia for trial. Some of Hamilton's critics charged that he planned this action to provoke a crisis that would require the use of federal troops. No direct evidence exists, but it is true that there was much talk among the federalists about the need of military action to establish the authority of the federal government.[23] In any case, "liberty poles" signifying a call to rebellion began to appear.

Among the incidents that occurred was the attack on the house of a federal inspector by a mob of approximately 500 people, including many members of the state militia. Several of the attackers were killed and the house was destroyed. This incident was followed by a mail robbery carried out by the rebels in an effort to secure letters bearing upon the disturbance. Several letters contained material that the rebels considered objectional and an effort was made to call up the militia to seize and imprison the writers and to seize the magazine at Fort Fayette in Pittsburgh. After much confusion, a rather disorganized army of protesters, estimated to number somewhere between 1,500 and 5,000 men, marched on Pittsburgh.

Faced with an open challenge, President Washington issued an order to call 13,000 militiamen from Pennsylvania, New Jersey, Maryland, and Virginia. As the companies were being gathered, Washington spent three weeks in the field reviewing troops.

The army, three times as big as the one Washington commanded at Valley Forge, was nominally commanded by Governor Henry Lee of Virginia, but Alexander Hamilton accompanied the army and is said to have made many of the decisions. When the army arrived at the site of the rebellion, a small number of prominent rebels were arrested and three weeks later most of the troops started home. About 1,500 troops remained until spring. One group of twenty prisoners was taken to Philadelphia and tried, but no one was convicted. In another group, two were convicted but later pardoned by the president.[24]

The military action effectively ended organized resistance to the tax, but receipts from the excise never turned out to be an important source of revenue and the cost of collection was very high. The tax was repealed in 1802, on the suggestion of President Jefferson. Ironically, his new Secretary of the Treasury, Albert Gallatin, who had been secretary of the Pittsburgh protest meeting, initially objected because he believed that repeal of internal revenues should take second place to retiring the debt.

FEDERAL TAXATION OF PROPERTY

In 1798 the federal government made its first attempt to impose a property tax. This was an important event in the history of American taxation for several reasons:

1. It was the federal government's first use of direct taxes.
2. It illustrated the magnitude of the problem that the apportionment provision of the Constitution presents.
3. The debate over the structure of the tax revealed the possibilities and problems inherent in property taxation.
4. The attempts to structure the tax called forth the Wolcott report, which is a prime source of information about state property taxes of the time.

In 1794, a special committee on public credit recommended imposing a direct tax that would raise $750,000 and also the imposition of certain stamp taxes. Neither proposal was accepted, but interest in the subject was revived two years later when Congress asked Secretary of the Treasury Oliver Wolcott to develop a plan to raise $2,000,000. Wolcott's challenge was to draft a law that would meet the constitutional requirement and still adjust to the conditions in the various states. As a first step, he undertook an inquiry as to the methods of taxation used in the various states. A great deal of variation from state to state was found. The revenue systems of the New England states were similar to each other and some of the Southern states also had many features in common. Despite the similarities, Wolcott noted that there were great differences among the regions. He commented that the more one studied the matter, the more differences one found, even within the same region of the country. Years later, Professor Henry Carter Adams summarized Wolcott's findings about the property tax.[25] Part of the table is reproduced in Table 3.1. It reveals that all five of the New England states, North Carolina, and Georgia levied a capitation (poll) tax. Only four states—Rhode Island, Delaware, New York, and Maryland—taxed the mass of property. Other states designated the specific items that were to be taxed. Land was taxed in a variety of ways. Only New Hampshire and Massachusetts used the English system of taxation according to annual (rental) value. Several states divided land into some kind of class or district and taxed uniformly by acreage within those divisions. Others used an ad valorem approach.

Table 3.1. State Tax Systems According to the Wolcott Report, 1796

	Uniform Capitation Tax	Tax on Horses, Cattle	All Farm Stock Valued	Taxes Imposed on Mass of Property[3]	Mode of Taxing Lands
Vermont	X	X	—	—	According to quantity, if enclosed
New Hampshire	X	X	—	—	According to annual rent
Massachusetts	X	X	—	—	According to annual rent
Connecticut	X	X	—	—	Included in mass of property
Rhode Island	X	—	X	X	According to state of cultivation
New York	—	—	X	X	Included in mass of property
New Jersey	—	X	—	—	Ad valorem, according to value in different counties
Pennsylvania	—	X	—	—	Ad valorem, according to triennial assessment
Delaware	—	—	X	X	Included in mass of property
Maryland	[1]	—	X	X	Ad valorem, upon valuation in different counties
Virginia	—	X[2]	—	—	According to permanent valuation
Kentucky	—	X	—	—	Uniformly by quality, all lands divided into three classes
North Carolina	X	—	—	—	Uniformly by quantity
South Carolina	—	—	—	—	Uniformly by quantity
Georgia	X	—	—	—	Uniformly by districts

1. A poll tax was contrary to the Constitution of Maryland.
2. Cattle excepted.
3. Other states designated taxable objects.
Source: Henry Carter Adams, *Taxation in the United States, 1789–1816* (New York: Burt Franklin, 1970, originally published 1884), 52.

A part of the table, not reproduced here, deals with the way tax collectors obtained their positions. Clearly, the preference was for electing these officials. In eight states tax collectors were elected by the people. In three states the sheriff was appointed, "if able to qualify." If not, the collector was elected in Kentucky, appointed by the state executive in Virginia, and by a court in North Carolina. In Delaware and Maryland the collectors were appointed by county officials.

Because of the great diversity that he found, Wolcott decided that a federal property tax should be independent of the state system. In 1798 he submitted a second report outlining his proposal. He proposed to tax three classes of property: houses; slaves; and lands. Houses were to be divided into nine classes according to value, with each house in a class bearing an identical tax. Slaves were to be taxed uniformly at $0.50 per head. Lands were to be taxed ad valorem at whatever rate was necessary to make up the state's allotment, after the revenue from the tax on houses and slaves had been considered.

The rates to be applied to houses were:

House Value ($)		Tax ($)
80 to	200	.50
200	600	1.50
600	1,200	3.00
1,200	2,000	6.00
2,000	4,000	12.00
4,000	6,000	20.00
6,000	10,000	30.00
10,000	25,000	60.00
25,000+		120.00

Although Wolcott and Hamilton were personally close, Hamilton did not approve of Wolcott's plan for taxing houses. He proposed a plan based upon the number of rooms. Under Hamilton's plan, the tax per room rose as the size of the house increased. The schedule was as follows:

Kind of House	Tax per Room ($)
Log house	.20
Two-room house	.25
Three-room house	.33⅓
Four-room house	.40
Five-room house	.60
Six-room house	.75
Seven-room or larger house	1.00

Hamilton's plan would have been the easiest to administer because it required only that the number of rooms be counted. The plan was a progressive tax in the sense that the tax per room would have been higher on larger houses. Whether it would have been progressive in relation to value is not clear.

Wolcott's plan took value into consideration, but it did not require the exact value of the house be determined—only the value class to which it belonged. It appears that the tax levied would have been in approximate proportion to value. If the tax on the central value of each class is computed the results are:

Value ($)	Rate per $1.00 of Value
140	.0036
400	.0038
900	.0033
1,600	.0036
3,000	.0038
5,000	.0040
8,000	.0038
17,500	.0034

The property tax was imposed under conditions of war hysteria. In 1797 French harassment of American shipping had been stepped up as a tactic in the war with Britain. France expelled the American envoy and stated that no American representative would be welcome until America met its demands regarding trade with England. President Adams asked for limited preparations for war and suggested that additional taxes would be required.

The modest moves requested by Adams were not sufficient for the war wing of the Federalist party, which included Hamilton, now retired as Secretary of the Treasury. When an American delegation was sent to France in an attempt to resume relations, they were humiliated before breaking off talks with secret French agents, designated as X, Y, and Z. The country was electrified. Congress appropriated funds for warships and created an army of 50,000 men with George Washington in command. Congress also enacted the Alien and Sedition acts, which empowered the president, in time of war, to arrest, imprison or banish aliens with whose motherland the United States might be at war. It was made a high misdemeanor to interfere with an officer or to abet insurrection, riot, or unlawful assembly. The publication of false or malicious writing against the nation, president, or Congress was punishable by imprisonment. These highly unpopular acts were used chiefly against Republican editors who criticized President Adams.

In July 1798, only a few days after the Alien and Sedition acts were passed, Congress passed the direct tax. Southern representatives objected to the tax on slaves and frontier leaders opposed any tax on land, but the bill passed comfortably. The tax on houses was not based on either Wolcott's or Hamilton's proposal. Instead, the law provided for a progressive percentage tax that is attributed to Albert Gallatin.[26] The schedule was as follows:

House Value ($)			Rate per $1.00 of Value
100	to	1,000	.002
1,000		3,000	.004
3,000		6,000	.005
6,000		10,000	.006
10,000		15,000	.007
15,000		20,000	.008
20,000		30,000	.009
30,000+			.010

The system adopted was similar to *l'impot progressive* proposed by the French revolutionists. This is a very rare example of a progressive property tax.[27] The administrative arrangements involved both federal and state officials. Federal officials were to assess property and collect the tax, but each state was to create a board of commissioners and these boards were given the right to make assessment rules that would reflect local custom.

Opposition to the property tax of 1798 was muted, as compared to the protest over the Alien and Sedition acts or the excise tax of four years earlier, but there was some protest. Many of the petitions that complained about the Alien and Sedition acts also added a few words of opposition to the direct tax. In Massachusetts, liberty poles appeared and the list of slogans included, "No Land Tax." Protest also came from the south. Jefferson complained that the tax would crush the agrarian economy of Virginia and that its share was far too large.[28]

There was one example of overt opposition known to history as Fries' Rebellion. In Bucks County, Pennsylvania, a group of assessors evaluating houses were captured and briefly detained by a small group of local militia led by John Fries, an auctioneer. Some of those in Fries' group were then captured by federal marshals. A group of about 140 men were organized to free them, but the marshals released their prisoners without violence. A week later, President Adams proclaimed that opposition to the law was too great to permit its enforcement by ordinary means and organized a military force to crush the rebellion. Residents of the area then agreed to cease resistance and permit the assessment of their property, but Adams deployed troops, who quickly captured about thirty alleged rebels including Fries himself. Most of the prisoners were accused of treason and tried. Some were convicted, but their convictions were set aside and they were held for retrial. A year later Fries and two others were again found guilty and were sentenced to death.

Adam's cabinet split when he asked for advice as to how to deal with the question of pardoning the men. Some wanted to execute all three, others thought that killing Fries would be enough. Adams disregarded their advice and pardoned everyone connected with the incident.

Table 3.2. Federal Government Finances, 1789–1836 (revenue and surplus in thousands)

Year	Customs	Internal Revenue	Sale of Land	Miscellaneous	Surplus
1789–91	$4,399,473			$19,440	$149,886
1792	3,443,071	$208,943		17,946	(1,409,572)
1793	4,255,307	337,706		59,910	170,610
1794	4,801,065	274,090		356,750	(1,558,934)
1795	5,588,461	337,755		188,318	(1,425,275)
1796	6,567,988	475,290	$4,836	1,329,416	2,650,544
1797	7,549,650	575,491	83,541	480,099	2,555,147
1798	7,106,062	644,358	11,963	138,113	223,992
1799	6,610,449	779,136		157,228	(2,119,642)
1800	9,080,933	809,396	444	957,976	62,674
1801	10,750,779	1,048,033	167,726	968,793	3,540,749
1802	12,438,236	621,899	188,626	1,747,031	7,133,676
1803	10,479,418	215,180	165,676	203,824	3,212,445
1804	11,098,565	50,941	487,527	189,274	3,106,865
1805	12,936,487	21,747	540,194	62,265	3,054,459
1806	14,667,698	20,101	765,246	106,886	5,756,314
1807	15,845,522	13,051	466,163	73,283	8,043,868
1808	16,363,551	8,211	647,939	40,961	7,128,170
1809	7,296,021	4,044	442,252	31,156	2,507,275
1810	8,583,309	7,431	696,549	96,926	1,227,705
1811	13,313,223	2,296	1,040,238	67,772	6,365,192
1812	8,958,778	4,903	710,428	127,024	(10,479,638)
1813	13,224,623	4,755	835,655	275,377	(17,341,442)
1814	5,998,772	1,662,985	1,135,971	2,383,897	(23,539,301)

Although Fries' rebellion appears to be an isolated example of overt opposition to the property tax, the tax was unpopular. A number of contemporary observers, including Jefferson himself, identified internal taxes as one of the causes of Jefferson's victory over the federalists in the election of 1800.[29] In 1802 Jefferson's administration made good on its pledge and repealed all internal taxes, both direct and indirect. As shown in Table 3.2, internal revenue collections from 1804 through 1813 were insignificant. Collections from customs duties, sales of land, and miscellaneous collections such as earnings of the post office were sufficient to produce surplus revenues until 1812. Clearly, Hamilton's vision of a strong, financially dominant federal government had not been achieved. Jefferson had started the process that would make state and local governments the fiscally dominant level governments in the first century of the American nation.

In 1812, war again required additional revenue. The tariff was doubled and the following year a system of internal revenue was reestablished. Included among the taxes was another property tax designed by Albert Gallatin, now Secretary of the Treasury. The new property tax was much simpler than the 1798 tax. The law provided for a levy on all taxable property according to its money value. As required by the Constitution, the tax was apportioned among the states in proportion to population, but apportionment to counties within the state was according to the assessed value of property in each county. As a concession to state sensibilities it was provided that any state legislature might change the apportionment among the counties. Also, the

Table 3.2. (Continued)

Year	Customs	Internal Revenue	Sale of Land	Miscellaneous	Surplus
1815	7,282,942	4,678,059	1,287,959	2,480,064	(16,979,115)
1816	36,306,875	5,124,708	1,717,985	4,528,103	17,090,980
1817	26,283,348	2,678,101	1,991,226	2,146,375	11,255,230
1818	17,176,385	955,270	2,606,562	846,951	1,760,050
1819	20,283,609	229,594	3,274,423	815,749	3,139,565
1820	15,005,612	106,261	1,635,872	1,132,925	(379,957)
1821	13,004,447	69,028	1,212,966	286,939	(1,237,373)
1822	17,689,762	67,666	1,803,582	771,418	5,232,208
1823	19,088,433	34,242	916,523	501,468	5,833,826
1824	17,878,326	34,653	984,418	483,806	(945,495)
1825	20,098,713	25,771	1,216,091	500,283	5,983,629
1826	23,341,332	21,590	1,393,785	503,727	8,224,637
1827	19,712,283	19,886	1,495,845	1,738,350	6,827,196
1828	23,205,524	17,452	1,018,309	522,345	8,368,787
1829	22,681,966	14,503	1,517,175	613,983	9,624,294
1830	21,922,391	12,161	2,329,356	580,208	9,701,050
1831	24,224,442	6,934	3,210,815	1,084,630	18,279,170
1832	28,465,237	11,631	2,623,381	765,312	14,576,611
1833	29,032,509	2,759	3,967,683	945,476	10,930,875
1834	16,214,957	4,196	4,857,601	715,182	3,164,367
1835	19,391,311	10,459	14,757,601	1,270,716	17,857,274
1836	23,409,941	370	24,877,180	2,539,305	19,958,632

Source: U.S. Bureau of the Census, *Historical Statistics of the United States, 1789–1945* (Washington D.C.: United States Government Printing Office, 1949).

states were permitted to pay the apportioned amount from their treasuries at a discount of 15 percent. These taxes were clearly labeled as war taxes. The words "war taxes" were printed in italics in the legislation and provisions for automatic repeal within one year after the war were included. Yield from this tax was excellent and administrative costs were moderate. Seven states availed themselves of the opportunity to pay the tax directly from their own treasuries in 1814 and four states did so in 1815 and 1816. By paying the tax from their treasuries, they secured the discount and avoided having federal property tax collectors within their boundaries.

TOWARD THE GENERAL PROPERTY TAX

Those charged with implementing the U.S. Constitution clearly understood the connection between government structure and finance. The federalists, who favored a strong central government, wanted to assume all revolutionary war debts and to impose internal taxes to service the debt. The existence of the debt would ensure the loyalty of wealthy bondholders. Taxes would produce revenue to service the debt, to expand central government activities, and would contribute to a sound currency. The existence of an administrative bureaucracy would create a class with a vested interest in the government and the collection of taxes would solidify the federal government's authority to deal with individuals rather than with the states. The early anti-federalists, and later members of Jefferson's Republican party, opposed assumption of debt and internal taxes because they opposed a strong central government.

The early victories of the federalists pointed toward a strong federal government. Armed opposition to the federal excise tax and the first federal property tax was quickly put down, but memories of these incidents remained as reminders of the opposition to federal internal taxation. Federal indirect taxes and apportioned direct taxes fell unevenly on taxpayers in a geographically and economically diverse nation. Additionally, the stationing of federal tax collectors in every state and community was offensive to many. The election of Jefferson as president in 1800 confirmed the declining popularity of the federalist position and support for state and local rather than federal government.

The success of the second federal property tax can be attributed to the desire to support the second war against Great Britain, the clear declaration that it was a temporary tax, and to the optional provision for state assessment and collection. After the War of 1812, federal internal tax collection dwindled to insignificant and it appeared the peacetime business of government in the new federal system would be carried on by states and their local governments.[30] The next great question for the American constitutional order was whether or not the states would be able to develop a tax system that would produce the revenue necessary to carry on essential government activities without losing political support. Out of that effort would come another political invention—the general property tax.

4
Constitutionalizing Uniformity: The Nineteenth Century

One American historian has interpreted American history in the first half of the nineteenth century from the clashing perspectives of land and market. On one side were the subsistence farmers. Cheap land owned in fee simple made possible a degree of economic self-sufficiency and political independence that was unthinkable in the Europe from which settlers or their forefathers came. To them, the newly created word "democracy" meant government that was "weak, cheap and close to home."[1] On the other side were individuals who were dependent on the market for the sale of their labor or the sale of products produced by their enterprises. The market orientation favored a much more active government providing a sound system of money and banking, transportation systems, and a tax or tariff system favorable to American industrial and commercial development.

The clashing perspectives focused upon three, interrelated questions:

1. How democratic—how responsive to popular mandates—would government be?
2. Would government power be extensive and concentrated at the federal level or limited and diffused among the states?
3. To what extent and in what ways would government promote economic growth?[2]

The defeat of the federalists in the election of 1800 represented a setback for the market interests and a victory for those who opposed concentration of power at the federal level. Because the constitution vested control over foreign affairs and the currency in the federal government, tariff and banking policies would continue to be debated at the national level, but many other aspects of economic and tax policy would be focused at the state level.

The dichotomy between market interests and subsistence farming took somewhat different forms in different states. Generally, Democrats opposed internal improvements, banks, corporations, and tariffs and approved decentralized government. The market-oriented Whigs usually supported banks, local improvements, and tariffs, but party lines were fluid. Personalities and regional interests sometimes caused major deviations from the "party line." For example, the Democrats in New York, a major commercial state, joined the Whigs in supporting state-financed local improvements.

All of the issues listed above were linked to the tax question, but intense debate over state taxation was postponed by the relative affluence of the states and widespread borrowing for public improvements that followed the War of 1812.

TAX-FREE FINANCE, 1820–1840

Federal assumption of the Revolutionary War debts enabled states to pay off most outstanding obligations. In 1792 Hamilton calculated that remaining state debts amounted to about $8.3 million. Delaware and Connecticut were entirely free of debt, while New Hampshire, Massachusetts, New York, and New Jersey had only nominal debts. Several states had to borrow to finance military activities during the War of 1812, but most of that was reimbursed by the federal government.[3]

By the beginning of the 1820s, states were in good financial condition. With the exception of New York, states had only nominal debts and expenditures were limited. Land sales, license fees, and interest on investments provided revenue. Several states received income from dividends or bonuses from state chartered banks. In a number of states revenue from these sources made taxes largely unnecessary. The favorable financial situation set the stage for the expansion of state entrepreneurial activity as states borrowed to build transportation systems and to establish banks.

Explanations for heavy state borrowing in the 1820s and 1830s include the shift of political power from the federal government that accompanied the rise of Jackson's Democratic party. Another factor was the need for transportation and communication facilities created by the westward movement of population. Private capital was in short supply and market-oriented commercial interests raised little objection to the use of public capital for financing of development-related enterprises. After President Andrew Jackson weakened and eventually killed the Second Bank of the United States, state banks multiplied. Several states issued bonds to subscribe to bank stocks or to create state banking systems. The banks responded to the shortage of capital by issuing large quantities of paper currency, which created inflation. Profits and the price of land and securities rose, creating a feeling of prosperity and encouraging state policymakers to further expand their entrepreneurial activities.[4]

The first big work of internal improvement was a resounding success. In 1825 New York state completed the Erie Canal at a cost of approximately $7 million. The results were immediate and sensational. Before the work was finished, tolls exceeded interest charges and economic benefits were enormous. The cost of shipping a ton of freight from Buffalo to New York City dropped from $100 to $15 and the time required fell from twenty to eight days. Completion of the Erie Canal ensured that New York City would be the premier port on the eastern seaboard and increased the price of farm produce and the value of land in a vast area north of the Ohio River.[5]

The success of the Erie Canal became exhibit number one for a host of promoters who were able to enlist the enthusiastic support of merchants, brokers, land speculators, and farmers for canals in other states. The appearance of the railroad added to the boom by offering the possibility of opening areas that could not be served by canals. State bonds found a ready market in the United States and in Europe. European investors were impressed by the prosperity of the growing nation and the repayment record of both the states and the federal government.[6]

Table 4.1 shows the rapid escalation in state borrowing during the 1820s and 1830s. Pennsylvania, New York, and Louisiana were the largest borrowers. In almost all of the states there was a sharp acceleration in borrowing after 1835. Total borrowing in the years 1835 to 1838 was almost two and a half times the amount borrowed in the preceding five years.

Table 4.2 shows the state debts outstanding in 1838 and the purposes for which the money had been borrowed. These data disclose that more than one-third of the total had been borrowed to support the building of canals. Lumping railroad, canal, and turnpike borrowing together reveals that the predominant reason for borrowing was to provide transportation facilities. Most of the remainder went to the support of banks.

Table 4.1. State Borrowing, 1820–38 (in thousands)

	1820–25	1825–30	1830–35	1835–38	Total
Alabama	$100		$2,200	$8,500	$10,800
Arkansas				3,000	3,000
Florida			1,500		1,500
Illinois			600	11,000	11,600
Indiana			1,890	10,000	11,890
Kentucky				7,369	7,369
Louisiana	1,800		7,335	14,000	23,135
Maine			555		555
Maryland	58	$ 577	4,210	6,648	11,493
Massachusetts				4,290	4,290
Michigan				5,340	5,340
Mississippi			2,000	5,000	7,000
Missouri				2,500	2,500
New York	6,873	1,624	2,205	12,229	22,931
Ohio		4,400	1,701		6,101
Pennsylvania	1,680	6,300	16,130	3,167	27,277
South Carolina	1,250	310		4,000	5,560
Tennessee			500	6,648	7,148
Virginia	1,030	469	686	4,133	6,318
Total	$12,791	$13,680	$41,512	$107,824	$175,807

Source: B. U. Ratchford, *American State Debts* (Durham, N.C.: Duke University Press, 1941), p. 79.

Table 4.2. State Debts Outstanding in 1838, by Purpose (in thousands)

	Banking	Canals	Railroads	Turnpikes	Miscellaneous	Total
Alabama	$7,800		$3,000			$10,800
Arkansas	3,000					3,000
Florida	1,500					1,500
Illinois	3,000	$900	7,400		$300	11,600
Indiana	1,390	6,750	2,600	$1,150		11,890
Kentucky	2,000	2,619	350	2,400		7,369
Louisiana	22,950	50	500		235	23,735
Maine					555	555
Maryland		5,700	5,500		293	11,493
Massachusetts			4,290			4,290
Michigan		2,500	2,620		220	5,340
Mississippi	7,000					7,000
Missouri	2,500					2,500
New York		13,317	3,788		1,158	18,263
Ohio		6,101				6,101
Pennsylvania		16,580	4,964	2,596	3,167	27,307
South Carolina		1,550	2,000		2,204	5,754
Tennessee	3,000	300	3,730	118		7,148
Virginia		3,835	2,129	355	343	6,662
Total	$54,140	$60,202	$42,871	$6,619	$8,475	$172,307

Source: B. U. Ratchford, *American State Debts* (Durham, N.C.: Duke University Press, 1941), p. 88.

In 1837 there was a severe panic, but this did not stop state borrowing. Many projects were unfinished and stopping construction would have eliminated any possibility of a return. Many investors thought the panic was merely a financial phenomena that would have little effect on basic economic conditions but, in the autumn of 1839, a second banking crisis revealed the seriousness of the depression and the weaknesses of the banking and financial system. Further borrowing was impossible and work on uncompleted projects came to a halt. Banks that had been established with state borrowing could not pay the interest on the bonds.[7]

In 1840 and 1841 legislatures wrestled with the problem. Most states had little in the way of a revenue system. There was talk of repudiation. The taxpayers, who had expected the enterprises to provide a profit for the state, were in no mood to pay taxes to bail out the bondholders—many of whom were foreigners or eastern moneyed interests. Legislators used available funds, confiscated trust funds, liquidated investments, and issued treasury notes to provide temporary relief. Illinois levied an additional property tax of $.10 per $100.00 and pledged state bonds to secure a bank loan. Indiana tried to relieve taxpayers by reducing taxes and issued treasury notes and scrip. Maryland used the income and later the principal of a trust fund set up for schools.

Pennsylvania enacted a tax bill estimated to yield $600,000, but it brought in only $33,000. Another tax bill the following year also proved to be disappointing. Then Pennsylvania issued "relief notes" and authorized banks to buy them by issuing their own notes. The notes quickly depreciated and were used primarily to pay taxes and other obligations to the state. Finally, the state sold its bank stock at prices far below cost and required banks to make loans to it. This exhausted Pennsylvania's bag of tricks and it defaulted. One writer wryly commented that "every expedient has been resorted to short of taxation."[8] Another said, "Speculation and hatred of all forms of direct taxation were the causes of the downfall of Pennsylvania's credit.[9]

In all, nine states defaulted and several others came close. Pennsylvania's default was notable because over two-thirds of its bonds were held overseas and a deluge of bitter protests came across the Atlantic. Letters to a London newspaper from an English clergyman were widely reprinted in both countries. In one letter he asserted that Americans

> prefer any load of infamy however great, to any pressure of taxation however light. . . . I repeat again, that no conduct was ever more profligate than that of the State of Pennsylvania. History cannot pattern it: and let no deluded being imagine that they will ever repay a farthing—their people have tasted the dangerous luxury of dishonesty, and they will never be brought back to the homely rule of right.[10]

In 1842 European bankers joined in refusing to bid for a U.S. government loan and one English firm said the United States could expect no aid unless the federal government assumed the debts of the states. There were even rumors of another war with Great Britain. In 1843 a committee of the U.S. House of Representatives made a voluminous report advocating that the federal government assume all state debts, but the report was tabled.[11]

The defaults led to a flurry of political activity by bondholders who were frightened by the strength of demands for repudiation and by the reluctance of legislatures to deal with the problem. Thousands of dollars were contributed, especially by English bankers, to pay lobbyists. Attempts were made to enlist prominent men to write and speak in behalf of the bondholders. Bankers and others wrote to legislators and other public officials. Unsuccessful efforts were made to secure diplomatic help.[12]

In the end, four of the nine states that were in default repudiated bonds totaling approximately $13,770,000. Several states did levy taxes to pay interest, but opposition to higher taxes was widespread. In Maryland, for example, local governments often refused to appoint tax collectors and finally the governor was empowered to make the appointments. Illinois was unable to obtain a loan to complete the Illinois and Michigan canal until it levied a tax to pay interest on outstanding debt. Indiana refunded canal debt to cut interest payments in half, but bondholders suffered losses and the issue remained controversial until 1871, when a constitutional amendment prohibited the state from paying the claims.[13]

STATE TAX POLICY AFTER 1840

If the widespread use of state financial power to support banks and public improvements represented a victory for the interests favoring government promotion of economic growth, the failure of those enterprises favored the advocates of limited government. It also brought about a renewal of the debate over taxation and strengthened the hand of those concerned about tax equality. As one author put it:

> The quest for a tax-free system of state finance was a central feature of pre-Civil War America, yet tax revision, in particular the adoption of ad valorem taxation was widespread as well. State after state in North and South alike, finding that reliance on taxes could not be avoided moved to ad valorem. Replacing the previous systems of specific taxes, which had featured various rates for each carriage, slave, or one hundred acres, ad valorem systems taxed according to value. *Everywhere tax reform resonated to the rhetoric of equality of burdens.*[14]

In Georgia the state property tax rate had been slashed by half in 1824. Further reductions followed until 1835 when Georgia levied no poll or property taxes to support state government. By 1838, however, nontax sources of revenue had dried up. Several Georgia newspapers acknowledged the widespread aversion to direct taxes and anticipated strong opposition to substantial tax hikes, but urged Georgians to pay sufficient taxes to support the government until they could be eliminated without injury to the public.[15]

The renewed interest in taxation made Georgians increasingly aware of inequities in the state's tax laws. Property taxation at specific rates resulted in tax burdens unrelated to value. For example, town lots and merchandise were valued at less than one-tenth the value of rural lands and slaves, but paid half as much in taxes. These inequalities led to a long controversy over the proposals to adopt ad valorem taxes, which were finally adopted in 1852.

The author of a financial history of New York state points out that the principal sources of revenue in the first fifty years were receipts from the sale of public land, revenue derived from investment of public funds, lotteries, peddlers' licenses, and fees. There was a property tax system that seemed to be based upon a taxpayer's ability to pay as measured by property owned, but during the first forty years of the state's history, a state property tax levy was made in only fourteen years. In those years, the state tax was apportioned to the counties and the county supervisors added the sum required to the amounts to be raised for town and county purposes. In 1842, after a fourteen-year lapse, state taxation of property was resumed to enlarge the Erie Canal, to pay interest on the debt, and to pay the current expenses of government. By 1850 the question of taxation became vexing and continued to be a matter of much controversy as tax levies increased.[16]

In 1823 New York attempted to make the tax more general by amending it in an attempt to reach banks and incorporated companies. The comptroller made an investigation of bank and corporate taxation in other states and, as a result, the legislature passed a law including bank stock, notes, bonds, and mortgages as taxable property. The tax was to be divided among the counties in proportion to the amount of stock held by stockholders residing in each. The law was strongly opposed by banks and, although the law remained on the statutes book, efforts to enforce it soon ceased.[17]

CONSTITUTIONAL LIMITATIONS

The fiscal crises brought on by the default of internal improvement debt, the controversies over tax policy, and the political success of the Jacksonians with their philosophy of limited government contributed to the strength of the movement for constitutional limitation on legislative power. These limitations included both tax uniformity clauses and direct limitations on the amount of debt that a state could incur. Uniformity provisions not only limited the way that the tax burdens could be distributed, but discouraged tax increases by making it more difficult to target politically weak groups. As one author put it, "The magic words *uniform* and *proportional* were to be a spell against excessive tax freedom."[18]

Several of the original thirteen states, including Georgia and New York, modified their statutes in an attempt to make the property tax more uniform, but none of them incorporated a uniformity provision in their constitutions until after the Civil War. It was in the new states, being formed to the west, that the constitutional uniformity movement developed and spread. This was partly because the need to write a new constitution provided the opportunity to incorporate a uniformity provision, but it also reflected the political climate in those states. In thinly populated, newly settled states, the Jacksonian doctrines of equality and limited government were widely accepted and the idea of limiting legislative action by requiring that taxes be uniform in relation to value found a congenial environment.

The Northwest Territory

The Territory Northwest of the River Ohio, more commonly known as the Northwest Territory, was established by the Continental Congress in 1787. Government was initially in the hands of a governor and judges appointed by the Continental Congress and, after the ratification of the United States Constitution, by the president of the United States. Territorial expenses were largely paid from the proceeds of fees and by the national government. Consequently, taxation played an insignificant role in early territorial public finance. Local governments, on the other hand, were financed by taxation. The expenses of each county were estimated by the court of quarter sessions, and the amounts needed were apportioned among townships by commissioners appointed by the judges. The commissioners were to list all male persons over eighteen years of age, their stocks of cattle, and the annual value of lands and other property. Assessors, appointed by the judges, were to assess each individual in proportion to his wealth in the county and ability to pay in money or specific articles. The tax was to be paid in money or articles useful for public use. The tax was to be collected by the sheriff. Delinquents could be arrested and their property could be seized and auctioned.[19]

In 1795 the governor and judges revised the territorial laws, copying most of the new laws from the statutes of Pennsylvania. Property subject to assessment remained practically the same, but emphasis was upon the income earning capacity of the property. Taxes were to be distributed according to the yearly value or profit of a property owner's holdings. Unimproved and unsettled lands were exempted. The estimate of county expenses was made by a county board composed of elected and appointed officers. There was a tax limit of $.75 for each $200.00 of valuation and a provision for a poll tax not to exceed $1.00 on those males over twenty-one years of age having less than $100.00 in taxable property.[20]

In 1798 the governor and judges copied a law from Kentucky adding unimproved and wild lands to the list of property subject to taxation. Unimproved lands were to be divided into three classes or grades. Lands of the first grade were to be taxed at the rate of $.30 per hundred acres; second grade lands were taxed at $.20 per hundred acres; and third grade at $.10 per hundred acres. Because unimproved lands produced no income, taxing them was a departure from the idea that annual income or the ability to earn income was the proper measure of one's ability to pay taxes.

In 1799 the first general assembly of the territory provided that all taxes from lands were to be used by the territory for general expenses of the territory and the taxes on all other kinds of property were to be used for county government purposes. Property made taxable for county purposes included houses in town, mansion houses in the country worth more than $200, out lots, water and wind mills, ferries, horses, mules and asses over three years old, neat (ordinary domestic) cattle, and bond servants over twenty-one years of age. Able-bodied, single men with less than $200 in property were subject to a head tax. The rates to be applied to livestock and bond servants were specific, per-head taxes. Other property was to be taxed according to values fixed by the appraisers appointed by the county court.[21]

Property Taxation in Ohio

Ohio was the first state to be created out of the Northwest Territory. Ohio's constitution, adopted in 1802 without a popular referendum, contained no provision dealing with taxation, but the terms under which Ohio was admitted to the Union provided that 5 percent of the proceeds of public land sold by the United States government were to be granted to the state for the provision of roads.[22]

The first legislature, meeting in March 1803, provided for a slightly modified version of the territorial tax laws. Later that year, the legislature met again and revised the revenue system. The main reliance was placed on land taxes that were borne mostly by nonresidents. Two-thirds of the taxes collected were to be paid into the state treasury and one-third paid to county governments. County commissioners were given power to assess additional taxes within their jurisdiction.

Lands were to be listed by their owners in one of three classes, each of which was taxed at a uniform rate per hundred acres. The system did not work well. The classes in which land was to be listed were based entirely on the fertility of the soil. For example, bottom land was usually placed in the highest class, although some bottom land was worth little because it was subject to flooding or located far from markets. Self-assessment meant that land owners were strongly tempted not to list land or to place it in a lower class.

Collection of taxes from nonresidents proved to be a problem. Residents were to list their lands with township listers and nonresidents were to list their lands in the county where located. This listing requirement, combined with the frequent changes in county boundaries, imposed a heavy burden upon nonresident owners, especially if they owned property in several counties. Often nonresident owners found it necessary to employ a land agent in each county. In 1806 the legislature responded to this problem by creating six large collection districts for the taxation of the lands of nonresidents.

In the early years of statehood, Ohio passed a variety of laws providing penalties for the failure to list property and for the sale of property on which taxes were not paid. However, liberal redemption provisions made tax title uncertain. As the author of a comprehensive history of Ohio finance put it, "The purchase of a tax title was speculation which involved a certain loss if unsuccessful, and a title of doubtful validity if successful."[23] It was not until 1822 that an effective tax sale law was adopted. Even then there was much confusion and controversy over the status of lands with earlier delinquencies. The controversy was not settled until 1829, when it was required that all previously delinquent taxes be paid but the penalties were forgiven.

During the War of 1812, the Ohio state government assumed responsibility for the property tax levied by the federal government. This resulted in a discount on the amount due and avoided having federal officials assess and collect the tax within the state, but it substantially increased state taxes and fueled criticism. Several studies of the tax system were made, but none had a significant impact until a joint committee of the legislature made a lengthy report in 1825. This report, issued in response to the governor's suggestions for tax reform, stated that the system of land taxation had been suited for the condition of the country at the time of its adoption, but condemned it as unsuitable in a more advanced stage of development. The report pointed out, for example, that towns had grown up and the value of property was affected by nearness to public highways, navigable streams, and other local advantages. As a result of the suggestions in the governor's message and in the legislative committee report, the 1825 legislature adopted legislation that has been said to mark the beginning of the general property tax in Ohio.

Actually, the 1825 tax was not a uniform ad valorem property tax even though the list of taxable property was long. Real estate was to be taxed by valuation, while livestock was to be assessed at per-head figures stated in the statutes. Merchants and brokers were to be assigned to classes by the associate judges and their capital was to be assessed according to the class to which they belonged, rather than by the amount of capital actually employed. The list of exempt property was long. The law exempted lands and buildings used for religious or educational purposes and most mills and factories. Part of the revenue was used for the construction of canals and the excitement of this venture muted criticism of the new law.

In 1831 there were major amendments to the tax law that moved Ohio closer to a uniform ad valorem tax. Intangible property and capital used in manufacturing were added to the list of taxable property and the list of exemptions was greatly reduced. More kinds of property were subject to appraisal, but some property was still taxed at values fixed in the statutes.

A Uniformity Clause in Illinois

Illinois Territory was separated from Indiana Territory in 1809. The territorial governor and judges adopted the Indiana territorial law for the taxation of land, but for the next three years it appears to have been scarcely used. A levy of $.10 per $100.00 valuation was imposed in 1809, with the proceeds apparently going to the counties to build buildings. Evidently, funds from fines and fees provided sufficient revenue for the territorial government until 1812.

In 1812 the territorial legislature imposed a land tax for territorial use. Rather than taxing by valuation, the law reverted to the earlier system of taxing land by class. This law remained in force with little change until Illinois became a state in 1818.[24]

A provision in the Illinois constitution of 1818 has a strong claim to be called the first to require uniform and equal taxation of property. Strangely, its origins are unclear and it was ignored for many years after its adoption. The provision in the bill of rights stated:

> That the general, great and essential principles of liberty and free government may be recognized and unalterably established, we declare: . . . That the mode of levying a tax shall be by valuation so that every person shall pay a tax in proportion to the value of the property that he or she has in his or her possession.[25]

Apparently, this provision received little attention or debate in the constitutional convention. It was included in the first draft of the constitution and remained unamended throughout the entire convention. The closest approximation to the wording of this provision in prior constitutions was in the Maryland constitution of 1776. The Maryland provision read:

> The levying of taxes by poll is grievous and oppressive and ought to be abol-

ished; that paupers ought not to be assessed for the support of the government; but *every person in the State ought to be assessed for the support of the government, according to his actual worth, in real or personal property, within the State*; yet fines, duties, or taxes, may properly and justly be imposed or laid, with a political view, for the good governments and benefit of the community. [Emphasis added.][26]

A clear difference between the Illinois provision and the Maryland provision is that the Illinois provision suggested that the uniform property tax was to be the only form of taxation. The Maryland provision, in contrast, gave unlimited permission for other forms of taxation, except the poll tax.

If the origin of the uniformity provision in the Illinois constitution is strange, so was its history in the first years of its existence—it was ignored! The land tax continued to be based on a rough classification of land into classes rather than on value, although there was considerable tinkering with the classification. Under the law of 1819, the method of determining class was changed to include considerations other than fertility as determined by geographic location. This method of taxing lands was in clear violation of the constitution, but a semblance of a general property tax did emerge. Not all property was taxed by each governmental authority, but nearly all objects of value were taxed by some authority. Land was the principal source of tax revenue, but several kinds of tangible personal property were taxable. The first tax on intangible property, a tax on bank stock, was imposed but it was abandoned in 1823, primarily because of administrative difficulties.[27]

The Illinois tax law of 1839 was a complete revision of the property tax system. It eliminated the old system of land classification and specified that both land and personal property should be taxed on the basis of their true value. It did not include a general definition of property, but contained a list of taxable personal property that included such tangible items as livestock, wagons, stock in trade, and all other species of personal property. In addition, there was specific mention of money actually loaned and the stock of incorporated companies. Exemptions were narrowed, but lands belonging to the United States, or the state, or exempted by terms of compact between the state and the United States were exempt as were burying grounds, church grounds, and grounds used by literary institutions not exceeding ten acres. The 1839 law eliminated the old system of making some kinds of property taxable for state purposes and other kinds taxable for local purposes. Instead, the state rate was fixed at $.20 for each $100.00 of value and the county maximum rate at $.50.[28]

Almost immediately after the passage of the 1839 act, Illinois was plunged into financial crises because of internal improvement debts. There was resistance to increased taxes and calls for repudiation, but the crises was weathered, and in 1845 the legislature replaced the list of taxable property in the tax law by the phrase, "all property, real and personal within the state, shall be liable for taxation." With this act, the statutory law of Illinois was finally in conformity with the constitutional provision enacted some twenty-seven years earlier.

SPREAD OF UNIFORMITY CLAUSES

Two years after Illinois put a uniformity clause in its first constitution, Missouri adopted its first constitution. Missouri's bill of rights contained a provision that "all property subject to taxation in this state shall be taxed in proportion to its value."[29] Unlike the Illinois provision, Missouri's did not require that all property be taxed.

The original constitution of Tennessee, adopted in 1796, included a limitation based on quantity rather than value. It required that no 100 acres of land be taxed higher than any other and that a town lot not be taxed higher than 200 acres of land. Poll taxes could not be more than the tax on 100 acres of land and taxes on slaves could not be more than that on 200 acres of land. In 1834 this provision was changed to one requiring uniformity according to value.

In the quarter of a century beginning with Tennessee's adoption of a uniformity clause and ending with the Civil War, fourteen states adopted constitutional provisions requiring that property taxes be uniform. All except five contained universality provisions, requiring that all property except for governmental, religious, educational, and charitable property be taxed. Nine of the fourteen provisions were in newly adopted constitutions, while the other five provisions were in revised constitutions or constitutional amendments. Two uniformity clauses were adopted during the Civil War and a number of southern states added uniformity clauses to postwar constitutions.

One of the most elaborate uniformity provisions was adopted in Ohio in 1851. An effort was made to ensure that all types of property including rapidly growing forms of tangible and intangible personal property would be taxed. This was done by spelling out in considerable detail just what should be taxed:

> Section II. Laws shall be passed, taxing by uniform rule, all moneys, credits, investments in bonds, stocks, joint stock companies, or otherwise; and all real and personal property according to its true value in money; but burying grounds, public schoolhouses, houses used exclusively for public worship, institutions of purely public charity, public property used exclusively for any public purpose, and personal property, to an amount not exceeding in value two hundred dollars, for each individual, may, by general laws, be exempted from taxation; but all such laws, shall be subject to alteration or repeal; and the value of all property, so exempted, shall, from time to time, be ascertained and published as directed by law.
>
> Section III. The general assembly shall provide by law for taxing the notes and bills, discounted or purchased, money loaned, and all other property, effects or dues, of every description, without deduction, of all banks now

existing or hereafter created, and all bankers, so that all property employed in banking shall always bear a burden of taxation equal to that imposed on the property of individuals.[30]

The Ohio provision required both uniform and universal taxation. It made clear that all property except charitable, religious, and public property was to be taxed.

Table 4.3. Nineteenth-Century Uniformity Provisions (first appearance in state constitutions)

	Year	Universality Provision
Illinois	1818	Yes
Missouri	1820	No
* Tennessee[1]	1834	Yes[2]
Arkansas	1836	No
Florida	1838	No
* Louisiana	1845	No
Texas	1845	Yes
Wisconsin	1848	No
California	1849	Yes
* Michigan[3]	1850	No
* Virginia	1850	Yes[4]
Indiana	1851	Yes
* Ohio	1851	Yes
Minnesota	1857	Yes
Kansas	1859	No
Oregon	1859	Yes
West Virginia	1863	Yes
Nevada	1864	Yes[5]
* South Carolina	1865	Yes
* Georgia	1868	No
* North Carolina	1868	Yes
* Mississippi	1869	Yes
* Maine	1875	No
* Nebraska	1875	No
* New Jersey	1875	No
Montana	1889	Yes
North Dakota	1889	Yes
South Dakota	1889	Yes
Washington	1889	Yes
Idaho[6]	1890	Yes
Wyoming	1890	No
* Kentucky	1891	Yes
Utah	1896	Yes

*Indicates amendment or revised constitution.
1. The Tennessee constitution of 1796 included a unique provision requiring taxation of land to be uniform per 100 acres.
2. One thousand dollars of personal property and the products of the soil in the hands of the original producer were exempt in Tennessee.
3. The Michigan provision required that the legislature provide a uniform rule of taxation, except for property paying specific taxes.
4. Except for taxes on slaves.
5. Nevada exempted mining claims.
6. One provision in Idaho requires uniformity as to class, another seems to prescribe uniform taxation.
Source: Glenn W. Fisher, "The Evolution of the General Property Tax in the Nineteenth Century: The Search for Equality," Property Tax Journal, Vol. 6, No. 2 (June, 1987), 105.

Intangible property, especially that owned by banks, was singled out for specific mention. The Ohio provision became the model for the Minnesota constitution of 1857 and for several later constitutions.

Except for the post–Civil War constitutions of the southern states, most uniformity provisions were adopted in states that were on the frontier at the time and most were in new constitutions. Table 4.3 shows the spread of uniformity and universality clauses in the nineteenth century. A uniform property tax is defined as one levied ad valorem at uniform rates on all property *subject to taxation*. A provision requiring uniform classification within a class does not qualify unless there is also a provision requiring that all property be in the same class. A provision is classified as "universal" if all property, other than religious, governmental, charitable, and educational property, must be taxed. Small "family" exemptions or the exemption of small amounts of property owned by widows or paupers does not disqualify a provision from being classified as requiring universal taxation.

There is, of course, room for differences of opinion as to how particular provisions should be classified. The wording of property tax provisions differs considerably and sometimes two or more provisions must be read together to determine the effect. Newhouse defines nine types of tax uniformity clauses, but some relate to nonproperty taxes and not all of the others would be classified as uniformity clauses under the definitions used for Table 4.3. Court decisions in some states are complex. In some states interpretations have developed that would, to the layman, seem to be contrary to the plain meaning of a constitutional provision. In preparing the table, emphasis was on the constitutional wording. No attempt was made to analyze the line of cases interpreting each provision, but in a few instances, early court opinions were used as an aid to classification.[31]

THE ORIGINS OF UNIFORMITY

In an important article on tax uniformity, William L. Matthews stated that it is difficult to find the beginnings of the idea of uniform taxation in the history of this country or abroad.[32] There were sporadic demands for tax uniformity in the colonial and revolutionary periods, but in the early state constitutions there was far more concern that taxes should be levied according to law and for a public purpose. Matthews finds little evidence that the concept of uniform taxation had a definite legal meaning or existence prior to its appearance in state constitutions. Matthews also points out that few definite origins for the concept can be found in the literature of political economy.

The Spirit of Equality

The paucity of debate seems to indicate that the idea of uniform property taxation was so much in harmony with prevailing opinion that debate was unnecessary.

One writer states that the dominant political concept of democracy was expressed in the demands for uniformity and universality. He identifies the uniformity and universality movement as one of the most significant interplays of economic and political forces in U.S. history. Certainly uniformity fit well with the passion for equality that has been identified with the nineteenth century.[33]

One manifestation of the prevailing opinion was the political success of the Jacksonian Democrats. Adherents to the Jacksonian cause believed in limited government administered by "the people" rather than by an elected or appointed elite. Democracy was to be brought about by frequent elections, long ballots, and the elimination of property qualifications for voting. Jacksonian principles were compatible with the "spoils" system because that system resulted in high turnover in elective and appointed office. Demands for equality focused on equality of process rather than equality of results, especially if equality of results could be obtained only by expert or centralized administration.

The Jacksonians were practical people who depended on experience and common sense rather than theory.[34] Apparently they accepted the equality and justice of the general property tax as an obvious truth, not something that had to be proved by reason. Many workingmen's newspapers of the Jacksonian period included among the slogans on their masts, "Equal Taxation of Property," but rarely was there any discussion of the issue.[35]

One of the few surviving statements concerning the property tax by a prominent Jacksonian is found in Robert J. Walker's classic statement against protectionism. Walker was Andrew Jackson's Secretary of the Treasury and would later be one of the territorial governors of Kansas. Walker, without elaboration, adopts taxation in proportion to property owned as the proper standard of justice in taxation and denounces the tariff as class legislation for the benefit of manufacturers:

> Legislation for classes is against the doctrine of equal rights, repugnant to the spirit of our free institutions, and, it is apprehended by many, may become but another form for privileged order under the name of protection instead of privilege—indicated here not by rank or title, but by profits and dividends extracted from the many by taxes imposed on them for the benefit of the few.[36]

The Jacksonian attack on the tariff was part of a larger theme that saw tariffs, excise taxes, and borrowing for public improvements as part of a scheme by the market-oriented Whigs to advance the interests of large corporations and monopolies at the expense of the masses. In his fourth annual address, President James K. Polk, a Democrat from Tennessee, declared that the Whigs' "American System" was designed to "encourage large and extravagant expenditure, and thereby to increase the public patronage, and maintain a rich and splendid government at the expense of taxed and improvised people." It would alter the government from the "plain, cheap, and simple" confederation of states conceived by the founders into "a consolidated empire, depriving the States of their reserved rights and the people of their just power and control in the administration of their government."[37]

There was a tendency among the Jacksonians to believe that complexity in public affairs was a camouflage for injustice. One democrat newspaper argued that the reason the Bank of the United States was so bad was that its operations were so extended that they could not be understood. The intricacies of the tariff were also seen as a conscious effort to defraud. In 1842 one Democrat paper stated that indirect taxes were attempts to disguise the weight of the tax. The *Bay State Democrat* put it succinctly: "Indirect taxation is a cheat. Unequal taxation is an injustice. Unnecessary taxation is robbery." In the same year, another paper put it another way: "So many miserable drains are devised by the cunning and invention of modern private purloiners, through Government means, that it requires vast intelligence and application to detect the devices by which wealth is abstracted by those who do not work, out of those who do."[38]

One of the important functions of Jacksonian rhetoric was to help the individual order the complex world. To individuals coping with the massive changes in society and in their lives resulting both from residence on a frontier and from the changes in society, this message had an intuitive appeal. It simplified complex issues and identified and personalized an "enemy" in a way that facilitated decision-making by practical men, many of whom lacked the background and all of whom lacked the time to study political economy. To those individuals, the general property tax had an obvious attraction. Taxing all property in proportion to its value seemed to promise both simplicity and fairness and it could be levied and administered at the local level. As an added bonus, a requirement that tax revenue be obtained from a uniform tax on property tended to limit expenditures. Legislatures could not hide taxes or impose taxes disproportionately on politically weak groups. These ideas were to be important in American politics long after the defeat of Jackson's Democratic party.

In 1851, the year that Ohio revised its constitution to include a comprehensive uniformity clause, the *Cincinnati Enquirer* editorialized:

No distinction should be made in different kinds of property. The State has no more right to tax real property than personal or any other kind of property: its right of taxation is just the same in reference to them all, and no stronger as to one than another. The right comes from the same common source, the consent of the people. The people are all equal—they partake equally of the blessings of the government, and their property should share equally in its burdens—In short, equality all round, equal burdens for equal rights and privileges, is the true rule and morality of taxation.[39]

A member of the West Virginia constitutional convention of 1861–63 said that he regarded the principle of equality of property taxation as second only to the great principle of equality in representation. A member of the Nevada constitutional convention of 1864 declared that the failure of any political body to make every species of property subject to taxation had the effect of creating a political class.[40]

Although uniformity clauses limited legislative policy choices, the property tax provided a sound basis for financing a constitutional order in the new states. Property was visible, it existed within the boundaries of every governmental subdivision, title could be attached to secure payment and there was a connection between property ownership and the need for government. Many state constitutions adopted after the fiscal crises brought on by the internal improvements boom contained provisions limiting state involvement in internal improvements. They also recognized government's role in registering and protecting property rights and in the provision of schools. The governor of Ohio in 1828 said, "The revenue, the internal improvements, and the school systems, are each essential links in the chain of our state policy: and by contributing to one, strength is communicated to all."[41]

In 1827 the governor of Kentucky made the case for taxation as a payment for the protection of property: "Property affords the only means of paying taxes, and for the protection of property most of the institutions of society have been established. It would seem, therefore, but right that men of property should pay for sustaining them."[42] In 1849 the governor of California said: "The law protects every man in his person and property. For the protection it gives his person he ought to pay a capitation or poll tax; and for the protection it gives his property, he ought of right to pay a tax in proportion to its amount and value."[43]

A strong statement of the spirit of the property tax was given in the final review at the Oregon constitutional convention in 1859:

> The article upon finances so provides that every citizen shall bear his equal proportion of the burdens of government—equal and uniform taxation. It has been complained, or it has been urged as an argument . . . against the formation of state government at this time, that the population is comparatively scarce, and that the wealth of the country is in a comparatively few hands. It is true that the population of the country is comparatively small, but the wealth of the country is comparatively great. And is it a burden that a man should pay taxes upon the property he really possesses? Sir, give me the wealth—and I will consent the most cheerfully to pay the taxes to meet the expenses of government.[44]

SUMMARY AND CONCLUSIONS

Federalism may have been invented by the delegates to the federal constitutional convention in 1787, but they provided only the outline of the new system of government. Many details remained to be worked out and many evolutionary changes would occur in the following years. Alexander Hamilton and his fellow federalists attempted to use finance as an instrument for strengthening the federal government, but opposition to federal internal taxes was a major element in their failure. By the end of Jackson's administration it was clear that most of the ordinary business of government would be carried on by state and local governments. Tax and expenditure policy-making shifted to the state level, but created little controversy at first. In 1820 the states were in good financial condition. They had little debt and taxes were low, but they soon moved aggressively to promote state banks, and to build canals, turnpikes, and other transportation facilities. Optimism was high and it was widely believed that profits from these enterprises would keep taxes low. The low-tax dream was shattered late in the 1830s as financial crises and the failure of many of the enterprises made it necessary for a number of states to default on their bonds and, reluctantly, to raise taxes. Tax policy became an important political issue in established states as legislatures moved toward a broad-based ad valorem property tax.

At roughly the same time, property tax uniformity clauses began to appear in the constitutions of newly admitted states. The reasons for this are not entirely clear. The legal concept of tax uniformity was not well developed and there is little discussion of the concept in the political or economic literature. Apparently the ideal of uniform taxation of all property was so much in the spirit of the times that it seemed self-evident. Uniform taxation of all property appealed to the spirit of equality, which was a strong influence long after Jackson's Democratic party lost the presidency.

The movement for constitutional uniformity clauses can also be seen as part of a broader movement to place limitations on legislatures. The writers of the earliest state constitutions, remembering problems with the British governors, provided for weak executive branches and strong legislatures. As time passed, faith in the legislative branch was weakened. The internal improvements boom of the 1820s and 1830s and its aftermath raised many doubts about the collective judgment of legislators. Property tax uniformity provisions limited the power of the legislature to determine the structure of taxation and complimented debt limits by making it more difficult to raise taxes on the politically vulnerable.

The nineteenth century constitutional tax provisions were generally quite brief, although, beginning with Ohio in 1851, some states lengthened the provision in a effort to make clear that all forms of intangible property were to be taxed. Administrative arrangements were left for legislative determination. In the spirit of Jacksonian democracy, it was assumed that competent administration would result from frequent election of local officials. It remained to be seen whether that kind of administration would produce uniformity under frontier conditions and in the evolving commercial economy.

5
Writing a Uniformity Clause: The Case of Kansas

The conditions under which the first state constitution was written differed from state to state, but there were many similarities, at least among the new states to the west. All of these territories were thinly populated, there was little in the way of public or private infrastructures, and there were no governments except for the rudimentary system of territorial government established by Congress. The delegates to the constitutional conventions were anxious to write constitutions that would serve as the basis for admission as states and would provide basic government services. They wanted a government that would maintain law and order, provide for the recording and protection of land titles, develop a road system, and establish schools, prisons, and other essential institutions. Taxes were recognized as a necessary, if unwelcome, component of the package.

Kansas was admitted near the middle of the constitutional uniformity movement—after years in which the constitutional provisions had been modified and refined, but before administrative problems had created widespread doubts about the feasibility of uniform taxation of all wealth. It is a good case study because the two sets of revenue laws and the four proposed constitutions written during the territorial period are a sample of the constitutional provisions and statutes then in effect in the states west of the Appalachian Mountains.[1]

Kansas was admitted to the Union less than three months before Fort Sumter surrendered and the Civil War began. In the decade preceding the Civil War, arguments over the formation of the Kansas Territory and the terms under which Kansas was to be admitted to statehood were important events in the polarization of attitudes and opinions that led the nation to war.[2] The Kansas-Nebraska Act (1854) changed the rules for determining whether new states would be slave or free and focused national attention upon Kansas Territory as the inhabitants struggled, sometimes violently, to establish a government and write a constitution that would lead to the admission of Kansas as a state.

THE KANSAS-NEBRASKA ACT

In January 1854 a bill to organize the territories of Kansas and Nebraska came before the U.S. Senate. Introduced by Senator Stephen A. Douglas of Illinois and supported by President Pierce, the bill proposed to replace the Missouri Compromise of 1820 with a policy of "popular sovereignty" as a way of deciding whether newly admitted states should be slave or free. The Missouri Compromise resulted in the admission of Missouri as a slave state, but prohibited slavery in any other territory acquired by the Louisiana Purchase north of 36 degrees, 30 minutes (the southern boundary of Missouri). The Kansas-Nebraska Act explicitly repealed that provision and stated:

> it being the true intent and meaning of this act not to legislature slavery into any Territory or State, nor to exclude it therefrom, but to leave the people thereof perfectly free to form and regulate their domestic institutions in their own way, subject only to the Constitution of the United States.[3]

The fight over the bill was bitter. The free-soil newspapers of the North made violent attacks on the bill, while supporters of the bill replied in kind. It was largely a sectional fight that polarized viewpoints and accentuated the differences between North and South. When the bill was passed and signed by the president late in May 1854, free-soil advocates lamented and proslavery forces rejoiced, but the battle for Kansas had just begun. Before Kansas was admitted as a state, four different constitutional proposals would be drafted. Each of the proposed constitutions contained different tax provisions. In addition, the territorial legislature drafted two different revenue laws and made extensive revision to one of them, but very little revenue was collected.

When Kansas territory was established, the country was occupied by Indians, most of whom had been moved into Kansas by earlier treaties. The only legal white residents were a few missionaries, traders dealing with the Indians, Indian agents, and the army with its civilian employees.

The Indians had been moved into Kansas with the understanding that the area was to become their permanent abode, but as population pressed westward, agitation for their removal began. As a result, the Indian commissioner negotiated a series of treaties in 1854 and 1855 by which the Indians ceded all or part of their lands. In many cases smaller reserves were retained in trust by the Indian Office or given as allotments to individual Indians. White settlers sometimes bought the Indian allotments or simply occupied land before the Indian claims were extinguished. This and later acts of Congress granting a large part of the state's lands to railroad companies created problems of land titles that plagued Kansas and complicated property taxation for many years.[4]

The problems of land title could wait. The organization of the territory and the attempts of proslavery and antislavery forces to win the state created a population boom. Settlers from Missouri moved west, either because they saw the possibility of opening Kansas to slavery or simply because they were looking for economic opportunities. The towns of Atchison and Leavenworth were settled primarily by Missourians and were centers of proslavery sentiment.

At the same time, there were organized efforts by abolitionists to colonize the state with free-soil settlers. The Massachusetts Emigrant Aid Company, soon to become the New England Emigrant Aid Company, raised money to recruit and support abolitionist emigrants to Kansas. Settlers sent by this company were largely responsible for founding the towns of Lawrence and Topeka. Wabaunsee was founded by settlers aided by the New Haven congregation of the famous abolitionist preacher, Henry Ward Beecher. Because the congregation had contributed both rifles and Bibles, the colony was known as the "Beecher Bible and Rifle Colony."

Feelings ran high and inevitably turned to violence. The national interest in Kansas was heightened as journalists popularized the term "Bleeding Kansas" and instances of violence were widely publicized. This complicated the task of governing the territory and obtaining the admission of Kansas as a state.

TERRITORIAL TAX LAWS

The organic act provided that the federal government would pay the salaries of the executive and judicial officers. The federal government also paid the salaries of the legislators and specified employees of the legislative branch and certain incidental expenses of the legislature, such as for a library and printing expenses. There was also an appropriation for the costs of buildings at the seat of government.[5] The only provisions dealing with territorial taxation were that no tax could be imposed on the property of the United States, and that lands or other property of nonresidents could not be taxed higher than the property of residents.[6] Additionally, sections sixteen and thirty-six of each township were set aside to be used for school purposes.

The first of the ten territorial governors to serve during the territorial years arrived in 1854. Governor A. H. Reeder was from Pennsylvania and was antislavery in his sentiments. He called an election in November 1854 to elect a delegate to Congress and one in March 1855 to choose members of the legislature. In both cases large numbers of Missourians crossed into the state to elect proslavery candidates. The governor was unhappy about the results but recognized the elections as valid.[7]

Governor Reeder chose the town of Pawnee on the Fort Riley military reservation as the territorial capital. His choice of this location, well west of the settled area, was evidently caused by his interest in the Pawnee Town Company. The Pawnee Town Company had erected a forty-by-eighty-foot stone capital building that was two stories in height, and an army major had built a boarding house large enough to accommodate forty people. The legislature met there for four days and, defying the governor, adjourned to Shawnee Methodist Mission near the Missouri border. The legislators' motives were no purer than the governor's. Many had interests in and, perhaps, were actually residents of Missouri.

Governor Reeder realized that many settlers were occupying lands to which they did not have clear title but, with inordinate optimism, addressed these words concerning taxation to the legislature: If you should find it necessary to levy and collect taxes for county or other purposes, I have no doubt the pre-emptor, who claims inchoate title in his quarter section, could be assessed thereon for his share of the public burden."[8] The laws passed by the first legislature, called the "bogus laws" by the abolitionists, were based on Missouri laws. These included the Missouri slave code and a provision decreeing the death penalty for anyone aiding a slave in escaping or promoting a slave rebellion. Imprisonment was prescribed for anyone speaking out against slavery or trying to have it abolished in the state. It was further provided that no one conscientiously opposed to holding slaves should sit on a jury trying anyone for violating these provisions.[9]

The abolitionists were outraged and in the fall of 1855 organized a separate government. A convention was held at Topeka, a constitution was adopted, and state officers were elected. This created two governments, the "bogus" government recognized by the federal government and the free-state government headed by Governor Charles Robinson. In July 1856, the Topeka government came to an end as the legislature was dispersed by federal troops.[10]

TAX LAWS OF 1855

Chapters 137 and 138 of the laws enacted by the 1855 legislature dealt with revenue. Many sections were copied word-for-word from the Missouri statutes.[11] Other sections were changed only to substitute the word "territory" for "state" or to reflect the difference between Kansas and Missouri local government. The tax statutes included a long list of types of taxable property. The list was comprehensive and clearly reflected a desire for a broad tax base. The specific mention of various kinds of intangible property, such as leaseholds over ten years, shares of stock, bills of exchange, and money loaned at interest, indicates recognition that intangible property constitutes wealth that should be taxed. In an attempt to avoid double taxation, the value of a corporation's capital was deducted from the value of its property. Apparently the word "capital" referred to the original investment in the corporation by shareholders. Such capital was to be taxed, probably at face or par value, by levying a tax on the stockholders to be paid by the corporation. The corporation could recover the amounts paid by billing the stock owners or by subtracting it from dividends paid.

The territorial taxes were established, by rate, in the statutes. All property subject to taxation was taxed at a rate of one-sixth part of 1 percent (1⅔ mills) of assessed value. This meant that a farm worth $1,000 would be subject to a territorial tax of $1.67. The tax on free male persons between 21 and 55 years of age was

$.50 cents. Although included in the property tax statute, this was a capitation or poll tax.[12]

Counties were permitted to add a county levy to the territorial levy. The county levy could not exceed the territorial tax by more than 100 percent (twice the territorial rate or 3⅓ mills). Unlike the territorial tax, the county tax was not levied at a fixed rate. The law provided that after the tax books had been prepared county tribunals would "ascertain the sum necessary to defray the expenses of their respective counties, and fix the rates of taxes on the several subjects, so as to raise the required sum and cause the same to be entered in proper columns of the tax book."[13]

Chapter 155 of the law adopted in1855 provided for the incorporation of towns and gave the trustees the power to appoint assessors and collectors. Apparently, it was contemplated that municipal taxes would be administered separately from the territorial and county taxes. The law also authorized the town collector to sue for nonpayment of taxes and provided that the taxes of nonresidents might be collected from the tenants, who then were allowed to collect from the owner or to offset the taxes against amounts owed to the owner.

The statute contained a rather complete set of procedures for administering the tax. Instructions for preparing the tax book detailed how property was to be classified and listed. There were instructions for handling omitted property and it was required that a duplicate copy of each assessment be signed by the assessor and delivered to the head of the family, or, in his absence, to another member of the family. There were provisions for appeal of assessments to the county tribunal and instructions for delivery of the completed book to the county clerk.

The sheriff was the collector of revenue and there were detailed instructions as to how the tax book was to be delivered to him, how he was to demand payment, and procedures for seizing and selling goods for the nonpayment of taxes. There were also instructions regarding the time and procedures for the collector to settle accounts with the county treasurer.

The assessor was to be paid $3 per day worked, but the collector was compensated by fees based on the percentage collected. The fee ranged from 2 to 7 percent depending on the type of tax, the person or organization from which it was collected, and the amount collected.

A separate chapter of the 1855 laws provided for a poll tax of $1 on every person entitled to vote in the territory.[14] This $1 tax was in addition to the permanent poll tax levied in the property tax chapter. It was a one-time tax to be collected on or before the first Monday in October 1855 (election day) and was not a revenue measure but an attempt to facilitate voting by Missourians. The election laws allowed free white male citizens, and certain Indians, who were residents of the territory and had paid a tax to vote.[15] The sheriff was required to have his tax books at the place where elections were held to receive taxes tendered. Anyone offering to vote was presumed to be eligible and, if the judges challenged this right and examined the prospective voter under oath, no evidence contradicting his testimony was received. If, on the other hand, the judges first received other evidence of the taxpayer's ineligibility, the voter's oath would not be conclusive. Section 11 added other provisions denying the vote to those convicted of violating the fugitive slave acts and requiring challenged voters to swear to uphold those acts.[16]

These requirements enraged those who wanted Kansas to be a free state. A convention of free-staters meeting in Lawrence when this bill was being considered denounced members of the "bogus legislature" as:

> having now before them a bill which they will probably enact into law, making the right of suffrage in the Territory dependent upon the payment of the sum of $1, without reference to the matter of inhabitancy, thus attempting to give the ballot-box by law for all future time to persons from foreign states.[17]

The controversy engendered by this act is indicated by the fact that the Committee on Finance in the 1857 legislature, still controlled by proslavery advocates, considered a bill to repeal the 1855 poll tax law even though it was no longer in effect. The committee report rejected the idea of repeal on the ground that it would appear to the world like a "valorous attack on a dead lion."[18] The report went on to point out that attacks on the law had come from both the east and north, but that in Maine, New Hampshire, Vermont, and Massachusetts taxation was an elementary and fundamental principle in the basis of representation and that Rhode Island had an identical "dollar law" in its constitution. After citing other examples of poll taxes in northern states the committee report concluded: "The Committee deems it a waste of time to defend the policy of law that expired by its own limitation more than a year ago, nor are they disposed at this late date to enter the tomb and dissect its carcass."[19]

Little revenue was collected under the laws enacted by the "bogus legislature." There was both active and passive resistance to the taxes imposed by the proslavery legislature. In the spring of 1856 a protest meeting in Osawatomie fell into a bitter debate, which resulted in the withdrawal of the more conservative members. The more-radical group that remained passed resolutions repudiating the territorial government and laws, the tax laws in particular, and pledged to resist if enforcement was attempted. About the same time military companies, including one led by John Brown, Jr., were organized in Franklin and Anderson counties.[20]

The failure to collect revenue under the 1855 laws was not only due to resistance from free-staters, but also to demographic and economic factors. The population was only a few thousand people, few land titles were perfected, and cash to make payment was scarce.

TAX LAWS OF 1858

In the fall of 1857 territorial elections were held in Kansas. Proslavery forces appeared to have carried the legislature, but investigation revealed massive fraud.

After Governor Robert J. Walker rejected the fraudulent ballots, the free-state forces were in control of the legislature. In 1858 this legislature replaced the revenue law enacted in 1855 with a completely new law.[21] The new statute followed the Wisconsin statutes even more closely than the 1855 law had followed the Missouri statute.[22] The only substantive difference in the definition of taxable property was that the Kansas statute contained a provision, not found in the Wisconsin version, that allowed debts to be deducted from the amount of personal property.

The organization of local government provided for by the 1855 legislature reflected the southern orientation toward the county as the principal local government. The laws enacted in 1858, by contrast, reflected the New England influence and emphasized the town form. This was not the pure town government of New England in which counties either did not exist or were largely geographic, not governmental, entities. Instead, it was the hybrid that grew up in many of the northern states and which is now referred to as "township government." Town or townships (both terms were used in the statutes) were rural subdivisions of the county. Municipalities were cities and were subdivided into wards. The law provided for town assessors or, within cities, ward assessors, rather than county assessors. Town assessors were to be elected for one-year terms at the annual town meeting. As in the case of the 1855 law there were detailed instructions for administering the tax. These included directions as to the headings to be placed on the assessment roll, and dates on which the rolls were to be completed. The secretary of the territory was given the power to prescribe forms and issue instructions. The board of supervisors of each county was given the power to adjust the aggregate value of real estate in any town or ward to produce a just relationship between the valuations of real estate in the various towns of the county.

An interesting feature of the 1858 laws was the strong self-assessment provision. Section 27 provided that an owner of personal property could, before the assessor had finished his work, file an affidavit stating the value of his personal property, less the value of any stock in a corporation liable to taxation on its capital. An owner of real estate could file an affidavit signed by himself and a disinterested resident of the same ward or town stating the value of his real estate. It was the duty of the assessor to value the property at the amount specified in the affidavit.

The assessor was to assess at its true cash value all property not assessed by its owner. When submitting the assessment roll, he was to attach an oath stating that all property not covered by an affidavit had been assessed at what was believed to be the true cash value.

The county board of supervisors, at its annual meeting, was to determine and estimate the amount of money to be raised in each town and ward in their county for school purposes.[23] In addition, the board was to determine the amount to be raised for county purposes and to apportion that amount, together with the territorial tax, among the several towns and wards in proportion to the valuation as equalized by the board of supervisors. Township taxes were to be levied at the annual town meeting.

The town clerk, after receiving notice of the amount of territorial, county, and school tax apportioned to the town, was to calculate the amount of these taxes, plus the local taxes and 5 percent for expenses, to be charged against each property on the assessment rolls.

The township collector could seize any goods and chattels of a person owing taxes and sell them to satisfy either personal or real estate taxes. If the township collector failed to collect the tax, the county treasurer could order the sheriff to sell "goods and chattels, lands and tenements" to satisfy unpaid personal property taxes.[24]

The 1858 legislature repudiated the actions of the pro-slavery legislature by providing that no revenue raised was to be used to pay appropriations previously made or to redeem warrants issued prior to January 1, 1858.[25]

1860 AMENDMENTS TO THE TAX LAWS

The 1860 legislature changed back to the county assessor system and made several other changes. The statement of taxable property and definitions thereof were in the same general form as in 1858, but some changes were made. Among them was the addition of a definition of money as "to mean and include gold and silver coins, and current bank notes in actual possession, and every deposit which the person owing, holding in trust, or having the beneficial interest therein is entitled to withdraw, in money, on demand."[26] Probably, the word written as "owing" should have been "owning," but, in any case, it clearly was the intent that coins, currency, and bank deposits should be taxed.

An addition to the law was a section providing the assessors with some guidance as to the meaning of value:

> Sec. 11. Each parcel of real property, outside of any town, city or village, mentioned in section second, shall be valued at its true value in money, excluding the value of the crops growing thereon and improvements; but the price for which such real property would sell at auction or at a forced sale shall not be taken as a criterion of such value. Personal property of every description shall be valued at the usual selling price of similar property at the time and place of listing; and if there be no usual price, then at the price that is believed could be obtained therefor in money.[27]

The new law eliminated self-assessment. Property owners were still required to swear to the list but it appears that this referred to the completeness of the list rather than to the value of the property.

Many of the differences between the laws of 1858 and 1860 were the result of the reduction in the role of towns in the 1860 law. Undoubtedly, the township form of organization was too elaborate and required too many officials in a thinly populated frontier area. The return to county assessors and collectors in the 1860 law resulted in a much shorter and simpler procedure.

FINANCIAL CONDITIONS IN THE TERRITORIAL PERIOD

Although the territorial legislatures passed two lengthy revenue laws and extensively amended one of them, territorial tax collections were minimal. The territory was in a turmoil over the slavery question, land titles were not well established,[28] coins, currency, or other forms of circulating median were scarce, and population was unstable. New settlers arrived and then moved on because of disputed claims or the appearance of better opportunities elsewhere. Territorial officers complained that reports from county officers were often not made and only a small percentage of the territorial taxes were paid. There is little evidence as to how much of the local levies were collected.

As the territorial period drew to a close, there was a severe drought in Kansas. From June 1859 until November 1860 very little rain fell. Streams, lakes, and wells dried up, crops failed, and Kansans were without money. Several counties failed even to levy 1860 territorial taxes. Believing it impossible to collect unpaid taxes for 1855, 1856, and 1857, the state auditor recommended that counties be released from payment, but that unpaid 1858 taxes be added to the territorial taxes for 1861 in those counties that had not paid. The counties would be permitted to retain any of the 1858 territorial taxes they had collected.[29]

The principal business of the territorial government was to frame a constitution and secure the admission of Kansas as a state. Both purposes are reflected in a tabulation of the expenditures made by the territorial legislatures. The chief objects of expenditure, in order of importance were:

1. Investigation of election frauds
2. Holding of constitutional conventions
3. Territorial roads
4. Legislative expenses[30]

The first, second, and fourth of these objects of expenditure are obviously related to the business of establishing the governmental machinery and writing the constitutional documents necessary for statehood. The provision of roads had a dual purpose. Roads were necessary for commerce, but they also facilitated the movement of elected officials and of citizens who needed to transact business in the county seat or territorial capital.

FOUR KANSAS CONSTITUTIONS

Kansas is unique in that four different constitutional documents were drafted before the territory was admitted to statehood. This circumstance, like so much of Kansas' early history, was related to the conflict over the slave question.

The Topeka Constitution of 1855

The first round in the battle over slavery went to the proslavery forces when Governor Reeder recognized the so-called bogus legislature elected with the help of Missouri voters. The action of this legislature in passing a slave code and providing severe penalties against any interference with slavery or advocacy of its abolition led to the convening of a convention in Topeka on October 23, 1855, in order to draft what became known as the Topeka constitution. Presided over by James H. Lane, it adopted a constitution that prohibited slavery but excluded the Negro and the mulatto from the state. This convention had no legal status as it had not been authorized either by the territorial legislature or Congress. The constitution was submitted to an election and on December 15, 1855, it was approved 1,731 to 46 by those free-state partisans who voted.[31]

State officers and legislators were elected under the provisions of the Topeka constitution. Charles Robinson was elected governor and the state legislature elected Governor Reeder and James Lane to the U.S. Senate. Troops sent by the territorial governor dispersed the legislature before any laws were enacted. This effectively ended the Topeka constitution and the Topeka government.[32]

The property tax provision of the Topeka constitution was found in Article XI—Finance and Taxation. It read as follows:

> Sec. 1. The general assembly shall provide by law for a uniform and equal rate of assessment and taxation, and taxes shall be levied upon all such property, real and personal, as the general assembly may from time to time prescribe; but all property appropriated and used exclusively for municipal, literary, educational, scientific, or charitable purposes, and personal property to an amount not exceeding one hundred dollars for each head of a family, and all property appropriated and used exclusively for religious purposes, to an amount not exceeding two hundred thousand dollars, may by general laws be exempted from taxation.

The bill of rights contained a provision stating that the payment of a tax should never be a qualification for voting. A public debt and public works section prohibited the loan of the state's credit to private individuals or corporations and limited the state debt to $100,000, except to repel invasion or suppress insurrection.

The Lecompton Constitution of 1857

The second attempt at constitution-making was authorized by the territorial legislature, which was still controlled by pro-slavery men. This convention met at Lecompton on September 7, 1857. The results of its deliberations were submitted to the people, who were also given the opportunity of voting for a "no-slavery" provision. This provision, however, protected slave property already in the state and the natural increase. The free-state men refused to vote and the vote on December 21, 1857, was 6,226 for the constitution and 569 against. In the meantime, territorial elections had been held in October 1857. After Governor Stanton had thrown out the fraudulent votes, these elections gave control of the legislature to free-state men. This new legislature then passed a law providing for another vote on the constitution. The proslavery advocates refused to vote and, on January 4, 1858, the constitution lost 10,266 to 164. President Buchanan was unwilling to accept the result and send the Lecompton constitution to Congress. After considerable debate, Congress ordered another vote that was taken on August 2, 1858, and the constitution again lost 11,812 to 1,926. This vote signaled the defeat of slavery in Kansas, but Kansas was still without a constitution on which it could be admitted as a state.[33]

The Lecompton constitution had both a revenue and a finance article and both made reference to property taxation. Pertinent sections read:

Art. IX—Finance

Sec. 1. The rule of taxation shall be uniform, and taxes shall be levied upon such property as the legislature shall, from time to time, prescribe.

Sec. 6. The property of the State and counties, both real and personal, and such other property as the legislature may deem necessary for school, religious, or charitable purposes, may be exempted from taxation.

Art. X—Revenue

Sec. 2. Taxation shall be equal and uniform, and all property on which taxes shall be levied shall be taxed in proportion to its value to be ascertained as directed by legislative enactment, and no one species of property shall be taxed higher than another species of property on which taxes shall be levied.

Sec. 3. The legislature shall have power to levy an income tax, and to tax all persons pursuing any occupation, trade, or profession.

Sec. 4. The legislature shall provide for the classification of the lands of this State into three distinct classes, to be styled respectively class one, two, three; and each of these classes shall have a fixed value in so much money, upon which there shall be assessed an ad valorem tax.

Sec. 5. The legislature shall provide for a capitation or poll tax, to be paid by every able-bodied male citizen over twenty-one years and under sixty years of age; but nothing herein contained shall prevent the exemption of taxable polls in cases of bodily infirmity.

Sec. 6. The legislature shall levy a tax on all railroad incomes, proceeding from gifts of public lands, at the rate of ten cents on the one hundred dollars.

Although this constitution provided for ad valorem taxation of most kinds of property, Section 4 of the Revenue Article provided that there were to be only three classes of land, each with a fixed value. This was a return to a method used earlier in other states but which had generally been abandoned in favor of having assessors determine the assessed value. Unusual for the time were the explicit provision for a general income tax, the mandatory poll tax, and the mandatory one-mill tax on certain railroad income.

The Leavenworth Constitution of 1858

The third constitution written in Kansas, the Leavenworth Constitution, was written because the more radical wing of the free-state forces in Kansas believed there was need for an alternative document if the national administration's efforts to have the Lecompton constitution approved began to make headway. The convention met in Minneola on March 23, 1858, and adjourned to Leavenworth. The constitution written by the convention was submitted to a vote and approved 4,346 to 1,257 with proslavery forces not voting. Little interest was shown in this constitution and the movement on its behalf was abandoned when it became apparent that the Lecompton constitution was not going to be approved by Congress. The finance and taxation article began with a section prohibiting a poll tax. The second section deals with the property tax:

Sec. 2. Laws shall be passed taxing, by uniform rule, all real and personal property, according to its true value in money, but burying grounds, schoolhouses, and other property used exclusively for educational purposes, houses used exclusively for public worship, not exceeding fifty thousand dollars in value, institutions of public charity, public and municipal property used exclusively for public and municipal purposes, and personal property to an amount not exceeding in value two hundred dollars for each head of a family, may, by general laws, be exempted from taxation; but all such laws shall be subject to alteration or repeal, and the value of all such property so exempted shall, from time to time, be ascertained and published as may be directed by law.

The Wyandotte Constitution of 1859

The fourth and final constitutional convention met in Wyandotte on July 5, 1859. In earlier conventions leaders of one or more of the political factions in the state had taken a prominent part, but at Wyandotte all were absent. Most of the delegates did not have a statewide reputation and were largely unknown to each other although five had been delegates to the Leavenworth convention and three were members of the Topeka convention.[34] They were generally "middle-class," with lawyers and farmers being the predominant group. The occupational breakdown was:

Lawyers	18	Surveyor	1
Farmers	16	Mechanic	1
Merchants	8	Printer	1
Physicians	3	Land agent	1
Manufacturers	3		

The delegates came from a wide geographic area. The places of birth of the delegates were:

Ohio	14	Massachusetts	2
Indiana	7	Maine	2
Pennsylvania	6	Virginia	1
Kentucky	5	England	1
New York	4	Scotland	1
Vermont	4	Germany	1
New Hampshire	3	Ireland	1

Although much attention has been given to the role of New England abolitionists in the early settlement of the state, few of those at the convention were from New England. Most of the delegates had probably come to Kansas seeking economic opportunity rather than to crusade against slavery.

The Wyandotte convention was unique in that it was the first in which both proslavery and free-state factions were represented. There were a number of Democrats among the delegates. Although they were not given any committee chairmanships and ended up not signing the completed documents, they participated actively in the work of the convention.

Several issues related to finance were highly controversial. Among them were the banking provisions and the questions dealing with territorial debt. Jacksonian mistrust of banks and bankers was reflected in Article 13, which, among other rules for the chartering and regulation of banks, prohibited the state from being a stockholder in a bank and required that all laws governing banks be submitted to a vote of the people. A provision requiring that no territorial debt be assumed without a two-thirds vote of each branch of the legislature was stricken from the proposed constitution, but the "Resolutions" sent to Congress asked it to assume the territorial debts.[35]

Given the strength of local boosterism and the importance of land speculation at the time, it is not surprising that two of the most hotly debated issues had to do with the location of county seats and the state capital. After debate, the convention adopted a provision that stated that neither county boundaries nor the location of county seats could be changed without the consent of a majority of the electorate. This debate was mild, however, as compared to the controversy over the location of the state capital. There were many accusations of corruption and on one occasion a near riot on the convention floor. Delegate William Hutchinson was charged with offering another delegate "a good lot" in return for a vote for Lawrence. After he denied the charge a committee of five was appointed to investigate a charge of perjury against him. The committee split. Two declared him guilty, two innocent, and the fifth member declared that both Hutchinson and his accuser were guilty of perjury. This led to a commotion on the floor with threats of violence, sleeves rolled up, and loaded canes raised in the air. Order was restored without a blow being struck and the matter was dropped.[36]

The truth will never be known but there seems to be little doubt that corruption was involved. The *Topeka Tribune* published a letter stating that a paper was circulating in Lawrence asking for contributions in money and property for the purpose of buying votes from members of the constitutional convention. Later it was reported that $50,000 had been raised and taken to Wyandotte. The report may or may not have been true, but it is of interest that $50,000 is considerably more than the total amount of taxes collected by the territorial government in more than six years of existence. C. K. Holliday, a railroad promoter who later became president of the Atchison, Topeka, and Santa Fe Railroad, was active in lobbying for Topeka. He was elated when Topeka was chosen, but lamented that he had killed himself politically. On a brighter note, he added that present pecuniary good was worth more than a prospective political position.[37]

In contrast with the debates over banking and the location of seats of government, there was relatively little debate over the provisions prohibiting the state from engaging in works of internal improvement or from contracting debts of over $1 million without a vote of the people, except for the purpose of suppressing rebellion or repelling an invasion. Obviously, the lesson taught by the bond defaults of the 1830s had been well learned.

Likewise, there was little controversy over the revenue clause. The delegates to the Wyandotte convention, like the delegates to other constitutional conventions of the period, felt little need to debate the uniformity question. Sections 1 and 2, dealing with the property tax read:

Art. 11—Finance and Taxation

Section 1. The legislature shall provide for a uniform and equal rate of assessment and taxation; but all property used exclusively for state, county, municipal, literary, educational, scientific, religious, benevolent and charitable purposes, and personal property to the amount of at least two hundred dollars for each family, shall be exempted from taxation.

Sec. 2. The legislature shall provide for taxing the notes and bills discounted or purchased, moneys loaned, and other property, effects, or dues of every description, (without deduction) of all banks now existing, or hereafter to be created, and of all bankers; so that all property employed in banking shall always bear a burden of taxation equal to that imposed upon the property of individuals.

Both of the above sections were taken from the Ohio constitution. The wording of Section 1 was changed somewhat, but Section 2, dealing with the taxation of banks and bankers was taken verbatim.[38]

The Wyandotte constitution was adopted on July 29, 1859, and ratified by the people on October 4, 1859. Congress did not approve the admission of Kansas as a state until January 29, 1861. On March 4, 1861, Abraham Lincoln was inaugurated president and on April 15 he issued the proclamation that officially began the Civil War.

FOUR CONSTITUTIONS COMPARED

Although only the Wyandotte constitution actually went into effect, the property tax provisions of all four have been reported here because they all tell a great deal about the property tax as it existed at the time in the United States. The provisions in all four constitutions were borrowed from other states. The Ohio constitution was adopted as the model for the Wyandotte convention, but many other constitutions were in the hands of the delegates. Other constitutions drawn upon include: Michigan (1850), Iowa (1857), Wisconsin (1848), Illinois (1848), Indiana (1851), Minnesota (1857), New York (1846), Pennsylvania (1838), Kentucky (1850), and the three earlier Kansas constitutions.[39]

Although all four constitutions accepted the general property tax idea, there were some differences. Some of the most important of these are summarized in Table 5.1. All required uniform taxation of property, except for the modification for land in the Lecompton constitution. Only the Leavenworth constitution appears to require universal taxation of property. The Topeka and Lecompton constitutions specifically give the legislature power to choose the property to be taxed.

Table 5.1. Provisions of Kansas Constitutional Documents Compared

| Document | Uniform | Universal | Exemptions | | Limits |
			Government, Charity, etc.	Family	
Topeka, 1855[1]	Yes	No	Optional	Optional, $100	No
Lecompton, 1857[3]	Modified[2]	No	Optional	No	Cities
Leavenworth, 1858[4]	Yes	Yes	Optional	Optional, $200	Cities
Wyandotte, 1859	Yes	No[5]	Yes	At least $200	Cities

1. The bill of rights prohibited a poll tax as a requirement for voting.
2. Taxation was to be uniform, ad valorem, but the legislature was to divide land into three classes with each class having a fixed value upon which ad valorem taxes were to be levied.
3. The legislature had power to provide for an income tax and to tax occupations. The poll tax was mandatory.
4. Payment of taxes was not to be a qualification for voting.
5. There was no requirement that all property be taxes, but a separate section directed that all property of banks and brokers, including intangibles, should be taxed.

The Wyandotte constitution is not so specific. The word "all" does not appear as a modifier, but there was a provision requiring that all the property of banks and bankers, including intangible property, be taxed.

All except the Wyandotte constitution make the exemption of property of governmental and charitable organizations optional. In the Wyandotte constitution it is mandatory. The Topeka and Leavenworth constitutions made exemption of family personal property optional. The Wyandotte constitution requires the exemption of at least $200.

SUMMARY AND CONCLUSIONS

The history of Kansas taxation in the territorial period illustrates: the widespread acceptance of the general property tax as a source of state and local revenue and the difficulties of implementing the idea in a new territory.

The two tax statutes and the four proposed state constitutions drafted during the territorial period provided for a broad-based, ad valorem property tax. All contemplated the taxation of real estate, tangible personal property, and at least some kinds of intangible personal property.

The revenue laws copied from Missouri and Wisconsin were typical of the general property tax laws then in vogue. They laid out an administrative structure that was far too elaborate for the thinly populated frontier of territorial Kansas. The local officials who had responsibility for administration often had minimal education and no experience in tax administration. They received no instruction or training and in some cases did not even have a copy of the laws that they were to administer. Land titles were uncertain and the conflict over slavery added to the problem of establishing a tax system.

At the end of the territorial period, indebtedness, excluding claims against the territory, was about 2.7 times the total amount of taxes that had been collected in the six years in which the territory had been organized. Some counties had paid little, if any, territorial taxes.

Some progress had been made. By the end of the territorial period thirty counties had made at least a partial report and the total assessed value, after equalization, totaled $32.7 million. The Territorial Board of Equalization had successfully asserted its right to change county assessments in order to prevent competitive undervaluation of property. Hopes and speculative fever were high. The board's report shows that 135,328 lots, more than two for every inhabitant, had been platted.[40] The governor commented that the value of platted lots was probably more than twice the value of farm lands actually under cultivation and suggested that if something was not done to stop the mania of town speculation there would soon be no land left for farms in the territory.[41]

6

Defining and Valuing Taxable Property, 1860–1900

Determining tax policy is a multi-step process. At the constitutional and statutory levels, policy is debated in broad terms. Symbols and catch phrases are common weapons in the debate and examples are chosen selectively to make the point. In these debates success will often go to the one who can sell a policy by using symbols that are in tune with the times.

The general property tax was in tune with the times in mid-nineteenth century America. A rapidly expanding nation was being built by common people who were willing to brave the rigors of the wilderness in order to improve their economic position and station in life. The political symbols of the European class system were under attack. Equality was the watchword and the uniform general property tax symbolized equality in a very important area of political and economic policy. The moderate level of controversy accompanying the spread of this new form of taxation indicates that it was an "easy sell" for those who advocated its inclusion in constitutional and statutory provisions.

Implementing the tax so that, in fact, all forms of wealth were taxed at a uniform percent of value was a very different matter. Inherent administrative difficulties were compounded by political opposition from those who discovered that equal taxation meant an increase in their own taxes. To compound the problem, administration of the tax became more complicated as the economy became more complex and people and property became more mobile.

IMPLEMENTING A GENERAL PROPERTY TAX

The history of the property tax is both a history of symbiotic relationships between the property tax and local government and a case study of the inherent contradictions of Jacksonian—and American—values. In order to understand either, it is helpful to consider the steps required to implement a property tax:

1. *Define taxable property.* A legal definition of property must be formulated. Property, in a legal sense, is a "bundle of rights." Often the rights related to a particular physical object are divided among several persons or organizations. For example, the rights of an "owner" of a given parcel of real estate may be limited by the fact that others hold surface leases, mineral leases, easements, mortgages, or other interests in the property. Tax uniformity can be achieved only if these are sorted out so that the underlying wealth is taxed once and only once.

   It has been said that this problem was not of great importance in a simple agricultural economy, but problems arose early in the history of the American property tax. Statutes listed items of intangible property to be taxed and were changed frequently in response to complaints of double taxation or tax avoidance.

   For constitutional reasons, certain types of government property cannot be taxed and it has generally been regarded as good policy to exempt property owned or used by charitable, religious, or educational institutions. This makes it necessary to define exempt organizations and to decide whether the exemption is based on use or ownership, which inevitably creates controversy.

2. *Define value.* Early tax statutes said little about the meaning of value. Definitions were generally short statements making some reference to "selling price" or "usual price." Sometimes there were attempts to clarify the meaning of value as applied to particular kinds of property, such as currency or notes selling at a discount. In the twentieth century, appraisal theory has become more sophisticated, but ambiguities remain.

3. *Define jurisdiction to tax.* The jurisdiction to tax real estate is determined by its location, but jurisdictions other than the one in which it is physically located may claim the right to tax personal property. To achieve uniform taxation, it is necessary that the jurisdiction be defined so that all property has one and only one tax location. The U.S. Supreme Court, aware of the importance of an independent tax power in a federal system, has been reluctant to interfere with the taxing power of the states. The Court has denied jurisdiction in clear-cut cases, but it has not been willing to adopt rules to ensure that property is not subject to taxation in more than one place. As a result, certain kinds of property, especially intangible property, can be subject to taxation in several jurisdictions.

4. *Establish a tax date.* Tax day must be established. To eliminate the possibility of double taxation or escape from taxation of mobile property, the same tax day should be used in every jurisdiction or rules should be established to ensure that all property is assessed and taxed in one and only one jurisdiction. This requires coordination of legislation and administrative cooperation among assessing units within and without the state.

5. *List taxable property.* All taxable property must be listed and assigned to the

proper taxing district. Real estate can be discovered by physical inspection. Complete cadastral (ownership) maps aid the process, but many kinds of tangible personal property can be discovered only by physical inspections inside homes and other buildings. This is a sensitive matter. Public records of certain kinds of intangible property exist, but often not in the locality or state that has jurisdiction to tax.

6. *Value every parcel or item of property.* Determining the value of property is a difficult task. Commonly, statutory definitions of value reflect the economists' emphasis on market value, but appraisers have had to develop an elaborate set of rules and procedures in their attempt to determine the market value of property types that are seldom sold. Even so, the best appraisers may differ as to the value of particular properties.

The problem is complicated by the fact that assessing property for taxation is more than a technical problem in appraisal. It is a political problem that must be solved in such a way as to maintain support for the constitutional order. The issue is compounded by divergent geographic interests. Assessed values established by local assessors are utilized for distributing the taxes of overlapping units of government and there is pressure on local assessors to keep total assessments low. To prevent competitive undervaluation the state must establish boards of equalization or provide strict state supervision of local assessment.

7. *Levy taxes.* The tax levy is the official act of imposing the tax. The governing body of each governmental unit is responsible for the tax levy, but state legislatures specify the procedures to be followed. The states may also limit the amount of taxes that local governments may levy for particular purposes.

8. *Compute tax rates and tax bills.* Taxes levied in dollar amounts must be converted to rates. Tax rates for the various funds and tax jurisdictions must be added, and the total multiplied by the assessed value of each parcel of property to determine the tax due.

9. *Collect taxes.* Taxes levied in rem become an automatic lien on the property and good title cannot be passed until taxes are paid. This has proved to be a powerful aid to real estate tax collection. If taxes are not paid, tax sales may be held. At the sale, the successful bidder agrees to pay the taxes and penalties due and receives a "tax certificate," which can be converted into a title unless the original owner redeems the property by repaying taxes, interest, and penalties. Because personal property may wear out, die, or be removed from the jurisdiction, collection of personal property taxes may be more difficult. It may be necessary to take legal action against the owner or to seize property that is about to be removed.

10. *Distribute the proceeds to local governments.* If the tax collector collects taxes for units of government other than his own, the collections must be distributed to the proper governmental unit.

A CASE STUDY

The next three chapters deal with the administration of the property tax and the interaction of tax policy and tax administration in Kansas. Some readers may find the descriptions overly detailed, but property tax administrators will experience many moments of deja vu. Most of the problems faced in Kansas, and the attempted solutions, were paralleled in other states. Many of the problems have persisted to the present.

This chapter focuses on attempts to clarify the meaning of uniformity, to define taxable property, to define taxable value, to determine jurisdiction, and to establish the assessment date. These were largely state, rather than local, responsibilities. It was the state legislature that defined taxable property, established jurisdiction rules, defined value, established local government, and designated administrative responsibilities. The courts interpreted the statutes and determined whether they were consistent with state and federal constitutions.

The forty-year period from 1860 to 1900 was a period of rapid change and development in Kansas. The state grew from a newly admitted frontier state with a population of 107,000 to a well established state with a population of 1,470,000.[1] In 1860 there were forty-one counties, but only thirty were organized well enough to report tax information to the territorial board of review.[2] Transportation still depended on wagon trails. Bridges were absent and streams had to be forded or crossed via privately operated ferries. The only operating railroad when Kansas was admitted to statehood was the twenty miles of the Atchison and St. Joseph road that had been completed on February 29, 1860. The St. Joseph to Topeka railroad was under construction at that time.

The lack of transportation meant a lack of markets for Kansas products. The immigration to the Colorado gold mines had helped the price of products in the immigration centers like Leavenworth and Kansas City, but the *Neosho Valley Register* predicted that wheat would never be grown in Kansas beyond the needs for home consumption because the state was too far removed from markets.[3] Under these conditions, it was not to be expected that a smoothly functioning administrative system could be quickly established.

The state was in no position to establish "branch offices" in the various parts of the state. Instead county and township governments were established and locally elected officials were required to swear that they would uphold the constitution and execute the laws of the state. The legislature also provided for the chartering of city governments and the establishment of school districts to provide additional local services. These local governments were created by, and were subject to, the will of the legislature, but they were the governments with which most citizens had contact and they often commanded the loyalty of the average citizen.

REFINING THE CONCEPT OF EQUAL TAXATION

The Kansas constitution directed the legislature to provide for a uniform and equal rate of assessment and taxation. The wording in these and other uniformity provisions implied that the tax rate would be a flat, uniform percentage applied to the value of the property.

That principle was widely accepted and its definition created relatively few controversies, but one early Kansas case did turn on the meaning of uniformity. This case grew out of the attempt of the 1863 legislature to collect unpaid territorial taxes. The legislation required counties which had not paid territorial taxes under the tax laws of 1860 to levy and collect those amounts in 1863. In *State of Kansas v. Leavenworth County Commissioners*[4] the Kansas supreme court held that this requirement violated the Uniform and Equal Clause. The opinion of the court pointed out that the act imposed uncollected taxes according to the 1863 assessment roll, which varied considerably from the assessment roll on which the original taxes were levied. Therefore, the provision was not an attempt to collect back taxes but to levy a new tax upon certain counties. The Leavenworth case made it clear that the Kansas property tax was on individuals or individual properties, not on a geographic area or local government.

In *Hines v. City of Leavenworth*[5] the owners of a number of lots, which had been assessed the cost of macadamizing the adjacent streets, claimed that the assessments were invalid because they were not uniform and equal. The court agreed that the state constitution required property to be taxed at uniform and equal rates and that such uniformity could only be achieved if the tax was levied on value. It also interpreted uniformity to mean that state taxes must be uniform throughout the state and county taxes uniform throughout the county. However, the court decided that assessments to pay for improvements on adjacent streets were not taxes to which the uniformity provision applied.[6]

DEFINING TAXABLE PROPERTY

It turned out that determining which property was taxable was a difficult and controversial matter. The tax law based on Wisconsin statutes, passed by the territorial legislature in 1860, continued in effect after statehood and was included with slight changes by the 1862 legislature. All real estate and personal property was declared to be taxable and several different kinds of intangible property were specifically listed and defined. Exemptions included federal, state, and local government property, property used for charitable, educational, scientific, and religious purposes, libraries, and the property of widows to the value of $500.[7]

It is clear from reading the lengthy sections that the legislature went to some lengths to ensure that the definition of taxable property was broad. The major departure from the concept of universal taxation was the exclusion of buildings and other improvements on real estate located in rural areas.

Problems with Land Titles

Ordinarily, it makes no difference how the bundle of property rights pertaining to real property is divided. The tax is levied against the real estate and if not paid the property is sold at a tax sale. An exception to the rule exists when some of the ownership rights are in the hands of a tax-exempt organization. The liability of the property to taxation may hinge on the nature of those rights.

The immunity of federal property from taxation is implied in the U.S. Constitution and was explicitly stated in the organic act establishing the Territory of Kansas. The act also required that all treaties, laws, and other engagements made by the government of the United States with the Indian tribes inhabiting the territories should be faithfully and rigidly observed.[8] The act admitting Kansas as a state also contained a provision that the state should never tax the lands or property of the United States, and the rights of Indians would be unaffected by the admission of Kansas as a state.[9] Confusion arose from uncertainty as to the meaning of the Indian treaties and as to when title passed from the federal government.

Many of the policies of the U.S. government providing easy means of acquiring land were modified in the decade before the Civil War. For example, the period of time during which one could occupy land without payment was limited to one year. Settlers were often forced to borrow at high interest rates to buy the land on which they had been residing. A revival of the treaty-making method of disposing of Indian land also complicated the process. Through treaties lands were placed in trust. The trust lands were then sold for the benefit of the Indians, allocated to individual Indians, or held in reserve for some future time. The most productive one-fourth of the area of Kansas—the eastern part of the state— passed by the treaty process from Indian ownership to ownership by individuals, land companies, and railroads without ever becoming part of the public domain. This land never came under congressional control and was not subject to the Homestead Act.

The scramble for trust land created confusion over titles and much litigation.[10] Many early tax cases involved land titles and the taxability of lands that had belonged to Indians or to the federal government. One of the first cases of this type was *Blue Jacket v. Johnson County Commissioners,*[11] which was decided in 1865. By the treaty of May 10, 1854, the Shawnees ceded to the United States the whole of their reservation containing about 1,600,000 acres. The government re-ceded 200,000 acres and gave them $829,000. The 200,000 acres were to be selected within thirty miles of the Missouri line. Individual Indians or family heads were allocated 200 acres per person. Blue Jacket, the head of a family consisting of himself and five others, selected land and obtained a patent with the restriction that it could not be sold without the consent of the Secretary of the Interior. Johnson

County levied taxes on the land and the personal property of Blue Jacket and threatened to sell it when the taxes were unpaid.

The opinion in the *Blue Jacket* case is long. It includes a summary of testimony that attempted to establish whether or not the Shawnees retained their tribal identity or were "civilized." Several Indian witnesses testified as to whether they used public roads, sent their children to school, and were married in Christian ceremonies. In the end, the Kansas court held that the Shawnees did not hold the land severally—that the limitation on the sale of the land did not affect the title to the land, but was a personal disability similar to those imposed on a minor. The tax and the sale of the land for nonpayment was upheld.

The *Blue Jacket* decision, and a similar decision involving the Miami Indians, was promptly overruled by the U.S. Supreme Court.[12] The Court said the state was not entitled to regard the tribal organization as gone because the primitive habits of the Indians had been broken. Rules of interpretation favorable to the Indian tribe were to be adopted and the provision in the treaty that exempts lands from "levy, sale, and forfeiture" applies to the sale for the nonpayment of taxes.

Another problem involved the taxability of land to which clear title had not passed. The 1864 legislature provided that lands entered as homesteads, including improvements and improvements owned by persons on Indian trust land, or improvements on land belonging to another person should be taxed as personal property, but the land could not be sold for property taxes.[13]

The validity of the provision was tested in the case of *Parker v. Winsor*,[14] decided by the Kansas supreme court in 1870. This case involved land that had been purchased by the Central Branch Union Pacific Railroad from the Kickapoo tribe and then sold to Winsor, but not yet patented[15] to the railroad company or to Winsor. Winsor had made improvements to the land that the assessor had assessed as personal property. The attorney for the county argued that it was clearly beyond the authority of the U.S. government to exempt lands from taxation after a bona fide sale, even though the patent had not been issued. Justice Valentine wrote a denunciation of the way in which the treaty power of the federal government had been used:

It may seem to border very closely upon the ludicrous, if not upon the ridiculous, to see the government of the United States gravely treating with a few half-naked savages, as though these savages were a great nation, and then have it seriously claimed that the treaty, thus made, is part of the supreme law of the land, paramount to any act of congress, or to any constitution or law of any one of the states; and yet no one at this day will question the power of the government or the validity of the treaty.[16]

Justice Valentine's complaint about the treaty power of the federal government is only one of many such complaints in the history of federal-state relations, but he recognized that the U.S. Constitution provides for the supremacy of treaty provisions and that Kansas was bound by the Indian treaties. The opinion goes on to conclude, regretfully, that the land is indeed exempt from taxation until patented. The opinion also holds that the Kansas legislature has no power to tax the improvements as personal property. The lands and improvements could not be sold for taxes, no tax lien could be attached, and they could not be forfeited to the government.

Several cases decided by the Kansas supreme court involved the date on which government land became taxable to private owners. *Kansas Pac Ry Co v. Culp*[17] (1872) dealt with the simple question of whether or not railroad grant land was subject to taxation before patents were issued. The railroad had been completed and accepted by the president, but the railroad company had not paid the cost of the survey; therefore, the patents had not been issued. The Kansas court held that the right to a title existed and that the property was taxable. The U.S. Supreme Court reversed, saying that the right to a title did not exist until the survey costs were paid.[18] The railroad naturally took advantage of this ruling by failing to pay the small survey costs until the land had been sold and it was necessary to give title. The problem was to become particularly troublesome in the western counties where railroads, especially the Kansas Pacific, sold land to settlers on an installment basis, but did not apply for a patent until the land was totally paid for and title had to be delivered. The Kansas Pacific began sale of its lands in 1868, but no lands were patented and placed on the tax rolls until 1873. By the end of 1879, the Kansas Pacific had sold more than 1.5 million acres, but had patented less than half of them. In 1882, twelve years after construction was completed and twenty years after the lands had been granted to the Kansas Pacific, it had taken title to little more than one-sixth of its lands.[19]

Not all cases involving government land went against the county. In 1873 the Kansas supreme court rejected the claim that lands purchased from Indians were forever tax exempt, even after having been sold to a non-Indian.[20] In 1875 the state supreme court heard a case involving land purchased from the state from the tracts donated by Congress for the support of an agricultural college.[21] The plaintiff, Oswalt, had made a down payment and agreed to pay for the land in installments. He received a bond for the deed. The court decided that equitable title was in Oswalt and cited the statutory provision that all property not expressly exempt shall be subject to taxation. The court also emphasized that the constitutional exemption of state property requires exclusive use for state purposes.

Statutory Changes

The 1866 legislature rewrote the tax law that had been inherited from the territory.[22] Section 1 of Chapter 118 stated that all property in the state, real and personal, not expressly exempted should be entered on the list of taxable property. Section 2 defined real and personal property. As in the previous law, it was clear that intangible property, including an interest in corporations not forming a part of the capital stock, was to be taxed. Shares in vessels and various forms of money were to be taxable. There was a provision stating that pensions receivable from the United States and salaries or payments expected from the United States for services performed were not taxable. The exemption of improvements on farmland was eliminated.

Section 3 was a long list of exemptions. The distinguishing feature of the new wording was the frequent use of the word "exclusively." Property of governments and governmental agencies was exempted only if owned exclusively by government. Property of religious, charitable, or educational institutions and of some local governmental agencies was exempt only if used exclusively for the purpose named. The 1866 law included a $200 family exemption for personal property, as required by the state constitution, and added an exemption for wearing apparel and family pictures. There was also an exemption of $100 for family libraries and school books.The $500 exemption for widows was dropped.[23]

Two years later, in 1868, a special senate committee was created to consider a petition of sixty-six widows of Lawrence and Topeka, endorsed by four hundred citizens of the state, asking for the exemption of the property of widows on the grounds that taxation of women who could not vote was taxation without representation. The chairman and two members of the committee reported that such an exemption would be in conflict with the tax uniformity provisions of the constitution. The majority report reviewed the theory of representation as it applied to political communities and to individuals within a community. The authors argued that the slogan "No taxation without representation" properly applied to political communities and not to individuals within a political community. Expounding a theory of virtual representation, without using the term, the authors argued that a representative in Congress represents the interest of the common people collectively, not just those of one party or those who vote. Near the end of the report, the majority left the realm of political theory to declare they would be glad to transfer the pretended boon of representation to the widows and ladies of the state if they "would pay our taxes." The majority concluded its report with these words:

> Man is the sentinel around the camp of life; he wards off the approaching danger, and receives the blow—a protection created by God. Within is the family; although deprived of its head and depressed in sorrow, it is nevertheless within the fortress.
>
> Better far would it be for the females of the State to be thus dependant on the stronger sex, standing on the outer ring of a boisterous life, than to cut loose and swing from her orb, and sail through life as an independent being.[24]

The minority of two on the committee took an entirely different track. They recognized that the tax exemption would violate the uniformity clause of the constitution, but believed it unjust to impose heavy and burdensome taxes on any class without consent. The report recommended the constitution be amended so as to make no discrimination against persons on account of gender or race.[25]

The tax laws were rewritten in 1876, but the sections that defined taxable property were changed only slightly. The provisions dealing with annuities, credits for specific amounts of labor or property, and manufacturers' inventory were omitted and the family library exemption was reduced to $50.[26] By the time the tax laws were compiled and indexed in 1884, the definition of personal property specifically mentioned property used, occupied, or employed by a railroad company, telegraph company, or corporation that is situated on the right of way of any railroad. The definition of money had been expanded to include time deposits in banks. The exclusion of pensions and other sums due from the federal government had been eliminated.[27]

Exemptions

The exclusive use requirement was strictly enforced in the early cases. In 1871 the Kansas supreme court heard a case involving exemption of unimproved land held by Washburn College in Topeka. Although the land was intended as the future site of the college the court denied exemption.[28]

The following year, the court decided two other cases involving exclusive use. A dwelling house in Lawrence, owned by the Diocese of the Episcopal Church and used as a residence for the bishop, was denied exemption on the ground that it was not used exclusively for religious purposes.[29] St. Mary's college owned farm land and had a contract with the U.S. government to educate approximately eighty Indians in agricultural pursuits and the rudiments of reading and writing. The property was used to train the Indians in agricultural pursuits and the produce was consumed by students, employees, and missionaries, or sold to help support the school. The exemption was denied on the ground that the use was not exclusively educational.[30]

In 1882 the court interpreted the exclusive ownership provisions as they apply to state property. The case involved an attempt to tax property acquired by Kansas State Agricultural College, as the result of foreclosing an unpaid loan.[31] The property was exempt because it was exclusively owned by the state as required by the statute. The following year, the Kansas court held that land taken by a county in partial satisfaction of a debt owed by a defaulting county treasurer was exempt, even though the county had made no use of the land in the way of cultivation or as a site for buildings.[32]

In 1889 the legislature limited and clarified the provisions dealing with property held by exempt institutions. The amount of exempt land around schools and churches was limited to ten acres, not leased or otherwise used for profit; exempt land around parsonages was limited to one-half acre.[33] Exempt land around scientific, literary, or benevolent institutions was limited to five acres and could not be leased or used for profit. Moneys and credits belonging to educational, religious, scientific, benevolent, and literary organizations was exempted if appropriated solely to sustain such institutions and did not exceed any limit imposed by the charter of the institution. In 1892 the Kansas supreme court explicitly stated that tax exemptions were to be strictly construed.[34]

Taxing Intangibles

Equitable taxation of intangible property proved to be the most difficult part of the attempt to implement a uniform property tax. It is clear from the constitutional and statutory language adopted in Kansas and other states that intangibles were considered to be wealth that should be taxed. The statutes specifically mentioned many kinds of intangible property that were taxable. Typical of the early Kansas provisions was the 1866 provision:

> The term "personal property" shall include every tangible thing which is subject of ownership, not forming part or parcel of real property; also, all tax certificates, judgments, notes, bonds and mortgages, and all other evidences of debt, secured by lien on real estate; also, the capital stock, undivided profits, and all other means not forming a part of the capital stock of every company, incorporated or unincorporated, and every share or interest in such stock, profits or means, by whatever name the same may be designated; and, also, every share or interest in any vessel or boat used in navigating any of the waters within or bordering on this state, whether such vessel or boat shall be within the jurisdiction of the state or elsewhere. The term "money" or "moneys" shall include gold and silver coin, United States treasury notes and bank notes drawn in money on demand. The term "credit" when used in this act, shall mean and include every demand for money, labor or other valuable thing, whether due or to become due, but not secured by lien on real estate. Pensions receivable from the United States, or from any of them, salaries or payments expected to be received for labor, or services expected to be performed or rendered, shall not be deemed annuities within the meaning of this act. The words "personal property" when used in this act, in their general sense, shall include all taxable property other than real estate.[35]

Another section provided that debts owing in good faith could be deducted from the credits belonging to the taxpayer and the statement of personal property need only state the amount of credits remaining after such deduction.

This statute is interesting because it, like similar ones in other states, illustrates the problems involved in an attempt to tax uniformly. It is clear that the writers of this statute believed that a wide variety of intangible property should be taxed. Unfortunately, implementation of the statutes would have resulted in multiple taxation of much wealth. Bonds, mortgages, and capital stock of corporations are property interests in tangible assets that are also subject to taxation. Taxing both the tangible and the intangible assets at full value makes the tax burden depend on the form of ownership. A tangible asset owned free and clear by an individual would be taxed differently than the similar asset mortgaged or owned by a corporation.

It is very hard to reconstruct the logic that lay behind the treatment of intangible property. There is no evidence that a correct analysis of the problem of taxing intangibles to produce uniform taxation of wealth existed. Some years later Professor E. R. A. Seligman of Columbia University attempted to analyze the problem. He pointed out that double taxation results if real estate or personal property is taxed at its full value and the mortgage on the property is also taxed. The most satisfactory way of avoiding this result, according to Seligman, was to tax the property at its location and exempt the mortgage from taxation.[36]

According to Seligman, attempts to tax the mortgage and to allow the deduction of the amount of mortgage from the value of the real estate had not been very successful. Failures had resulted from jurisdictional problems or from the mortgagors' ability to charge higher interest rates or to include clauses requiring the land owner to pay the tax. Seligman warned that it does not follow that the value of outstanding mortgage bonds should be deducted when taxing corporations. In many cases bonds are merely substitutes for capital stock and it is necessary to tax both to reach the true faculty of a corporation. "In the case of individuals, indebtedness diminishes the capacity to pay taxes; in the case of corporations, indebtedness often augments that capacity because the so-called debt is in reality an integral and constituent part of the capital."[37] Seligman does not explain why a bond issued by a corporation differs from a mortgage given by an individual. He complicates the argument further by pointing out that, in some cases, corporations borrow to meet emergency needs and do not augment their capital. Strictly speaking, he argues, only so much of borrowed money should be assessed to the borrower as represents the capitalization of surplus profit. He concludes that separating the two kinds of borrowing would be impossible in practice.[38]

A much clearer explanation was written by Professor Jens Peter Jensen of the University of Kansas in 1931. Jensen discussed the legal point of view of property as rights or control over economic goods, but observed that courts have found it necessary to recognize the popular use of the term property to designate physical things. He then went on to observe that the economist faces the necessity of distinguishing between "wealth" and "property":

> Wealth consists of material things plus such incorporeal rights as do not diminish the rights of others in material things. Such rights as patents, royalties, trade marks, good will, franchises, do not represent an interest in particular things owned by particular persons; they do not diminish the rights or interests of anyone in particular material goods. It is convenient to designate such rights as nonrepresentative intangible property, or merely as non-representative intangibles. But the majority of rights in tangible or material things diminishes the rights of others in particular things. With land, where the most complete right or estate is that of fee simple, the debt of the owner secured by

mortgage on the land *pro tanto* diminishes the equity of the owner in the particular parcel of land.[39]

Jensen states out all rights have a value in exchange that can be, more or less, accurately determined in the market. A theoretically perfect property tax would result if every person were taxed on net equities. If one person holds all rights, that person should be taxed according to the full value, but if rights are divided, each should be taxed on the value of the rights held. Even the pyramiding of equities as the result of the corporate form of organization can be handled if the rule of taxing only net equities is adhered to. Each person would be taxed on the difference between assets and liabilities.

Jensen points out that there is another road to achieving the goal of uniform taxation of all wealth. Every tangible object and all categories of rights, such as patents and good will, that do not represent rights in particular tangible goods could be taxed.[40]

Practical considerations render the use of either of the approaches suggested by Jensen difficult. Many tangible assets are owned ostensibly by the person or corporation in possession, but the equities may belong to many different individuals or corporations. To use ownership as the basis of taxation, the tax administrator would have to value the net equities of every taxpayer. The problem is complicated further by the jurisdiction question. Both the tangible assets and the owners of the equities may be widely scattered. Many jurisdictions have an equitable claim to the tax contributions, but there would be administrative and legislative problems with any attempt to divide them.

The long list of intangibles made taxable by the statutes indicates that legislators were aware that many kinds of taxable property might constitute wealth or taxpaying ability. Unfortunately, attempts to avoid multiple taxation were inadequate and inconsistent.

A bill exempting mortgages from taxation was passed in 1873. The purpose of the act as expressed in the title was "to promote the improvement of real estate by exempting mortgages and other securities from taxation."[41] The mortgage exemption was immediately and overwhelmingly unpopular. The most prominent farm organization, the Grange, passed a resolution asking for its speedy repeal. Grange members felt it unjust for any form of wealth to escape taxation.[42] In 1874 Governor Thomas A. Osborn reported that the various assessors had paid no attention to the law and recommended it be repealed.[43] The legislature immediately obliged,[44] but, in his 1875 message, Governor Osborn again raised the subject. He said that many argue that real estate encumbered by a mortgage is doubly taxed because the lender of money on mortgage security likely increases the interest to cover the tax. He also reported that many believe the current law discriminates against Kansas citizens because personal property owned by non-residents escapes Kansas taxation. He optimistically concluded that the problem was not insurmountable and that if the legislature's attention were called to the problem, an act to deal with the problem would be passed.[45] Apparently, the legislature did not find it so simple; no such legislation was passed.

The first Kansas supreme court case involving intangible property concerned the deduction of debts.[46] The plaintiffs, in a case which reached the Kansas supreme court in 1870, had failed to list school district bonds worth $17,000 and notes against an individual named Walker in the amount of $50,000 held by a partnership. To secure the notes, Walker had conveyed a large amount of land to a partnership and the partnership had given Walker a bond to re-convey the land when the notes were paid. The partnership claimed to have debts of $80,000. It claimed that no taxes were due because the debts were deductible against the credits. The court rejected the argument, finding that the arrangement with Walker actually constituted a mortgage and the legislature had provided that debts were not deductible against mortgages. The plaintiff also argued that no value had been ascertained and that the face of a note is no proof of its value. The opinion of the court contains no mention of this claim.

There is no positive indication in the *Lappin* opinion that the arrangement had been entered into for the express purpose of avoiding taxation, but in the second case involving intangibles there can be little doubt. Plaintiff in *Mitchell v. Leavenworth County Commissioners*[47] withdrew $19,350 from a banking house on February 28, receiving the funds in nontaxable legal tender notes (currency). He placed the notes in a sealed envelope in the bank vault. After assessment day on March 1, he deposited the notes in an ordinary deposit. The county commissioners appointed a committee to inquire into the matter and as a result increased the plaintiff's assessment by $9,000. The case came to the court as a request for an injunction against the county commission. The court concluded that the transaction was for the sole and express purpose of evading taxation. The transaction was not a violation of the law, but the motive of defrauding the government and escaping the just burdens that society imposes is such that a court of justice, sitting as a court of equity, will not lend its aid. The request for the injunction was denied. This case was appealed to the U.S. Supreme Court, which upheld the Kansas court:

> We think the decision in this case was correct. United States notes are exempt from taxation by or under state or municipal authority; but a court of equity will not knowingly use its extraordinary powers to promote any such scheme as this plaintiff devised to escape his proportionate share of the burdens of taxation. His remedy, if he has any, is in a court of law.[48]

There are several important aspects of the *Mitchell* case. It originated as a request that a court of equity issue an injunction against the local officials.[49] Because those who appeal to courts of equity must have "clean hands," the request was denied.[50] Had the case been tried in a court of law rather than a court of equity, the outcome might have been different. The legal "technicality" is important because many of the early Kansas tax cases were actions in equity in which the taxpayer requested an injunction against official acts. The "clean hands" requirement places the plaintiff in a difficult legal position and does not always result in a definitive ruling on the meaning of the law.

Another important aspect of the *Mitchell* case is that there was no challenge to the fact that $19,350 in currency was assessed at $9,000, even though the law required that property be valued at its true value in money. This case is only one of many early cases in which the practice of fractional assessment was accepted or ignored by attorneys and court alike.

The *Mitchell* case illustrates another problem of taxing intangibles. United States notes had been ruled to be obligations of the federal government and, like U.S. government bonds, were exempt from state or local taxation. Other forms of money, such as coins, were taxable.[51]

The cases cited indicate a fundamental weakness in the theory of the general property tax. Property, a legal term, is not synonymous with wealth, an economic term. Authors of early property tax statutes understood that some kinds of intangible rights represented wealth, but were not able to separate those rights that were interests in taxable objects and those that had economic value apart from any particular tangible object. Even if they had been able to do so, jurisdictional problems would have made local taxation of intangible values extremely difficult.

JURISDICTION

In *A Treatise on the Law of Taxation* (1872), Thomas M. Cooley stated that protection of the government is the ᷈onsideration for which taxes are demanded and that all parties who receive or are entitled to that protection may be called on to render the equivalent. The protection may be either to the rights of a person or to the rights of property. It follows that a tax cannot be levied against property unless it has actual situs within the state so as to be under the protection of its laws. Real estate has situs only in the place where it is located, but personal property is often said to follow the owner *(mobilia sequuntur personam).* Cooley cited a long list of cases upholding that principle but also stated that personal property may he taxed where it is located. The case of the corporations is peculiar:

> They may be taxed for their franchise, and they may be taxed as persons where their business is carried on. And, as no state is under obligation to permit a foreign corporation to carry on business or exercise franchises within its territory, the permission to do so may be granted under such restrictions, or allowed on such conditions regarding taxation as the state may think proper or prudent to impose.[52]

This clearly opens the way for double or even triple taxation.

Cooley is emphatic in stating that debts owed to foreign creditors by either corporations or individuals cannot be taxed. The creditor cannot be taxed because he is not within the jurisdiction, and the debtor cannot be taxed because debts are not property of the debtors. Debts possess value only to the creditors.[53]

The 1860 territorial law carried over into the first years of statehood was not very clear regarding the place at which property was to be taxed. Apparently, real estate was to be listed and taxed at its location and personal property at the residence of the owner.[54] In *Griffith v. Carter*[55] the court was faced with a case in which the owners of a stock of goods located in Coffey County had listed the goods and paid the tax in Douglas County, their county of residence. Their agent in Coffey County also listed the goods in Coffey County and the authorities there had levied a tax and threatened to sell the goods for nonpayment. The court pointed out that the legislature had affirmed the *mobilia sequuntur personam* doctrine by specifically requiring personal property to be taxed at the residence of the owner.

The 1876 law expanded the directions as to where property was to be listed. Section 4 required that personal property was to be listed in the place where the owner resided unless otherwise provided.[56]

Section 7 provided that property listed on behalf of others should be listed in the township or city in which said property is located, and provided that toll bridges located in two townships or wards be listed as half in each township. Personal property not pertaining to a business was to be listed in the township where located on the first day of March, except that money and credits not pertaining to a business were to be listed in the township or city in which the owner resided. The property of banks or bankers, brokers, insurance or other companies, merchants, and manufacturers was to be listed and taxed in the county, township, city, and school district where their business is usually done. Animals and farm implements were to be listed where permanently kept, except that animals owned by persons living outside the limits of a city were to be taxed in the township where the owner resides. Animals or farming implements temporarily outside the state or in unorganized territory within the state were to be listed where the owner resided on March 1.[57]

The stock, coaches, wagons, harnesses, and other personal property of mail and express companies, telegraph lines, and telegraph instruments were considered personal property within the counties in which located. Corporations, except banks and banking associations, were required to list their capital stock in the township or city where the principal office was located. Owners of the stock were not required to list it. A separate section provided that stockholders in banks and banking associations were to be taxed in the city or township where the bank was located. The banking association was to pay the tax and recover it from the stockholders.[58]

Under the 1876 statutes, railroad property, except real estate not used for railroad operations, was to be assessed as personal property by the state board of railroad assessors and taxed where located.[59]

Real estate is taxable where located, but sometimes cases arise because the government, not the property, has "moved." In 1873 the Kansas supreme court dealt with a case resulting from a change in county boundaries. The legislature had detached a portion of Sedgwick County and attached it to the new county of Harvey. The court declared that portion of Harvey County liable for a proportionate part of the railroad bonded indebtedness previously incurred by Sedgwick County in order to build a railroad between Wichita and Newton. The court ordered Harvey County to apportion taxes sufficient to pay the portion of the debt equal to the portion of the railroad in Harvey County.

ASSESSMENT DAY

One of the common characteristics of the general property tax is that the taxable status of property is determined on a fixed day, called tax day or assessment day. Value, tax situs, and taxability are established on that day. Changes after that day have no effect. This arrangement simplifies administration but in some instances does not work well. For example, the stock of goods a merchant holds may fluctuate seasonally to the benefit or detriment of the owner. The rule encourages manipulation to reduce taxation, especially if adjacent jurisdictions have different assessment days. Another problem is that the principle requiring all property to be taxed once and only once each year may be violated as property is moved among jurisdictions having different assessment dates.

The 1860 law provided that during the period between May 1 and August 1 the assessors should list and assess property owned on May 1, but also contained a provision that the county board of equalization should add land to the tax roll if preempted or entered before the third Tuesday in August. This departure from the tax day procedure was upheld by the Kansas supreme court in 1871.[60] The following year, the court held that land which did not pass from the government until October 1 was not subject to taxation for that year.[61]

The May 1 assessment date was changed to April 1 in 1862, and then to March 1 in 1866. The 1866 law stated that transfer or sale of personal property subsequent to March 1 did not authorize the omission of the property from the list, even if the list was not made out until after the sale.

The 1868 law also contained provisions requiring that merchants average the value of personal property on hand during the year.[62] The merchant was directed to estimate the value of property on hand in each month of the preceding year, add the monthly estimates and divide by the number of months he may have been engaged in business.[63] It also provided that merchants beginning business after March 1, but before November 1, were to report the average value of property on hand. Manufacturers were subject to similar averaging provisions with regard to articles purchased for use in the manufacturing process.[64]

No averaging provision was applied to livestock. In 1872, F. W. Giles described the situation:

The cattle business, one of the most important in the State, and requiring the employment of a large portion of the moneyed capital of the State at some seasons of the year, almost entirely escape taxation. The merchant whose goods and wares are local is taxed for the average amount, but the merchant whose cattle in tens of thousands darken the plain for half the year, roving from county to county, having no fixed abode, bears no burden of State, county or town. The law does not inquire of him the average number of cattle held during the year, but only how many he owned in the State on the first day of March. Now, as the trade in cattle has not commenced at so early a day in the year, and there are none in the State but such as have wintered here, of course there are none other to tax. Immense herds may be ruminating in unorganized counties, or across the border of the State, lingering there from abroad, or driven there from within, for the sole purpose of avoiding taxation, and with entire efficacy.[65]

In 1881 a provision was added to Section 7 dealing with stock driven into a county from any unorganized county or beyond the boundaries of the state for the purpose of grazing. Such stock was made taxable if driven into the county at any time before December 1, just as if it had been in the county on the March 1 assessment day.[66] That provision was declared unconstitutional in 1884. Singling out one class of property for treatment different from that accorded other classes of property was held to violate the uniform and equal provision of the Kansas constitution.[67]

Banks were also subject to an averaging requirement for reporting the value of notes and bills discounted. The average value of "moneys, effects or dues of every description" loaned, invested, or otherwise used with view to profit was to be reported. Specie kept on hand for the purpose of redeeming its currency or meeting its liabilities to depositors and balances due from other banks on which no interest profit or other consideration was received could be deducted from the average of taxable intangibles.[68]

The 1876 statutes contained a provision to prevent escape of taxation by converting cash into U.S. government bonds just before assessment day. The provision required value of such bonds be divided by twelve and multiplied by the number of months such bonds were not owned during the year. The result was to be listed as money on hand on the first of March.

Special provisions dealing with the taxation of railroads required all personal property, including rolling stock belonging to railroads and cars making regular trips over railroads in the state, to be returned for taxation as of March 1. There does not appear to have been any provision for averaging or prorating.[69]

A law passed in 1899 provided that personal property brought into the state after March 1 and acquiring a situs before September 1 was to be listed by the assessor unless the owner could prove that the property had been assessed for taxation in another county or state.[70]

DEFINING VALUE

Economists had been debating the meaning of value for many decades before Kansas became a state. The classical economists had developed the labor theory of value and had attempted to distinguish between "value in use" and "value in exchange," but the development of marginal utility theory and the supply-demand analysis of Alfred Marshall was not developed until late in the nineteenth century. Supply-demand analysis was crucial to the development of appraisal theory, but in the mid-nineteenth century, those who drafted property tax legislation paid little attention to the finer points of value theory. Apparently, it was assumed that value and market price were equal and that an assessor would have no great difficulty in determining value. The first Kansas statutes contained a very simple, market oriented definition of value:

> Each parcel of real property, outside of every town, city or village, mentioned in section second, shall be valued at its true value in money, excluding the value of the crops growing thereon and improvements; but the price for which such real property would sell at auction or forced sales shall not be taken as a criterion of such value. Personal property of every description shall be valued at the usual selling price of similar property at the time and place of listing; and, if there be no usual price, then at the price that is believed could be obtained therefor in money.[71]

Aside from the awkward wording that might be taken to mean that the definition of value applied only to property outside of municipalities, the definition was straightforward, if unsophisticated. Value was the usual selling price in money or, in the absence of a usual selling price, it was the price the assessor believed it would bring.

The 1866 tax law contained language dealing with the standard of value to be applied to different kinds of property:

> Each parcel of real property shall be valued at its true value in money, excluding the value of the crops which may be grown thereon; but the price at which such real estate would sell at auction or a forced sale shall not be taken as the criterion of such true value. . . . Personal property shall be valued at the usual selling price at the place where the same may be held; but if there be no usual selling price known to the person required to fix the value thereon, it shall be valued at such price as is believed could be obtained therefor in money at such time and place. Money, whether in possession or on deposit, subject to be withdrawn on demand, shall be entered in the statement at the full amount thereof. Depreciated bank notes shall be entered in the statement at their current value. . . . If a credit calls for a specific labor or service, it shall be valued at the current price of such property, labor or service. Annuities shall be val-

ued at such prices as the person listing believes them to be worth in money. Manufactured articles remaining unsold in the hands of manufacturers, shall be valued at their market price at the time and place. No person shall be required to list a greater portion of an obligation given for the payment of rent than the amount which may then be actually due.[72]

It may have been of some help to the assessor to know that depreciated bank notes were not to be listed at face value and that credits calling for specific labor or service should be valued at the current value of that labor or service, but most of the added verbiage was probably of little help. The instruction to value unsold manufacturing articles at market price, at the time and place of listing, gives no indication as to whether the retail or wholesale market was meant, but even so, it may have been more helpful than the statement that annuities should be valued at the price the assessor believes them to be worth in money. Both provisions depended heavily on the judgment of the assessor.

Experience under these laws revealed that the judgments of assessors varied. Dissatisfaction with the tax laws was becoming more general, especially among the Grangers who were concerned about personal property being assessed at various percentages of its true value. In 1870 they were instrumental in securing legislation that they thought would improve the situation.[73] Chapter 120, Laws of 1870, provided: "The several township assessors shall meet at the county seat, in their respective counties on the third Wednesday of April of each year, and then agree upon an equal basis of valuation, of such property as they may be called upon to assess."

The intent of this law was to promote uniformity by allowing all the assessors in a county to come to a common agreement as to the values to be assigned to the various kinds of property. Actually, the new provision was to become a major source of confusion, an impediment to good tax administration, and a favorite target of writers attacking the property tax. In the year the new provision was passed, the assessors of Shawnee County met and agreed to assess all the personal property in the county, except moneys, credits, and shares in national banks, at one-third of its actual value, and to assess moneys, credits, and shares in national banks at full value. They also agreed to permit persons assessed to deduct the amount of their indebtedness from *moneys* and credits, even though the statutes allowed such deductions only from credits.

The action of the Shawnee County assessors was challenged by Daniel Adams and other owners of money, credits, and shares in a national bank. The plaintiffs had paid all their taxes except for two-thirds of the levy on the assessed valuation of moneys, credits, and shares of stock in the national banks owned by them. They asked that the court enjoin the collection of the unpaid portion of the taxes levied against them. The petition was denied in 1871 and then appealed to the Kansas supreme court.[74] The attorney for the plaintiffs pointed out that the assessors deliberately violated the law.

After rejecting the plaintiffs' appeal to a Wisconsin case on the ground that cases in Wisconsin and other states are divided, the court analyzed the dilemma posed by such cases. It found a difference in the way the assessor's action would affect state and local taxes. If a county, township, or municipal corporation in raising revenue for itself alone should intentionally attempt to collect less from one kind of property than from another, there would seem to be some reason for declaring the whole of the taxes void. However, the court goes on to point out that the assessor acts for the entire people of the state and not merely as agents of a county, township, or municipality. Reducing the taxes to be paid by the plaintiffs would have further reduced the portion of the *state* tax paid by taxpayers of Shawnee County.[75] The court added that the plaintiffs have not presented the case so that it is possible to declare the local taxes void and still declare the state taxes valid.

The decision in this case appears to be based on considerations of geographic equity. The evidence showed that the constitutional uniformity requirement had been violated as to the different classes of property within the county, but the court refused to intervene because setting aside the taxes would shift part of Shawnee County's state tax burden to the rest of the state. In making this decision, the court presumed, without evidence, that property in other counties was assessed at true value as required by the statutes.

The case illustrates one of the basic problems of property tax administration as it developed in the United States. Laws are written and interpreted by state government, but administered by local officials who are not subject to administrative supervision. After they have acted, the taxpayer's only remedy may be to sue to invalidate the tax levy, but, because of the way taxes are computed, it is difficult or impossible to do that without imposing inequities on others or completely crippling government. The court, as in the case just reported, can only say that the action was illegal but that nothing can be done about it.

The court made it clear that the assessors had misconstrued the laws:

> *But still they must have so construed said section, for it cannot be supposed that they willfully intended to violate the law.* This section means that the assessors shall meet and compare their various views and notions with regard to the values of all the different articles of property required to be assessed, and then from these various views and notions agree upon what should be the true and correct values as the basis of the valuations of the property that they might be called upon to assess. [Emphasis added.][76]

The emphasized portion of the above quotation may have been the statement of a legal principle, rather than an indication of naiveté on the part of the court. In any case, assessors continued to "misconstrue" the law and it would remain in effect for many years despite denunciations by state officials and other observers of the property tax scene. In effect, the assessors of each county replaced uniformity with a county classification system. This illegal exercise of local autonomy provided "cover" for legislators and local officials who found strict adherence to a uniformity provision personally objectional or politically dangerous.

SUMMARY AND CONCLUSIONS

In its attempts to implement uniform property taxation as specified in the state constitution, the Kansas legislature found it necessary to steer among a number of obstacles. Some were imposed by the federal constitution, laws, and treaties. Some were inherent in the nature of the administrative problem. Some resulted from the political clout of those striving to reduce their own tax burdens.

The process of determining what property was taxable in Kansas was complicated by the large amount of Kansas real estate that was federal property or the property of Indian tribes. This property was transferred to private ownership under a variety of arrangements—some legal and some involving various kinds of legal shortcuts or falsifications. Land was often occupied by claim jumpers and railroads found it possible to keep federal land grant land off the tax rolls for many years by delaying receipt of title from the federal government.

Early problems of defining taxable property foreshadowed the greater problems that were to come. It was widely agreed that some kinds of intangible property should be taxed, but neither the writers of the statutes nor the courts had a clear understanding of the relationship between the legal concept of property and the economic concept of wealth. With the benefit of hindsight and the thinking of later scholars, it is possible to think more clearly about this problem. However, it is by no means certain that a system capable of producing equal taxation of wealth could have been developed. The problem is made even more difficult by jurisdiction problems. The jurisdiction rules applied in the American judicial system do not prevent intangible property rights from being taxed in more than one location. To compound the difficulty, the problem of separating and valuing equities and the jurisdiction problem have synergistic relationships. Solutions to either problem are difficult, but solving both at once is even more difficult.

The jurisdiction problem is simpler in the case of tangible property, but even so, there are problems. Some kinds of tangible personal property are normally moved during the course of a year. Other kinds were moved to take advantage of different tax days in different jurisdictions. Attempts to eliminate these problems led to the adoption of averaging provisions, as a replacement for tax day assessment, for some kinds of property, but this approach created new inequities.

Another state responsibility was to define "taxable value." The legislature responded by making it clear that market value or usual selling price was to be the standard. Some attempts to give more specific directions for specific kinds of property were made, but in the end, much reliance was placed on the assessor's judgment. An ill-advised effort to improve the assessment process was made in

1870, when the township assessors of each county were required to meet annually to agree on the basis of valuation. These meetings were intended as opportunities for the assessors of a county to come to an agreement as to the value of common items, but the results can better be described as allowing a classification system in each county. This leads us to a discussion of the role of local government in the administration of the property tax.

7
Local Administration, 1860–1900

Alexis De Tocqueville found the emphasis on local government one of the important and unique features of American politics. He admitted that the complex system of local government was administratively inefficient and, on the surface, seemed to promote disorder, but he expressed admiration for the political results:

> The Americans seem to me to have overstepped the limits of sound policy, in isolating the administration of the Government. . . . As the State has no administrative functions of its own, stationed on different parts of its territory, to whom it can give a common impulse, the consequence is that it rarely attempts to issue any general police regulations.[1]

> It is not the *administrative*, but the *political*, effects of the local system that I most admire in America.[2]

In Kansas, governments were organized from the top down. Congress established the territorial government before there was any substantial non-Indian population in the area. Many parts of the state had no local governments when the state constitution was approved. Nevertheless, the system followed the pattern of older states in providing for local administration of such important functions as law enforcement and taxation. De Tocqueville's observation that the state had no administrative function of its own stationed in different parts of the territory was as true in Kansas as it had been decades earlier in states farther east. County officers swore obedience to the law, but did not owe their obedience to any superior officer.

A dichotomy between American state policy as expressed in legislation and as implemented locally was perceived by Frank J. Goodnow. In his pioneering work on public administration, Goodnow asserted that the will of American states could be modified by the local community through its powers of execution or nonexecution: "The result of such a system of local self-government is that state laws which are unpopular in specific communities are often not enforced or are enforced with such modifications as to make the same law quite different as a rule of conduct in different parts of the state."[3] The Kansas property tax provides an almost perfect example of this phenomenon.

ESTABLISHING THE TAX SYSTEM

First priority in the new state of Kansas was to establish a system of taxation that would produce revenue. The territorial government had achieved only limited success in this regard. Local governments were newly established, population was sparse and mobile, and communication was poor.

Evidence of problems was found on the abstracts of assessment rolls filed by the county clerks. In 1864 there was confusion as to whether the capitation (poll) tax was still in effect. The clerk of Dickenson County wrote: "There is [*sic*] eighty-one persons liable to capitation tax if one is levied. If so fix blank." There were two blanks from Jefferson County. The first, a hand-drawn replica of the printed blanks included the remark, "I am of the opinion that the personal property and capitation tax is much larger than can be collected." The second, on a printed blank, contained a note stating that the numbers were the same as on the original but that no plat was on file for one town. The note also reported that since the assessment, about 100 persons had gone into military service and were, therefore, exempt from the capitation tax.[4]

Communication problems are also illustrated by documents in the auditor's file of abstracts for 1865. A letter to the county clerk of Morris County reads:

> The law requires that immediately after the meeting of the County Board of Equalization you send to this office abstract of your assessment Roll. None has been received from your co. although a month has elapsed since the meeting and this is the day for the meeting of the State Board. If therefore your county should be charged an amount of tax greater than others, the blame must rest where it properly belongs. Send your abstract.

The clerk of Morris County replied on the back of the letter:

> I am sorry things are as they are. Our Board had been informed that the law was changed so that the return be made at the same time as the Census returns. We have had no equalization.
>
> Are we to be left without the Laws, and then to be blamed for not doing our duty. Have the laws been published? Why have they not? Let the printer that agreed to publish them see to his bond.[5]

The clerk of Atchison County reported that the work of the county assessor and his assistants had been delayed about one month awaiting census blanks and instructions from the Secretary of State. Davis County reported that "all the Law we have is Ch. 60 Sec. 13, Laws of 1863 and according to that the abstract will be on time if mail does not get lost in the mud." There were several letters that indicated confusion as to whether the capitation tax was still in effect or asking why some counties were exempt from the capitation tax. The clerk of Johnson County reported he had been sick a week, but understood that the 1863 law required the abstract to be forwarded by August 15 and that he knew nothing about a later law.

The 1865 state auditor's report indicated that fifteen counties had not filed abstracts when the state board met. The board determined that the average increase in taxable values in the counties that had filed was 20 percent and it added that percentage to the values for the counties that had not reported. The auditor recommended that there be a change in the date of meeting of either the state or county boards of equalization as the time between them was too short with existing mail facilities.[6]

The state did try to help counties discover taxable property. The auditor's report for 1865 included copies of his correspondence with the U.S. Secretary of the Interior requesting a list of lands embraced in the Sac and Fox, Kaw, and Ottawa Indian reservations that had passed into private hands. The list received was, "a little incorrect," but it was rearranged and forwarded to the clerks of the proper counties. The auditor expected that the state's revenue would increase by at least $10,000 as a result of these large additions to real estate.[7]

The problems with such elementary aspects of tax administration as getting assessment rolls completed and abstracts returned to the state by the legally specified date tended to disappear as local governments became better organized, tax laws more stable, and communication facilities improved.

In at least one instance, there was large-scale defiance of state authority. The message of Governor James M. Harvey in 1872 reported that Wallace County had never paid any revenue to the state; nor had Cherokee County since the Neutral Land League succeeded in electing the county officers there:[8]

> It is the duty of the State to provide for the protection of persons and property within its limits; for this purpose it has a proper and legitimate claim upon all the property in every county, for its due proportion of the necessary expenses. The Executive can, and will repress riotous demonstrations and secure the protection of persons and property by the interposition of military force when necessary; but under existing laws, cannot guarantee the assessment and collection of taxes in those anomalous cases where organizations, having purposes inimical to law, have succeeded, or may succeed, in the election of local officers so corrupt or incompetent as to be unwilling or unable to preserve the peace or assess and collect the revenue.[9]

The limitations on administrative action imposed by the division of responsibility between state and local governments are well illustrated by the governor's statement. The governor could use military force to quell a riot, but he could not guarantee the assessment and collection of the property tax.

LISTING AND VALUING PROPERTY

The 1862 law provided for the election of county assessors for a one-year term. The assessor, with the approval of the county commission, was empowered to appoint one or more deputies. Both the assessor and the deputies were to be paid by the county commission at a rate not exceeding $2.50 per day for time actually worked.[10] The 1866 law increased the county assessor's term of office to two years and raised the maximum pay to $3.00 per day.[11]

In 1869 the office of county assessor was abolished and the township trustee was made the township assessor. Incorporated cities of the first and second class were declared to be townships for the purposes of assessment and were required to elect an assessor.[12] Township trustees were elected for one-year terms.[13] Later, city assessors were appointed.[14]

The 1876 statutes placed the initial responsibility for listing personal property on the taxpayer or the taxpayer's agent. The taxpayer or agent was required to file a statement listing personal property in twenty-five specified classes. There were six classes of animals, eight classes of other kinds of tangible property, and eleven classes of intangible property. The statutes stated that the person listing the property could be required to verify the list by oath.[15]

It was the duty of the assessor to increase or diminish the value of any or all items of personal property as listed by any person, company, or corporation if he was satisfied that the return had been made above or below its true value. The change had to be made at the time the return was made.[16]

If the property owner or agent failed to deliver a list or refused to take the oath, the assessor was to proceed to make a list from available information and to take statements under oath from anyone who might have the necessary information. If any person having such information refused to take an oath or to testify under oath, the assessor could have him summoned before a justice of the peace where he could be forced to testify.[17]

Upon delivering the list to the county clerk, the assessor was required to take a long prescribed oath attesting that he had followed the law and had not in any way contrived in violation of the law. The assessor swore he had diligently and by the best means possible endeavored to list and ascertain the value of all items of personal property, moneys, credits, investments in bonds, stocks, joint stock companies, corporations, or otherwise.[18]

In every even-numbered year, the assessor was required to list all the real property in his township or city liable to assessment and taxation and to assess the same at its value in money.[19] The assessor was required to take an oath certifying the list and the value of each parcel of property.[20]

The county clerk was responsible for providing books and forms to the assessor. On or before the first day of March, in each year in which real estate was to be assessed, the clerk was to provide each township or city assessor with a list of taxable lands or town lots in the township or city. The list was to show the assessed value at the last preceding assessment. The clerk was also responsible for adding property that had been omitted by the assessor or that became taxable after the assessor had reported. For example, merchants who commenced trading after the first of March and before the first day of November were to report their property to the county clerk. The clerk was to certify the amount of railroad property assessed by the State Board of Railroad Assessors and the amount to be placed on the roll of each governmental unit. The clerk was also to add to the assessment roll any property that the assessor had failed to assess. If the taxpayer or taxpayer's agent refused to list personal property, the county clerk was to add 50 percent to the value returned by the assessor. The clerk was also required to correct errors in the quantity and description of land contained in the tax roll, but was to make no deductions in value except as specifically provided in the act.[21]

The county clerk and the board of county commissioners had the power, any time prior to final settlement of taxes with the treasurer, to compel the property owner and witnesses to attend a hearing for the purpose of determining the proper amount of taxes due. It was the duty of the county attorney to appear at such proceedings and examine witnesses or otherwise aid in determining the proper amount of taxes due.[22]

County Board of Equalization

Early in the history of the American property tax, it was realized that there needed to be review or equalization of the work of the local assessor. A board of equalization was created in the Massachusetts Colony in 1668. Commissioners representing the shires and towns were to meet to revise assessments; "so that there may be a just and equal proportion between county and county, towne and towne, merchant and husbandmen."[23] By the time Kansas was admitted to the Union, county boards of review existed in a number of states, but a careful student of the property tax reports that the boards were unable to exercise any significant influence upon the course of development of the general property tax.[24]

The boards of equalization in Kansas were composed of the county commissioners. In even-numbered years they were to equalize the assessment of real estate and personal property. In odd-numbered years, when real estate was not assessed, they were to equalize the assessment of personal property.

The statutory instructions were not models of clarity or consistency. The instructions for raising the valuation of property assessed at less than its true value in money required valuations be *raised to the level agreed upon by the assessors of the county*. The instructions for reducing the valuation of property assessed at more than its true value required valuations be reduced to *the average value in the county.* In view of the fact that the true value in money, the level agreed on by the assessors, and the actual level of assessment often differed, it is difficult to see how equal taxation could have been attained.[25]

Local violations of the constitutional uniformity requirement were tacitly accepted by the legislature and there was no intervention by the courts. The Kansas supreme court did rule on a number of procedural issues. For example, in an 1883 case the court decided that the 1876 law clearly gave boards the power to raise an assessment without notice to the property owner.[26] In *Atchison, Topeka & Santa Fe Railroad Co. v. Wilson*[27] the board's right to change the assessment of real estate in odd-numbered years was upheld. In a Marion County case, the court set aside actions of a county board of equalization because it had not met within the county.[28]

In *Fields v. Russell*, decided in 1888, the court stated that there was no requirement that the board receive evidence or hold a hearing. "Counties are divided into commissioner districts, and the board is supposed to know the value of property in the county."[29]

The attorney for the plaintiffs in an 1892 case was unrestrained in his indictment of a system that depended on the personal knowledge of the commissioners:

> It is only necessary to read it [the order of the county board of equalization] to discover its insincerity. What possible knowledge could the board have had that every piece and parcel of property in the city of Atchison was assessed 61 percent less than the basis agreed upon or, in Shannon township, 24 percent? This the order presumes. Can it be supposed that they were acquainted with each lot? What wonderful discernment enabled them to arrive at this particular number, 61? Equalizing presumes a comparison. It would puzzle the profoundest philosopher to establish a comparison between the valuations of the town lots and farm property. It would give a mathematician the nightmare to figure out how adding 61 percent to the total valuation of a precinct would enable him to find a "happy medium". Observe, also, the punctilious care with which the percent is figured out. Sixty percent would not suffice, it must be 61. Twenty-five percent would be to large; it must be only 24. An then, to complete the subterfuge and lend a mock air of justice to the whole farce, the board rebukes poor Walnut township also, saying:
>
> > "Nay, if the scale do turn
> > But in the estimation of a hair"
>
> and gravely adds 1½ percent to its valuation also. And this is called equalization![30]

Unfortunately for the plaintiff, this vivid language did not sway the court, which upheld the action of the county board of equalization raising the valuation of all property in certain townships and cities.

Another weakness of the board was its political nature. The author of a book on Kansas taxation published in 1900 stated that "individuals make free use of this opportunity to threaten and persuade the board to modify valuations. Often the privilege is a means of righting a wrong; often it is a means of shirking the payment of a just share of taxation."[31]

The State Board of Equalization

The purpose of state boards of equalization was to ensure that taxpayers in each county or assessment district paid a proper share of the state tax. Sporadic state equalization occurred in Virginia in 1782, and attempts at statewide equalization were made in Maine, Vermont, and Connecticut in 1820, but the first instances of regular statewide equalization appeared in the midwestern states in the 1850s. Michigan and Iowa established statewide boards in 1851 and Wisconsin and Indiana in 1852. The evidence shows that evasion and competitive undervaluation were important reasons for the creation of these boards.[32]

The Kansas State Board of Equalization was composed of the secretary of state, state auditor, and the state treasurer. The board was directed by the statutes to examine the abstracts of property assessed for taxation in the several counties, including railroad property. Real property was to be equalized by adding or deducting such percentages as the board deemed equitable, but the board could not reduce the aggregate state assessment. The board was to apportion the amount of taxes raised for state purposes among the several counties of the state in proportion to the valuation of taxable property as equalized.[33] An 1881 case upheld the right of the State Board of Equalization to increase the value of property assessed by the State Board of Railroad Assessors.[34]

The 1876 statutes provided that when the State Board of Equalization changed the valuation of any county, the county commissioners were authorized to use that valuation as the basis of making all levies—but apparently this was not done. Elbert J. Benton reported in 1900 that the practice was to use county valuations for local purposes and the valuations fixed by the state board for the purpose of allocating state taxes among the counties.[35]

The board had no staff and the only information provided was an abstract that the state auditor compiled from the reports of the county clerk. The abstract showed the aggregate and average valuation of major classes of property for each county. The 1871 report of the auditor noted that the work of the board was based on nothing more than conscientious belief and not on knowledge of facts.[36]

In spite of the lack of precise data, the State Board of Equalization made many changes in the valuation of farm lands. In 1860 the median increase or decrease in the county average value per acre was 19.4 percent, but by 1870 the size of the changes had declined to almost zero, then rose in 1871 and 1872. Later in the 1870s there were several years in which the board made relatively few changes, but changes were made in almost every county in 1886 and 1889.[37]

The proceedings of the 1897 board suggest that some things had not changed greatly since the early days of statehood. The board met on July 14, as required by law, and adjourned because many county clerks had not reported in time for the state auditor to complete the abstract of assessment. The board met again on July 21 and continued in session from day to day for the purpose of hearing the representatives of the counties relative to valuation. Before adjournment on July 25, they ordered changes in the assessed values of locally assessed property ranging from a 40 percent increase to a 50 percent decrease. In only five counties were the values certified by the county clerk accepted.[38]

TAX LEVY

The first state legislature made a permanent annual levy of one mill for the support of the common schools.[39] This levy continued in effect, even though it violated Article 2, Sec. 24, of the Kansas constitution, which required that no money be drawn from the treasury except in pursuance of a specific appropriation and that no appropriation should be for more than one year.[40] Constitutional challenge to this procedure did not reach the supreme court until after the levy was repealed in 1879.[41]

State tax levies were earmarked for specific use and the proceeds were segregated by an accounting device known as a *fund*. For example, the revenue act passed in 1869 levied seven mills for current expenses, one and one-half mills for interest on the state debt, and one-half mill for the sinking fund.[42] These levies plus the one-mill permanent school fund levy totaled ten mills, which was the highest mill levy levied by the state of Kansas until 1992.[43]

The county commission was directed to estimate and determine the amount of money to be raised for county purposes, the amount to be raised for school purposes, and the amount of other taxes they were required to levy.[44] In addition to general authority to levy taxes, the county was given specific, limited authority to levy taxes for specific purposes. For example, the poor law passed in 1862 provided that a tax could be levied to purchase or build an asylum, but if the amount was more than $500 the proposal had to be submitted to a vote of the people. The same law authorized a tax for the support of the poor.[45]

Each township elected two constables, two justices of the peace, one township trustee, and as many overseers of the highway as might be necessary. The trustee was to levy the tax subject to the concurrence of the board of county commissioners.

Chapter 76 of the Laws of 1861 required the county superintendent of schools to divide the county into convenient school districts. According to that law, the adult male and female inhabitants of the district, in the annual meeting, could vote to establish an annual tax not to exceed .05 percent to purchase or lease a school site. The inhabitants could also vote to levy a tax not to exceed .025 percent for teachers' wages and up to .025 percent to supply blackboards, outline maps, and apparatus for illustrating the principles of science, or to discharge debts or liabilities of the district. The provision of this chapter that allowed women to vote at the annual school meeting was one of the first examples of women's suffrage in the United States.

The 1862 statutes also contained a chapter permitting the incorporation of cities. Among the powers of the city council were the powers to levy a tax on the value of all property within the limits of the city as ascertained from the books of the county assessor. The tax was not to exceed ten mills. Of that amount, one mill could be for the general support of the common schools and one-half mill could be for furnishing real estate and buildings for the school. The council could also impose a poll tax not exceeding $1 on able-bodied male persons over the age of twenty-one and under fifty years of age. In addition, they could levy and collect a license tax on auctioneers, taverns, hawkers, peddlers, dram-shops, liquor sellers, pawn brokers, shows and exhibitions for pay, billiard tables, ball and ten pin alleys, hacks, drays, wagons, or other vehicles used within the city for pay, theaters, and theatrical exhibitions.[46]

The early legislative sessions passed many special bills dealing with the incorporation or powers of municipalities. By 1876, the number of special bills had been reduced and municipalities were designated as cities of the first, second, or third class. Cities of the first and second class were not part of townships, but the area encompassed by cities of the third class remained within a township. All cities were empowered to levy property taxes, subject to maximum mill or percentage rates. All were empowered to levy license taxes and cities of the second and third class could levy capitation taxes. All cities had power to impose special assessment, called special taxes in Kansas, for the purposes of making local improvements such as streets or sidewalks.

The first tax case decided by the Kansas supreme court involved the legality of a tax levy made by the city of Leavenworth in 1858. Leavenworth levied taxes in addition to the seven mills expressly authorized by its charter, arguing that authority to carry out other functions implied the right to levy taxes to finance them. The court disagreed, stating that the powers of municipal corporations are strictly limited and controlled by the will of its creator as expressly defined in the charter or act of incorporation.[47]

In 1871 the court heard a case in which it was claimed that the levy for the bond sinking fund was excessive. The court observed that the evidence indicated that the excess must have been slight and that it would have to be enormously great before the court would set aside a levy for this reason. In any case, the plaintiffs had not paid or offered to pay any part of the tax and therefore had not placed themselves in a position to receive relief from a court of equity.[48] This is only one of many cases that show the courts' reluctance to void a tax levy. Another example is the 1872 case, *Wyandotte & K.C. Bridge Company v. Wyandotte County Commissioners.*[49] The county commission, after an election, authorized the issue of bonds to assist the city of Wyandotte to build a free bridge. The plaintiff asked for an injunction to prohibit the levy of a tax to pay the bonds because such assistance was illegal. The court declined to issue the injunction because there was no way of knowing whether the plaintiff would own property and be taxed when the tax was levied and therefore the plaintiff had no standing before the court: "It has already been settled in this state that a private person cannot, by virtue of being a citizen and taxpayer merely, maintain an action against the county or its officers where the act complained of affect merely the interest of the public in general.[50]

McConnell v. Hamm[51] (1876) involved a tax levy to service bonds issued illegally to finance a woolen mill. The taxpayer paid the tax voluntarily, but the county treasurer refused to turn it over to the bondholders. The court refused to order the treasurer to pay, but said the matter of whom the money belonged to could not be decided until properly presented to the court.

A Marion County case grew out of a county seat dispute. A county seat election was held in 1866, but the board of commissioners erected county buildings in a different location. On August 8, 1878, the county commissioners, on or about midnight, with the doors closed, without the presence of the county attorney, and without public notice, directed the county clerk to advertise for bids to "repair" county buildings. In fact, the repairs were new permanent county buildings. The district judge upheld the commissioners, but the supreme court held that the erection of permanent buildings is not a normal county function, cannot be financed out of moneys levied for normal expenses, and that ample provision had been made for the creation of a special fund for buildings and for issuing bonds after an election.[52]

TAX COLLECTION

From the viewpoint of the governmental unit, one of the principal advantages of the property tax is the ease with which it can be collected. The tax becomes an automatic lien on the property and, in the case of real estate, owners are forced to pay the tax in order to keep a clear title or to transfer the title.

The 1876 statutes required officials of cities, school districts, and townships to certify tax levies to the county clerk to be collected by the county treasurer and paid into the treasury of the proper governmental unit.[53] The treasurer was required to accept state warrants and state bonds in payment of state taxes, county warrants in payment of county taxes, township warrants in payment of taxes of that township, and city warrants in payment of taxes of that city, but the warrants were to be received only in payment of the tax for the fund on which such warrants were drawn. Taxes were due on December 20, but could be paid in installments with the second half being due the following June 20.[54]

When personal property taxes remained unpaid on the first day of January or the first day of July, the county treasurer was to issue a warrant directing the sheriff to levy the unpaid taxes plus penalties and fees against the goods and chattels of the person to which such taxes were assessed.[55] The procedure for collecting delinquent real estate taxes was similar to that in use in many other states and did not differ greatly from that commonly used today. The county treasurer between the first and tenth of July was to make a list of all lands upon which taxes had not been paid by June 20. This list, accompanied by a notice that the lots would be sold at a sale beginning the first Tuesday in September, was to be published in a newspaper of general circulation and also posted in the county treasurer's office.[56]

At the sale, the person offering to pay the taxes and charges against a parcel of land or town lot for the smallest quantity of land off the north side of the parcel or lot became the purchaser. If there was no other purchaser, the property was to be "bid off" to the county treasurer in the name of the county.[57] It was specifically provided that lands and lots did not need to be sold in the name of any particular person and that no sale was to be invalid because the name of the owner was incorrect.[58]

The purchaser was required to pay the amounts due within twenty-four hours and was given a tax certificate. Tax certificates for lands bid off to the county were to be issued to any person willing to pay the taxes and charges due. The owner of land sold at tax sale had three years in which to redeem the land by reimbursing the holder of the certificate for all taxes, fees, and penalties paid, plus interest.[59] If the owner of the property did not redeem it, the holder of the tax certificate or his assignee was entitled to a tax deed. This deed granted an absolute estate in fee simple, subject to unpaid taxes and charges, and was prima facie evidence of regularity.

Many early tax cases heard by the Kansas supreme court dealt with tax collection or foreclosure.[60] Many involved procedural questions. For example, it was often claimed that tax certificates or tax deeds were not made out properly or that the tax sale had not occurred on the proper date or at the proper place.[61]

A perusal of early Kansas newspapers reveals that many parcels of real estate were sold for taxes. Settlers were mobile and sometimes abandoned land, taxes unpaid, and moved on to some other place. Capital was so scarce and interest rates so high that it was often cheaper to "borrow" from the government by leaving taxes unpaid than to pay the interest rates demanded by eastern capitalists.[62] If the interest rate charged on delinquent taxes was high, it made it difficult for an owner to redeem land sold by the sheriff for taxes, but too low a rate encouraged delinquency. The rate on unpaid taxes was 25 percent for several years, but in 1869 it was raised to 50 percent.[63] By the end of the century, it had been reduced to 15 percent.[64]

In spite of the great amount of property sold in tax sales and much controversy and litigation over the redemption procedure, the general approach to collecting real estate taxes did not change greatly. One major change was an 1879 law allowing the county to permit the owner to redeem property for less than the legal tax, penalties, and interest if land bid off to the county had gone unredeemed for three years and no one had offered to purchase the property for taxes, penalties, and costs. Alternatively, a tax sale certificate could be issued to a purchaser for less than the unpaid taxes, penalty, and interest.

CRITICISM OF THE PROPERTY TAX

It was clear at the end of the nineteenth century that Kansas had not succeeded in implementing uniform, equal taxation of wealth. County boards of equalization had the authority to correct assessments, but had no information about values except their own knowledge. The State Board of Equalization could adjust the aggregate value of real estate in the counties for purposes of apportioning the state tax, but was provided with no data about values except worksheets showing the average assessments per lot and per acre.

Criticism of Assessment and Equalization

The weakness of the property tax administration did not result from lack of critical attention. Almost every governor from the beginning of statehood until the end of the century denounced the tax or its administration. The state auditor's reports often contained even longer and more detailed criticism, and sometimes the state treasurer joined in with a word or two denouncing some aspect of the tax.

Criticism of assessment and equalization was not confined to the reports of state officials. In 1872, F. W. Giles published a forty-page booklet entitled, *Review of the Tax System of the State of Kansas.*[65] Giles was an early resident of Topeka. He had served as the first postmaster, as county recorder, county clerk, and had engaged in a variety of real estate and banking businesses. In 1872 he became the first president of Topeka National Bank. He was also one of the plaintiffs in the *Beman* case in which the supreme court had refused to provide any remedy to taxpayers whose property was overassessed as a result of the agreement of the assessors at their county meeting.[66]

Giles evidenced considerable sympathy with the assessor who is told to value property at its true value in money and also to value it at such equal basis of valuation as the several assessors of the county may agree upon. He noted that assessors have little data on which to base a decision. There are few sales and the assessor can only call to mind the price he has quoted a real or imaginary inquirer for his own farm. Thinking about the problem, the assessor holds council with his neighbors,

> in which the general subject and severity of taxes is discussed, the hard work and poor pay of farming lamented, and the disgusting announcement made that "that conscienceless scamp of an assessor, Jones, over in Hardscrabble township, is valuing property shamelessly low, to avoid taxation . . . so they say." In the despairing frame of mind consequent upon his many doubts and perplexities, the assessor finally gets about his work; makes entry of his first piece of land by the standard of "true value in money" which at that particular moment does not mark a high figure upon the scale, and which, under the surveillance of his tax-abhorring neighbors, drops lower and lower as piece after piece is added to the roll and the return made ready for exhibit. Thus after

seven day study of the science of political economy as applied to the subject of taxation, the work of the several assessors is complete and with feelings of men who have thrown dice, they stand before the county board, each curious to conceal his own work, and to discover that of his associate assessors, when the box is raised.[67]

Giles then presents data showing great variations and abrupt fluctuations in the average value per acre among townships of Shawnee County and similar data for other counties.[68]

Giles' analysis differs from many of the time in that he does not blame local officials for the poor quality of assessment. As the title of his work indicates, he believed the system to be at fault. The blame for the situation goes to those who make the laws, not those who try to apply them. The analytical part of his work ends: "What manner of men are those that make our laws."[69] Giles was not content to criticize. He proposed that the state tax be apportioned to the counties on the basis of the density of population of the county. He refers to the theories of economists M. Bastiat and Amasa Walker to support the view that it is population that gives value to land. County, city, and township taxes would continue to be based on value, but valuations would be determined by county assessors applying systematic methods of appraisal. The county assessor would prepare geographic and topographic maps and property would be classified with respect to the conditions that influence value. Giles referred to the way insurance companies classify property with respect to risk as an example of the way property could be classified for assessment purposes and mentioned the distance of a property from town, railroads, and highways as factors that would be considered.

To complete his reform plan, Giles proposed to eliminate the taxation of personal property. He based his argument on the impossibility of administering the tax on personal property. Referring to the use of the oath as a means of enforcing personal property taxation, he concluded that an oath loses it power and by common consent it is not deemed a lie when it is so palpable that none believe it. To those who objected that it would be inequitable to exempt personal property, Giles replied that there were other ways of reaching the individual that will restore the just burden of public duty. The work of David Wells and his associates on a special board of commissioners for the state of New York was cited, but no details were given.[70]

Giles was ahead of his time in Kansas and in the forefront of national opinion about the property tax. His ideas about appraisal methods, county assessors, and the exemption of personal property would be heard increasingly on the national and state scenes. Some of his suggestions were echoed by Kansas governors, but few were acted on.

In 1889 Governor John A. Martin reported that the Kansas laws for assessment and taxation had defects that were recognized as organic. He stated that it was absurd to expect that township assessors holding their office by election would not endeavor to secure all possible exemption of their neighbors from the burden of taxation. Governor Martin cited the contradiction between the requirement that property be assessed at true value and the requirement that the assessors of a county agree upon the basis of value and endorsed a resolution of the county clerks calling for a county assessor.[71]

In 1895 Governor L. D. Lewelling, a populist, tried a different tactic. He proposed that owners of property be given a strong and selfish motive for returning property at its actual value. He suggested that the legislature provide that in any controversy over the value of property, such as in disputes over value for insurance purposes, the valuation placed on the property for taxation should be conclusive as its actual value. Going one step further, he proposed that no kind of legal action, not even a criminal action, should be maintained without the production of a certified copy of the assessment list showing that the property had been listed for taxation and that no property had been removed to avoid taxation.[72]

Governor E. N. Morrill, speaking six days later as incoming governor, seemed uncertain as to whether there were organic problems with the system or whether problems could be cured by good administration. If every officer complied strictly with the laws relating to assessment and taxation, there would be little cause for complaint, but he added that it was impossible to get just valuation of property under the present system. He recommended that county assessors be appointed by the judge of the district court for four-year terms to replace the 1,600 city and township assessors elected for one-year terms.

Quantifying Inequities

As the century drew to a close, there was greater emphasis on quantifying inequities. In 1888, the *Queen City Herald* of Ottawa published a table based on questionnaires sent to county clerks. The clerks were asked the rate of assessment as a percent of real value. They were also asked the assessed value of national banks in their county. The answers were combined with data about the paid up stock and surplus of national banks as shown in the biennial agricultural report. Answers were received from seventy-one counties but "some were not clear." Answers from forty-one counties were compiled into a table that is not entirely clear either, but it is obvious that local officials did not hesitate to admit that assessment was not at true value. The answer to the question regarding the level of assessment ranged from 25 to 66⅔ percent, and the remarks column indicated that different classes of property were assessed at different levels. Many indicated that real estate was assessed at a percentage different from the "general level" of assessment. Often real estate was assessed lower. In one case, real estate was reported to be assessed at 16⅔ percent. The assessed values of the national banks ranged from 7½ percent of paid in stock and surplus to 60 percent.[73]

The Kansas Bureau of Labor also began to collect and publish quantitative data about the prevailing level of assessment. In 1897, for example, the bureau

Table 7.1. Basis of Assessment of Real and Personal Property for 1897 (as agreed upon officially by township and city assessors)

County	Realty (%)	Personality (%)
Atchison	25	25
Chase	50	33⅓
Cherokee	33⅓	50
Decatur	100	100
Gove	200	33⅓
McPherson	40	40
Rawlins	100	100
Republic	20	33⅓
Sedgwick	30	30
Wabaunsee	20	33⅓
Woodson	50	50

Source: Kansas Bureau of Labor as quoted in James Ernest Boyle, *The Financial History of Kansas* (Madison: University of Wisconsin Bulletin No. 247, Economic and Political Series, v. 5. no. 1, 1908), 117.

reported the level of assessment officially agreed to by the township and city assessors in a number of counties. Table 7.1 is from the report.

In view of the growing national sentiment in favor of exempting personal property or taxing it at a lower rate, it is interesting that a few counties reported taxing personal property at a higher rate. Perhaps the land hunger and speculative land mania resulted in favorable treatment of real estate.

An important advance in the effort to provide quantitative evaluation of the level and quality of assessment occurred when the Bureau of Labor began comparing assessed values with actual sales prices. The 1897 report included a chart based upon 1,648 sales. The chart shows clearly that different classes of property were assessed at different levels. Farm real estate was assessed at a higher percentage of value than personal property and small farms were assessed higher than were larger, more valuable ones. The following tabulation shows the assessment rates (by percent) for various kinds of property:

Farms worth $500 and under	56.0%	Packing houses	6.0%
Farms worth $500–$1,000	41.0	Money	2.0
Farms worth $5,000	25.0	Mortgages, notes, and bonds	0.9
Farms worth $10,000	17.0	Debts and accounts	0.0
Goods and chattels	10.0		

Commenting on these data, James Boyle explained that once an assessor breaks away from the 100 percent basis of valuation he no longer has any guiding principles except the considerations that come up in individual cases. "A small holding is assessed at something like its real value; but in the case of a large holding he is willing to knock off a few thousand since this still leaves a large sum. Another factor is the importance, prestige, and influence of a person with a large holding. He is more apt to be favored with a lenient assessment than his humble neighbor."[74]

Criticism of Local Expenditure and Debt Policies

As tax administrators, local officials acted as agents of the state. They were bound by state law to carry out policies established by the state. On the other hand, local governments were given authority, within limits, to determine the level and composition of local taxation, spending, and borrowing. These powers, especially the borrowing power, were the subject of frequent criticism. Governors and other state officials often mingled criticism of local expenditure and borrowing with their criticism of poor property tax administration.

The state constitutional provisions limiting state debt to $1 million and forbidding the state to be a party to any work of public improvement prevented the state from granting financial aid to railroads or other public enterprises. However, a way was quickly found to avoid that barrier.[75] An 1865 law, authorizing counties to subscribe to stock and issue bonds to railroad companies, was upheld by the Kansas supreme court in 1867.[76] By 1870, municipal aid to railroads amounted to more than $1 million, and concern about the level of debt began to rise. In 1876 new limits on subsidies to railroads included an overall limit of $4,000 per mile. However, the legislature voted many special bills exempting particular local governments from its provisions.[77]

Aid was also given to many enterprises other than railroads. Coal mines, flour mills, manufacturing, prospecting for coal, oil, and gas, and many other enterprises were given subsidies. In 1873 a federal court, in an opinion written by Judge John J. Dillon, held that taxation is a mode of raising revenue for *public* purposes. When it is prostituted to objects, such as the establishment of a bridge, manufactory, or foundry in no way connected with the public interest, it ceases to be taxation and becomes plunder. Bonds issued by a municipality in aid of such private enterprises are "void from the beginning, and void into whatsoever hands they may have come."[78] The attorney general, citing this decision, said that all bonds of this description were void. Money collected from the people to pay them was robbery, and no officer should levy and no person should pay such a tax.[79]

Surprisingly, this opinion had little lasting effect. Some debts were repudiated, but issue of new debts soon resumed. Much latitude was exercised in the interpretation of the phrase "private enterprise." Railroads were not considered in that class and many people considered flour mills as more than private enterprise.[80]

Governor James M. Harvey, in 1872, expressed concern about rising municipal indebtedness. Such obligations, if assumed for other than a public purpose, are illegal, and when legal, may become onerous. Governor Harvey recommended that the legislature strictly define the purposes for which counties, cities, townships, or districts could incur indebtedness. He warned that manipulators of questionable enterprises seeking municipal aid would question the legislature's authority, but thought the legislature would agree that it was a duty of primary importance. Governor Harvey also warned against the passage of special legislation to aid particular enterprises. In a statement that would be echoed by many economists today, he said:

> I recommend your discountenance of a manifest tendency to apply for special legislation to enable towns and cities to subsidize manufacturing establishments, or any kind of private enterprise. I believe the establishment of manufacturers to be conducive to the highest prosperity of the State, but special enactments subsidizing them are apt to contain provisions detrimental to the rights of citizens if not absolutely unconstitutional. The best way to encourage manufactures is to so legislate as to make taxes light and invite the influx of capital and its investment at reasonable rates.[81]

Governor Thomas Osborn made local government reform a major emphasis in his messages. He acknowledged that local governments were under local control and that magnificent school buildings had been erected, but thought that statutes regarding local finance should receive careful review. Governor Osborn believed county government management was an area in need of reform. He cited the expenses of holding courts and the boarding of prisoners as a great source of expense and recommended elimination of the fee system for compensating civil officers.[82] He attributed much of the extravagant expenditure of local governments to lack of proper interest in the selection of local officers and hoped that public sentiment could be created that would result in only the best men occupying office as members of school boards, township trustees, and county commissioners.

Governor Osborn expressed concern about the quality of persons elected as local officials, but in 1877 Governor Anthony attacked the entire system. He said:

> Our system of local and municipal government is both cumbrous and expensive. It provides for too many officers, and invests them with power to incur liabilities and levy taxes, altogether inconsistent with economy and safety. . . . I think it is your first duty to see if it is possible to simplify and cheapen local government machinery; to abolish city governments over rural communities—returning mayors, councilmen, and policemen to the field of productive industry.[83]

The governor then went on to say that if the affairs of the state had been conducted with the same disregard of ultimate results that had characterized local government, the state would be without hope.

Looking back, it is humorous that Governors Osborn and Anthony thought municipal debt was too high. The period of rapid growth in municipal debt still lay ahead. Railroads, stimulated both by federal land grants and municipal subsidies, were overbuilt. James Ernest Boyle points out that stimulating mills and factories from the public funds proved to be a complete and dismal failure. Like a lottery, the game was seductive to the public because there was a chance of winning.

Total debt outstanding in 1876 was about $13 million. Ten years later the debt issued in a single biennium exceeded that amount and by 1892 municipal debt outstanding exceeded $37 million. This was more than three times the annual taxes levied by local governments in the state.[84]

PROPERTY TAX REVENUES

In spite of all the criticism, the property tax produced revenue to establish and maintain state and local government in the period from the beginning of statehood until the turn of the century. Although the government sector of the economy was smaller in relation to the private sector than it is now, the government carried on numerous activities.

In addition to the general governmental functions of making and enforcing laws, a number of institutions were established and maintained during the period. These included prisons, asylums, and homes for soldiers and their orphans. Three universities were established and supported, and there were schools for the deaf and blind. There were a number of agencies for the promotion of agriculture or industry. Among these was a horticultural society, forestry stations, a silk station, a livestock and sanitary commission, and a board of agriculture.[85] The state maintained a library and a historic society. The state also managed the permanent school fund established with proceeds from the sale of school lands. Even so, the financial activities of state government were relatively small compared with those of local government.

In 1896 there were 9,284 school districts in the state.[86] There were 105 counties subdivided into 1,484 townships, and there were hundreds of cities.[87]

Table 7.2. Kansas State and Local Tax Levies, 1875–1899 (levies in thousands)

	State	County	City	Township	School	Total
1875	$729	$1,423	$515	$310	$1,365	$4,342
1880	883	2,061	364	565	1,882	5,695
1885	1,033	2,863	950	982	3,050	8,878
1889	1,515	4,145	2,055	1,458	4,239	13,412
1895	1,402	3,869	1,998	1,479	4,241	12,989
1899	1,799	3,753	2,015	1,602	4,148	13,317
(levies as percent of total)						
1875	16.8	32.8	11.9	7.1	31.4	100.0
1880	15.5	36.2	6.4	9.9	32.0	100.0
1885	11.6	32.2	10.7	11.1	34.4	100.0
1889	11.3	30.9	15.3	10.9	31.6	100.0
1895	10.8	29.8	15.4	11.4	32.7	100.0
1899	13.5	28.2	15.1	12.0	31.1	100.0

Source: Kansas Legislative Council Research Department, Summary History of Kansas Finance, 1861–1937 (Publication No. 60, October, 1937).

In 1875, the first year for which local government tax data are available, total state and local property tax levies amounted to $4,342,000. By 1899, total levies had increased to $13,317,000. In that period the population of Kansas had increased from 531,156 to 1,425,119. The per capita tax levies had increased from $8.17 to $9.34. Table 7.2 shows the breakdown of the levies by level of government. In 1875 county and school levies each amounted to almost one-third of the total. Beginning in 1885 schools became the major users of property tax revenue, a position that they have occupied ever since.

SUMMARY AND CONCLUSIONS

At the end of the nineteenth century, the property tax was the major source of state and local government revenue. Casual observation and rudimentary statistical analysis indicated that uniform taxation of property had not been achieved. Different classes of property were assessed at vastly different percentages of value as were different parcels within classes. The assessment of intangible personal property was particularly bad.

State officials often blamed local officials for poor administration, but some admitted that there were faults in the system. Local officials took an oath to support the constitution and faithfully administer the laws but knew that observing the oath would reduce their chances of reelection. The courts were blunt instruments of enforcement. They considered only those cases brought before them and were reluctant to take actions adverse to unrepresented parties or to bring the machinery of government to a halt by declaring a tax levy invalid.

As De Tocqueville so wisely perceived, the system of local administration did have political advantages. Political participation was maximized because thousands of local officials were involved in the administration of the tax and expenditure of the revenue. Support for the political system was so strong that local expenditures, especially for schools and economic development, rose rapidly. State officials warned of catastrophe ahead.

Although assessment was poorly done and complaints about administration rose, the property tax, especially on real estate, had some features that made it ideally suited to supporting the large number of overlapping taxing units that were formed. Every parcel of real estate is visible, in a fixed location, and even the smallest governmental unit had taxable property within its jurisdiction. The in rem character of the tax was another advantage. The tax was levied against the property, not against a person. It was unnecessary to know or locate the owner to levy the tax. Perhaps even more important, collection was quasi-automatic. Because good title to property could not be passed until all outstanding taxes were paid, the unpleasant and politically dangerous task of collecting delinquent taxes from one's neighbors was greatly eased.

In spite of its considerable success as a source of local revenue, complaints about the property tax were rising as the nineteenth century ended. This was due in part to the rising level of taxation and in part to better understanding of how poorly the tax was administered. Statistical measurement of the quality of assessment and the burdens of taxation became more sophisticated and more widely publicized.

In states farther east, many policy-makers and tax experts were urging that the property tax be modified and that other forms of taxation be used to reach certain kinds of wealth. Some states had already taken steps in that direction. Before Kansas followed those moves, however, it would undertake an ambitious, widely observed effort to improve administration of the tax.

8
Defective in Theory or Practice?

It is impossible to cite another tax that was accepted so widely with so little protest as was the American property tax. On the other hand, it is difficult to think of one that has been criticized so passionately.

At first, there were only intermittent criticisms by disgruntled taxpayers, but toward the end of the nineteenth century critiques of the tax began to be more systematic and better documented. A number of state tax commissions studied tax questions and academic writers began to give attention to state and local tax questions. In 1888, Professor Richard Ely cited tax study commissions in New York (1871), Massachusetts (1875), and Illinois (1886) as evidence of rising interest in the field of taxation.[1]

In 1908 Professor J. H. T. McPherson stated that there had been thirty years of rising criticism of the general property tax.[2] A year later Professor Charles Bullock stated that forty years of criticism had not shaken the belief of the average citizen that substantially all property should be taxed.[3] On the basis of these statements, it appears that systemic and organized criticism of the property tax began in about 1875. That was the year that Nebraska and New Jersey adopted uniformity clauses and it was several years before seven states in the northern and western parts of the country adopted constitutions containing uniformity provisions.

THE SCIENCE OF PUBLIC FINANCE

About 100 years earlier, Adam Smith and other members of the English classical school of economics began to write extensively about taxation. American economists gave tax matters, other than the tariff, little attention until the publication of Ely's book. After that time, there was rapid growth in the literature on state and local taxation. Important examples include Henry Carter Adams's *The Science of*

Public Finance[4] published in 1898 and a number of books and articles by Edwin R. A. Seligman.[5]

The literature was both descriptive and prescriptive. The authors described existing tax systems and prescribed changes in the tax system in the name of "the science of public finance." Often Smith's four canons of taxation served as a starting point. Ely, for example, accepted Smith's idea that the amount of tax should be in proportion to the ability to pay or the revenue a citizen enjoys, and added that this is called equality of sacrifice. Later writers were to expand the equality of sacrifice idea into an argument for progressive taxation, but Ely and his contempories generally interpreted ability to pay as justification for proportional taxation of revenue (income) or property. Ely defended direct taxation as promoting good citizenship, but argued that personal property taxation was becoming more and more unsuited to an industrial civilization. He pointed out that real estate was the chief source of great wealth and special privilege, and it should be the basis of every system of taxation.

Without using the term capitalization, Ely explained the theory of capitalization of a tax on land and added that the theory was applicable, to a lessor extent, to improvements to land. He discussed the problem of competitive undervaluation, suggested that real estate be exempt from *state* taxation, and argued that all assessors in a county should be placed under a single supervisor. He was emphatic in stating that the proper standard of value should be the selling price in an open market. Ely pointed out that the income tax had been successful in Europe and suggested that utilities and railroads be taxed on the basis of gross receipts. He also proposed a tax on the rental value of houses to replace the tax on household goods.

Seligman agreed with Ely on many issues.[6] He agreed that the general property tax is theoretically unjust and said that not a single scientist of note upholds the property tax as the sole or chief contribution to the cost of government. The famous quotation denouncing the general property tax that began Chapter 1 of this volume appeared in all ten editions of Seligman's book.

THE NATIONAL TAX ASSOCIATION

A national forum for criticism of the property tax was created with the establishment of the National Tax Association in 1906. The governor of Ohio invited governors of all states and the premiers of Canadian provinces to attend a conference on state and local taxation in Columbus in 1907. The president of the association invited state auditors, state comptrollers, members of tax commissions, boards of equalization, professors of economics, and presidents of universities to attend. Representatives of thirty-three states and three Canadian provinces accepted. The delegates included four governors and the premier of a Canadian province. Thirty-one universities and a number of associations sent representatives. A second conference was held in Toronto, in recognition of Canadian interest, and was called the Second International Conference on State and Local Taxation.

The papers delivered at both the first and second conferences addressed several different aspects of state and local taxation, but the underlying theme was that the property tax had failed. The delegates to the first conference unanimously adopted a resolution calling for abolition of constitutional uniformity provisions. The same resolution was passed at the second conference.

The attacks on the property tax differed in detail, but the following points were made in several papers:

1. Intangibles cannot be reached for property taxation and if they could it would be double or triple taxation.
2. Tangible personal property is very difficult to assess and self-assessment does not work. The use of oaths and other inquisitorial methods are not tolerable and do not work.
3. Real estate is poorly assessed, mostly because competition among assessment districts results in pressure on assessors to undervalue property. State boards of equalization have not been successful in stopping competitive undervaluation.

Few remedies for the difficulty of taxing intangibles were offered, but several speakers suggested using alternative taxes, such as the income tax. Alternatives for taxing tangible personal property included a tax on the rental value of residences and a proposal that businesses be taxed as a unit, thus capturing the total value of real estate and personal property.

The most popular proposal for dealing with the problems of taxing real estate was "separation of sources." Several writers believed the problem of competitive undervaluation would be eliminated if there was no state property tax, but Professor T. S. Adams reported that such an approach had previously failed in Wisconsin. He argued that inherent difficulties in appraising property and political interference were the main difficulties in appraising real estate.

Most of the speakers at the first two conferences were tax administrators and academic economists. Charles Merriam, prominent political scientist and reformer from Chicago, described how the tax debauches the political system. He saw the property tax system as a strong bulwark of political "machines." The machines used both overt favors and fear of overassessment to fortify their power.

At the third conference in 1909 less attention was given to castigating the property tax and more attention was given to specific tax problems, such as the taxation of insurance companies, utilities, merchants, and manufacturers. There was a session on intergovernmental relations in which the pending income tax amendment to the federal constitution was discussed.

An important event at the third conference was the appointment of a committee to determine whether the failure of the property tax was due to inherent defects or to poor administration. The committee reported to the fourth conference that the tax had failed because of defects in theory. This conclusion was adopted by the conference with the addition of the statement that the attempt to tax personal property was the reason for the failure.[7]

THE KANSAS TAX STUDY COMMISSION OF 1901

In 1901 the Kansas legislature passed legislation establishing a Board of Tax Commissioners consisting of two members of the senate, three members of the house, the state treasurer, the auditor of the state, and the attorney general. The eight-person commission was to consider the laws relating to assessment and taxation and to formulate bills for revision. Ten thousand copies of the report and the recommended bills were to be printed and distributed so that comments could be received before the 1903 legislature convened.[8]

The commission immediately asked Governor Stanley to appoint its members as delegates to the national tax conference to be held on May 24 and 25 in Buffalo, New York, under the sponsorship of the National Civic Federation. The five legislative members and the attorney general attended the conference. Present were state officials, members of tax commissions, and students of taxation from eighteen states.[9]

At the conference most delegates condemned their own state tax laws, but the delegates from Indiana declared that theirs was the best tax system in the United States. Corporate property was being taxed at fair cash value, and the assessment of personal property was increasing. The assessed value of the state had increased, and the rate of taxation proportionally lowered. The principal defect in the system, according to the Indiana delegates, was the elected township assessor, but they expected that to be corrected.[10]

After returning from Buffalo, the Kansas commission met for sixty-seven days and gave unanimous and unqualified approval to a proposed bill modeled after the Indiana system. The accompanying report pointed out that the time spent in preparing the bill proved that tax revision was a lengthy task that the legislature could not undertake. It also expressed the hope that the bill would be adopted without material change.[11]

The report began with a cogent criticism of the Kansas tax system. It stated that the laws relating to taxation constituted a Joseph's coat of many colors, each representing the temporary opinions of legislators or fluctuations in public sentiment. Assessments were made by a township or city assessor impelled by a desire to reduce his township's or city's shares of county and state taxation. The assessor was frequently, though perhaps unconsciously, influenced by considerations of personal friendship or the desire for reelection. No power was lodged in any state body to correct inequality between the different counties, except for the small state levy. The report repeated the charge that meetings of township and city assessors in each county, "had become schools in which they were taught the methods of releasing property from assessment, of lowering values, and generally evading the tax laws."[12]

PROPOSED LAW

The proposed law would have made no substantive change in the definition of property subject to taxation but would have made a radical change in assessment administration. A state tax commission, composed of the state auditor, state treasurer, secretary of state, and two elected commissioners, would be given power to supervise local assessors.

County assessors, elected for four-year terms, would not be eligible for re-election or to be candidates for any office during their terms. They were to appoint deputies, as needed, subject to confirmation of the county commission. No deputy was to assess in the township or district in which he resided. Deputies were to be responsible to the county assessor and serve at his pleasure.[13]

The form to be used in listing personal property was included in the proposed statute. The form was based on Indiana practice but was more specific and complete. The blank contained 102 lines for listing specific items of personal property. Six of these were intangibles: annuities, bonds, notes secured by mortgages, other notes, accounts, and other amounts due. There were ninety-six kinds of chattels. These included money on hand, merchandise or raw materials on hand, various kinds of jewelry, garden products on hand, various kinds of instruments and machines, and several different classes of livestock.[14] Appended to this form were four interrogatories regarding property controlled, disposed of, or converted, and a taxpayer oath. The commission stressed the advantage of requiring the taxpayer to list all his property or commit unmitigated perjury. The commission argued that it was not true that there was already a large amount of perjury; rather, the law was so full of loopholes that there was little difficulty evading it.[15]

The proposed law contained several provisions dealing with specific businesses such as banks, merchants, manufacturers, pawnbrokers, grain brokers, telephone and telegraph companies, express companies, pipelines, railroad and car companies, and a provision dealing with corporations in general. Banks were to continue to be taxed on the value of their capital stock, less the value of real estate assessed to the bank. The officers of the bank were to report the name and address of each shareholder and the value of shares held. The assessor was to examine the most recent report of the bank and, if necessary, the books of the bank to determine the market value of the stock, including surplus and undivided profit. Bank officers could be examined under oath regarding the value of the stock, but bank books were not to be examined for the purposes of discovering the amounts on deposit by customers.

Merchants' and manufacturers' inventories were to be assessed at their average value during the year. In order to encourage manufacturing, it was provided that manufacturers be assessed on the average value of their raw materials, not the value of their finished products.

The provisions for valuing telegraph, telephone, express, and pipeline companies were nearly exact copies of the Indiana statute. Assessment of intercounty telephone companies was to be made by the tax commission. The companies were to be valued as going concerns by determining the total valuation of the stock and bonds of the company. From that amount would be subtracted the assessed value of real estate owned by the company outside of Kansas, not directly used in the business. The fraction of the resulting value to be assigned to Kansas was determined by dividing the total miles and value of lines in Kansas by the total miles and value of lines of the company.

These provisions embodied two concepts that were becoming accepted by those wrestling with the problem of assessing corporation property. The first, known as unit appraisal, was based on the idea that the value of property, such as railroads and telephone companies, can best be determined by valuing the company's operating property as a unit rather than by having local assessors attempt to value the few miles of pipe or line in each assessment district. The unit value is apportioned to the state and to local taxing districts within the state on the basis of some physical measure, such as track miles or line miles.

The second concept was that a company may have value different from the value of all tangible and documentable intangible property owned. Additional value results from the ownership of public franchises, favorable leases or patents, established management systems, knowledge of the market, customer goodwill, and other intangible values. An assessor can use the market price of bonds and stocks as an indication of the total market value of a company and subtract the assessed value of the tangible assets that have been separately assessed to obtain intangible value. The commission stated that this plan of assessing utilities had worked well in Indiana and Ohio and had been sustained by the U.S. Supreme Court.[16]

The general approach to railroad assessment was unchanged. Railroads were to provide more complete lists and schedules and to give the amount and market value of their intangible property. If market value was not available, "true" value was to be given. The report argued that large increases in the assessed value of other property would not result in railroads paying a smaller share of the property tax. The state tax commission would ensure that railroad valuations were increased.

The commission reported that Kansas laws dealing with the collection of taxes had been working satisfactorily but recommended repeal of the provision allowing county commissioners to compromise delinquent taxes. This provision often led to compromise of taxes for far less than could have been obtained at a tax sale and, in some municipalities, it had become common practice for taxpayers to refuse to pay taxes and rely upon obtaining a compromise from the county.

A major innovation was the recommendation for a tax on inheritances and bequests. The tax of $5 on every $100 of the value of an estate would have applied only to amounts passing to collateral heirs. Amounts passing to direct heirs of the ascending or descending lines, or to a spouse or sibling, would not have been subject to tax.

The report of the tax commission concluded by pointing out that the subject of taxation had become increasingly important as the complexity of civilization swelled the expense of government. The tendency had been to abandon the general property tax because of failure to collect taxes on personal property and to substitute a tax on corporations. This was especially true in the eastern states where personal property had largely assumed the corporate form. Kansas could not do this because the constitution required the general property tax, but the commission added that the general property tax had never been fairly tried in the state by a modern, well-adjusted law. "Until such has been tried and failed, we still believe in the general property tax as the fairest that can be levied in a community like ours."[17]

DEBATE OVER TAX REFORM

The administrative recommendations were the commission's attempt to deal with highly controversial, but related, issues. One set of issues revolved around the question of local versus state authority and the relative role of politics and administration. The state versus local issue had always been an important one in American politics. Despite the wide acceptance of Dillon's rule as a legal principle, U.S. local governments enjoyed an unusual degree of independence. Local officials took oaths to support the state constitution and statutes, but enjoyed almost complete freedom from state supervision. Only judicial and electoral processes were available to interpret the law or to insure that the oaths were kept. The judicial process was slow and cumbersome and the electoral process often worked to encourage disregard of the law.

Distinct, but related, was the matter of the separation of politics and administration. This doctrine, as articulated by Frank Goodnow, defined politics as the expression of the will of the state and administration as the implementation of that will.[18] Although complete separation is impossible and, perhaps, undesirable, students of government were beginning to teach and write of the advantages of an impartial, professional bureaucracy. Such a bureaucracy is characterized by hierarchical organization in which specialized tasks are carried out by specialized personnel. The personnel are supervised by superiors dedicated to carrying out applicable laws and regulations.

Although falling short of what a modern administrator would consider ideal, the recommendations of the temporary tax commission contemplated a long step toward centralization and professionalization of property tax administration. The permanent tax commission would have been elected, but the two full-time commissioners would have had staggered, four-year terms at a time when one- or two-year terms of office were the rule. The provision that county assessors were to be elected for four-year terms without being able to succeed themselves was intended to insulate the office from politics. The elected assessors would have been able to appoint and assign work to deputy assessors, subject to county commissioners' confirmation and the proviso that deputies could not assess their own township. The tax commission would have been given administrative powers, such as the right to prescribe forms and records and to require county assessors to attend training schools. The tax commission would have had power to summarily remove county assessors, and deputies would have served at the pleasure of the county assessor.

The reforms did not find quick acceptance in the legislature. Bills were introduced in both the House and the Senate in the 1903 session. Amended versions passed in both chambers, but the conference committee failed to work out an acceptable compromise. In the years from 1900 to 1904, politics in Kansas were dominated by arguments over bossism and corruption within the Republican party. The failure of the bill to pass had less to do with the merits of the bill than with the fact that different factions of the Republican party controlled the two houses of the legislature.[19]

The 1904 Republican convention saw a bitter fight among the "machine" Republicans and factions of the reform-minded Kansas Republican League. Progressive Republicans Edward W. Hock and Walter R. Stubbs lost a struggle to nominate a spokesman for railroad users to the railroad commission and to keep pro-railroad candidates from dominating the Republican ticket. Nevertheless, Hock was nominated for governor and he and Stubbs succeeded in incorporating some of their reform ideas into the party platform. These included economy and anti-corruption planks and a promise to amend the railroad laws to eliminate discrimination, inequality, and extortion in rate-making. They also wrote the part of the document calling for equalizing and minimizing of state taxes.[20]

Hock easily defeated the Democratic candidate for governor, David M. Dale. In his January 1905 message to the legislature, Governor Hock proposed an extensive reform program. He did not advocate the tax commission bill, but decried the existing state of tax assessment and suggested that the legislature attempt to bring about an honest listing of personal property and the taxation of property at full value. He asked for severe penalties for those who failed to assess the value of franchises of such enterprises as telegraph, telephone, pipelines, and express companies at full value. He stated that a county assessor with deputies in each township would be an improvement and concluded that such things could be more easily agreed on than the more elaborate attempt made in the 1903 legislature.[21]

Hock, with the help of Speaker of the House Stubbs, forced much of the progressive Republican reform program though the legislature, but the only tax reforms passed were provisions changing the method of taxing telegraph, telephone, pipeline, and express companies and establishing a State Board of Assessors to assess such companies doing business in more than one county.

In his 1907 message to the legislature, Governor Hoch devoted only half a page to taxation. He said that Kansas tax rates seemed high because assessments were low, but that Kansas was actually a low-tax state. He pointed out that the bank commissioner reported $140 million in bank deposits, but that less than $5 million were reported for taxation. He asked that severe penalties for violating the tax law be enacted, but did not specifically mention the tax commission.[22]

THE TAX COMMISSION

Despite the governor's failure to push it, the 1907 legislature passed a tax commission bill. It did not contain the provisions setting up specific methods for taxing various kinds of property, but administrative changes were far-reaching.[23] The Tax Commission replaced the Board of Railroad Assessors, the State Board of Assessors, and the State Board of Equalization. The commission was composed of three persons appointed for four-year terms by the governor with the advice and consent of the Senate. Commissioners were to be persons known to possess a knowledge of taxation, were to serve full-time, were not to hold any other public office, and were not to engage in any occupation inconsistent with their duties as tax commissioners or to serve on any committee of any political party.

The commission was to provide a uniform method of keeping the tax rolls and other tax records in each county and in the office of the state auditor and state treasurer. It was to provide tax forms to county officers and visit each county to insure proper assessment and the keeping of tax records. The commission had general supervision of county assessors and was to require county assessors to attend a meeting in Topeka at least once in two years. It had power to require local officers, individuals, and corporations to provide information on the subject of taxation, to examine witnesses, and to require witnesses to produce books relating to tax matters. It was to investigate cases where evasion or violation of the laws of assessment and taxation had occurred, to recommend remedial measures, and to investigate the tax laws of other states and countries for the purpose of formulating and recommending legislation for securing just and equal taxation.

The commission had far-reaching powers of review and equalization and was to prosecute any member of any board of county commissioners and any county, township, or city assessor for violation of any rule, regulation, or statute. The Tax Commission was to prepare interrogatories and questions to be answered by taxpayers or other persons. Any person knowingly answering falsely was guilty of perjury and was to be sentenced to hard labor for not less than one year nor more than five years. Persons refusing to answer were guilty of a misdemeanor and could be imprisoned from six months to one year.

The board of county commissioners of each county was to appoint a competent resident of the county as county assessor. County assessors were to serve two-year terms and were not eligible to be a candidate for any other office. The county assessor and the county commission were to determine the number of deputies, and the county assessor was to appoint the deputies with the consent of the county commissioners to hold office at the pleasure of the county assessor.[24]

Appointment and Organization of the Commission

Governor Hoch moved quickly to appoint a quality commission. The first name announced was that of a distinguished Democrat, Judge James Humphery of Junction City. Judge Humphery was born in England. He came to Kansas in 1857 and held several offices including eight years on the controversial railroad commission. He was a regent and a lecturer on law at the state university.

Another appointee, Samuel T. Howe, was born in New York. He held several local offices in Kansas and was elected state treasurer in 1882. While serving in that position he recommended the establishment of a tax commission. In 1895 he became a member of the railroad commission. Although he had only a common school education, he was a member of the bar.

The third member of the commission, S. C. Crummer of Belleville, had been Republican state chairman and private secretary to Governor Hoch.

Judge James Humphery, the Democrat, was elected chairman by his two Republican colleagues, but he died on September 18. Governor Hock then offered the appointment to David W. Dale, his Democratic opponent in the 1904 election. Dale wrote a long, thoughtful letter declining the appointment. He agreed with the governor that this legislation was the most important in twenty years. He pointed out that accepting the appointment would be personally inconvenient, but his refusal was based on the belief that the commission would not be a success in the long run. He doubted that Governor Hoch's successor would be as broad-gauged and nonpartisan:

> The interests and politicians may demand a Board of Tax Commissioners subservient to their interests and demands. I know full well the law will be unpopular to the "tax dodgers" and certain corporate interests, and that before the law can be given a thorough trial, the "knockers" clamors for the scalps of the officials who are honestly and conscientiously endeavoring to properly and efficiently enforce the law will be heard throughout the State and some weak-kneed governor, as your successor, may deem it advisable to look upon this law in a different light than you do, and conclude in the interest of the "knockers" to change the policy adopted by you.[25]

The governor then named Judge W. S. Glass to the Tax Commission. Glass was born in Indiana and finished his legal education at the University of Iowa. He had served as a member of the Kansas legislature and was a county attorney. In 1906 he was the Democratic candidate for judge of the supreme court.

The commission elected Samuel T. Howe as chairman. He served until his death in 1922 and became a nationally known expert in the field of taxation, serving as president of the National Tax Association in 1915 and 1916.

Early Activities of the Commission

Upon organization on July 1, 1907, the commission, acting in its capacity as the state board of equalization, set to work equalizing property for the tax year 1907. The commission decided that it was impractical to change the "general basis of valuation" for 1907, but did make modest changes in the aggregate assessed value in many counties. These were percentage increases or decreases in the total value of lots, lands, or personal property. The total amount of locally assessed value returned by the counties was just over $348 million. Increases made by the tax commission totaled more than $21 million and decreases $10 million, for a net increase of $11 million.[26]

The commission finished equalization on July 26, 1907, and then began to prepare for the assessment of March 1, 1908. Under the law, county assessors could not be appointed until the January 1908 meetings of the boards of county commissioners. In the interim, the Tax Commission prepared a series of about thirty forms and sent them to the county clerks. These included assessment rolls, personal property tax statements for corporations and individuals, statements for the assessment of intracounty pipelines and telephone companies, forms for the appointment and qualification of county and deputy assessors, and special forms for providing statistical information to the tax commission. Circular letters explaining the required changes were sent to county clerks and boards of county commissioners. On December 2, 1907, a pamphlet of instructions to county and deputy assessors was mailed to county clerks, to county commissioners, and to township trustees.[27]

The commission members worried that a large increase in assessed values would result in large tax increases. No changes in tax limits had been included in the Tax Commission bill and the legislature was not scheduled to meet until January 1909. The commission considered the matter so important that it sent some 10,000 copies of a circular letter to the taxing officers of all counties, cities, townships, and school districts in the state. The letter pointed out that the legislature had not required that the mill rates be decreased proportionally to the increase in assessed values, but that it should be clear that the legislature did not intend to authorize an increase in taxes.

In January 1908, Governor Hock, in response to a campaign launched by supporters of a primary election law and a bank deposit guaranty law, reluctantly called a special session of the legislature. In his message to the legislature, the governor pointed out that the expected increase in assessed values had given rise to apprehensions that taxes would greatly increase.[28] The legislature responded by enacting a tax lid that prevented any taxing district from making a tax levy that would produce more than 102 percent of the amount that could have been raised in 1907. The Tax Commission, over its objection, was given the power to grant exceptions to the tax lid. Interestingly, this law was similar to a 1970 Kansas law that is often cited as an innovation in tax limitation.

The legislature amended the Tax Commission law to require that the township trustee be appointed by the deputy assessor for the township.[29] This action largely nullified the attempt to establish a normal administrative hierarchy and to insulate assessment from the local political process.

On January 14, the commission sent each newly appointed county assessor a letter of instructions and copies of forms designed to procure statistics regarding real estate sales. The county assessor was asked to report the date of sale, description of real estate sold, the assessed value of the property, and the ratio of assessed value to sale value. All counties responded to the request during January, and the commission built up a file containing more than 40,000 ratios from about 1,600 taxing districts for the years 1903 to 1907.

The commissioners called the county assessors to meet in Topeka on January 28, 1908. The commissioners attended a joint meeting of the state association of county clerks and county commissioners and made visits to the counties in an effort to prepare county officials for the 1908 assessment. Orders were issued prescribing the way various kinds of property were to be listed on the roll, and it was ordered that the county clerk, not the township assessor, list real estate on the tax roll. This was contrary to practice in some counties. Obviously aware of local sensitivity about such orders from Topeka, the commission expressed concern about imposing unnecessary duties on local government, but added that the commission's responsibilities and the interest of economy and efficiency required it.[30]

As railroad assessors, the commissioners toured the several railroad systems noting the condition of property. They also examined financial records for the preceding five years and carefully studied "everything which could be conceived of as bearing on value."[31] The result was a railroad assessment of $356,070,646. In a paper read at the National Tax Association meeting, the commissioners pointed out that the U.S. Census report of 1904 had estimated the value of railroads in Kansas at $356,356,000. This similarity was not, they stated, the result of any use of census data but was a remarkable result arrived at by two different valuation methods. The commission did admit that some local taxing districts had been unhappy because the value of some railroads had been reduced, placing a greater tax burden on local property.

In 1908, thirteen county boards of equalization were ordered to reconvene. Some were ordered to make specific changes, others were simply ordered to equalize assessments. The commission also heard 127 appeals from taxpayers.[32] Several reductions were granted. It does not seem that the commission adopted the politically expedient method of granting token reductions to all appellants. In fact, the commission indicated that the burden of proof was on those who wanted to overturn local decisions. In one case the commission stated:

> This appeal being unsupported by evidence sufficient to rebut the evidence inherent in the fact that the equalized value of the property in question was fixed by the unanimous action of the County Board of Equalization, therefore the appeal is dismissed.[33]

Several cases were dismissed for failure to provide evidence or to follow proper procedures, but in one case the commission used its general power to equalize on its own motion. In that case the appellant failed to appear before the County Board of Equalization and, because of high water, could not appear before the Tax Commission. Despite the appellant's failure to appear, the commission felt that the facts showed injustice and relief was appropriate.[34]

PROCEEDINGS OF THE FIRST ASSESSORS' CONFERENCE CONVENTION

Few documents give a clearer picture of the state of property tax administration at a given time than do the proceedings of the first biennial meetings of Kansas county assessors. The proceedings were informal. Members of the Tax Commission presented short papers on different aspects of property tax assessment, but most of the time was devoted to answering questions. The proceedings were recorded and published as a guide to assessment law and practice.

The first of these "conference conventions" met in Topeka on January 28 and 29, 1908. All 105 county assessors were present. Governor Hoch addressed the opening session of the meeting and pointed out the importance of the new law.[35]

After the governor had addressed the group, Chairman Howe read a short statement. It clearly reflected the view that tax policy should be made by the legislature and administered by impartial administrators: "How [a taxpayer] shall contribute and in what measure must be for the legislative body to determine. The rules laid down by that body must be observed by all officers charged with their administration."[36]

The transcript of the conference reveals that the county assessors found the implications of this statement difficult to accept. This was illustrated by a lengthy exchange between the assessors and the members of the commission over exemption of Masonic homes. The commissioners cited court cases from several states holding that an institution did not qualify as a charity unless it served the general public, not just members of the organization. The response suggests that many assessors were surprised, unbelieving, and outraged. After a lengthy exchange, Commissioner Howe admitted that lodges had not been taxed anywhere in the state and that, as a member of the Masonic order, his sympathies were with the protesting assessors.

Definition of Value of Real Estate

Chairman Howe read a statement setting forth the commission's position on the statutory meaning of value as applied to real estate. The statement pointed out that the statutes used the phrases "true and full cash market value," "actual and full market value," "actual value in money," and "true value in money." Section 14 of the law, which contained the only positive rule laid down for valuations, stated that "all property, real, or personal, shall be valued at its actual value in money." The commissioners had concluded that the same meaning must be given to all these expressions. The phrase "actual value in money" had been adopted by the commission as the distinctive expression of the law. This was defined by the commission as:

> such a value as a subject of sale would bring in money under ordinary circumstances when a person fully informed as to values wished to buy the subject of sale without any particular need for it, and on the other hand, where the owner, also fully informed as to values, wanted to sell, but was not obliged to do so.[37]

The commissioners admitted that it is easier to write a definition of value than it is to determine value, but the paper provided an amplification of the definition. It pointed out that sales of property cannot be taken as an absolute guide until analyzed and divested of all conditions not involved in the sold property. It was also pointed out that one person might, for a particular reason, be willing to pay more for a property than others would pay. In the absence of an absolute guide to actual value, all facts and circumstances tending to show that value should be considered. Among these are the considerations given in deeds covering local sales, earning values, local rental values, asking prices, prices offered, adaption to particular uses, more favorable conditions arising through the growth of cities, and better facilities for marketing. The commissioners stated that the most weighty of these is price, but added that neither speculative prices nor sales where the consideration is grossly inadequate are true measures of the actual value.

A relation exists between the rental value and the actual value in money. A marked disparity between rental values, treated as the income, and the selling prices of real estate, treated as the capital invested, suggests that such real estate is over- or under-valued, as the case may be. When using earning value of real estate to assist in setting value, the assessor should make due allowance for the personal equation. The earnings of the thrifty, energetic farmer must not be credited entirely to the earning power of the land, any more than lack of thrift and energy on the part of the slothful farmer should diminish the earning power of the land.[38]

The commission's statement was a rather good summary of valuation theory. The importance of market price and the warning that not every sale is at market price would be included in instructions to assessors today. The income approach to valuation was suggested in the discussion of earning capacity or rental value, and the warning that allowance should be made for the personal equation is echoed today in the rule that estimated income should be based on "average management." There was no clear reference to the cost approach to appraisal, but the recognition of possible disparities between selling prices and rental values suggests that the assessor of 1908 was being asked to "correlate" the results of the income and sales comparison approaches to value, just as is done by appraisers today.

The county assessors showed little interest in the fine points of valuation theory. Immediately following the reading of the paper, John T. Gray of Stevens

County stated that the commission had very plainly laid down its interpretation of the actual value of real estate and moved that any person having any question to ask on this subject submit it in writing to be answered by the commission. The motion was seconded and passed, and the discussion turned to other matters.

FIRST REPORT TO THE LEGISLATURE

In January 1909, the commission made its first report to the legislature. Much of the report was devoted to summarizing the literature on property taxation and describing property tax administration in Kansas.

A table showing the increasing tax burden in Kansas demonstrated that the per capita tax burden in Kansas was relatively stable from 1889 until 1903 and then rose sharply. The increases for the various governmental units from 1901 to 1907 were:

State	37.1%
County	31.9
City	64.8
Township	61.3
School	49.8
Total	46.4

The commission had attempted to determine the reasons for the increases by asking local officials to provide information or opinions. Replies from sixty-five counties indicated that there were a variety of causes. Increased costs of labor, fuel, and materials were often cited. The increase in school taxes was caused largely by an increase in teachers' salaries and longer school terms. Improvements of streets and highways, and the replacement or improvement of public buildings, were frequently mentioned as reasons for higher expenditure. The commission found it difficult to criticize expenditure for such purposes or for any public expenditure that "naturally follows the growth of population and the development of civilization," but warned that all public expenditure should be along lines of rigid economy.[39]

One section of the report was devoted to the organization and activities of the National Tax Association and another to special tax commissions in other states. Emphasis was on the conclusion reached by many of these commissions that it was impossible to administer the general property tax—particularly the tax on intangible property.

Another section described the assessment and equalization of Kansas property taxation. The enormity of the problem is indicated by the fact that there were 1,577 assessment districts in the state, each assessed by a deputy assessor. The commission stated that the opinion of the deputy assessors regarding values would vary considerably unless they were held to some proper standard of value. It went on to propose equality among taxpayers within the district, equality among taxing districts, and equality among counties. The county board of equalization could equalize among assessment districts, and the state board of equalization among counties. However, if the original assessments were not equal, it was not feasible for the state to correct them. The commissioners believed the county assessors' efficiency would increase with experience and recommended that the implicit authority of county assessors to revise the work of the deputies be made explicit. They also suggested that the Tax Commission be given authority, after summary hearing, to order reassessment of the real or personal property in any district in which assessment appeared not to have been in compliance with the law.[40]

PROCEEDINGS OF THE SECOND ASSESSORS' CONFERENCE

It is clear from the proceedings of the second assessors' conference that the commission's report to the 1909 legislature had not been well received. The 1909 legislature had changed the law to provide that in counties of less than 12,000 population county clerks were to be ex officio county assessors. Rather than the experienced core of county assessors that Chairman Howe had predicted at the previous conference, there were twenty-eight newly appointed assessors, forty-nine county clerks, and only twenty-eight assessors who had been appointed to succeed themselves. The legislature had also passed a law providing that the county assessor appoint two taxpayers from different political parties who, with the deputy, were to constitute a township board of review.

It was reported that Governor Stubbs would not be able to attend the conference, but Chairman Howe's opening statement was upbeat. He remarked that the county assessors' meeting two years earlier had been called the most momentous gathering of county officers in the history of the state and that remarkable results had been achieved. The last assessment under the old system in 1907 had resulted in an assessed valuation of $425,281,214. In 1908 the new plan produced a total valuation of $2,451,560,398. The average rate of taxation in the state had been reduced from 4.67 percent in 1907 to 0.865 percent in 1908 and 0.9447 percent in 1909.[41]

The first question had to do with when and where the newly created township boards of review would meet. Chairman Howe replied that they had hoped the question of boards of review would not come up. He added that the commission was studying the question, and that instructions would be provided in time to guide the assessors and the boards.

There was a lengthy discussion about what to do when a township is too big for one township trustee (deputy) to assess. The commission members insisted there was no legal authority to divide districts and no law making third-class cities separate assessment districts. Commissioner Glass stated that it was extremely unfortunate that the legislature had seen fit to wipe out laws on the subject and not substitute proper laws in their place. This subject came up again later in the conference and the discussion fills several pages in the transcript. Several assessors reported how they had tried to get around the problem. On several occasions one of the commissioners made comments to the effect that because silence might be construed as consent, the commissioners must state that they could not condone what had been done.[42]

War Stories

It is no surprise that a number of assessors related "war stories." Usually these were stories of a taxpayer's attempts to evade taxation and the assessor's attempts to outwit them. Some assessors indicated that they had taken shortcuts or revised the rule to fit the situation. One reported that a farmer had four good horses and one old, almost worthless one. Rather than reduce the average value and risk the possibility that the county board of equalization would raise it, he put the old horse down as a six-month-old and put a lower value on it. Howe commented that a sixteen-year-old horse is not a yearling! Another assessor reported that he had dealt with similar situations by adding lines to the assessment blank showing different ages and conditions so that cripples would not be assessed the same as good horses. Another wryly commented that in his county many horses go lame just before the assessor arrives.

PROCEEDINGS OF LATER ASSESSORS' CONFERENCES

The pattern established in the first conference of county assessors was continued through later ones. Most of the time was devoted to commissioners' answers to questions posed by those present. Many of the questions and answers were incorporated into the manual of instructions that the commission published for the guidance of assessors, deputy assessors, and others involved in property tax administration.

At the fourth conference Chairman Howe read a statement expressing concern about the unequal assessment of real estate by different deputy assessors. He presented a chart showing great variation in land values on either side of township lines. This led to a discussion of whether it was advisable or permissible for the deputy assessors to get together and discuss the assessments to be applied. Because there had been so much condemnation of the assessor meetings required under prior law, the subject was approached carefully. One county assessor reported that he suggested to the deputies that they should try to do something about the inequalities. He then added that he was not "officially aware" that they had gathered to discuss the matter, but that the inequalities did disappear and that little equalization among townships had been found necessary. The discussion of township-to-township variation led the county assessor of Shawnee County to suggest that favoritism could be eliminated by having deputies assess outside their own township. Chairman Howe replied that the 1907 law was originally designed so that county assessors could assign deputies outside their own townships, but was changed. Later, the legislature explicitly directed that township trustees be assigned to their own township.[43]

SUMMARY AND CONCLUSIONS

The report of the 1901 Kansas Tax Commission was a landmark in the effort to achieve the goals expressly or implicitly embraced by those who wrote the nineteenth century tax uniformity clauses. The 1901 report was accompanied by carefully drafted statutes based on the accumulated experiences of the eighteen states represented at the Buffalo conference. These statutes were based on the proposition that the best chance of achieving property tax uniformity required:

1. Statutory provisions specifically tailored for certain kinds of property, such as easily moveable tangible personal property and intangible property including intangible corporate value.
2. Centralized assessments of certain properties, such as railroads and utilities.
3. State supervision and training of county assessors.
4. State equalization and review of local assessment.
5. Deputy assessors selected by and responsible to county assessors.

The authors of the report were not unaware of the need for political accountability. They proposed that the state Tax Commission be composed of elected state officials, serving ex officio, and two elected, full-time commissioners. The county assessors were to be elected, but they could not engage in political activity and could not run for reelection. They were to have what was then an unusually long term of four years.

The history of the proposal is an excellent case study in the difficulties encountered by property tax reformers. Even in the midst of a period of political reform in Kansas, it took six years for an amended version of the 1901 proposals to be adopted. Few of the provisions dealing with specific kinds of property were included, but far-reaching administrative reforms were decreed. A reform-minded governor quickly appointed strong, progressive men to the commission, but even before all the administrative machinery was in place, a special session of the legislature began altering the law. The county assessor's power to select his deputies was replaced by the requirement that the township trustee be appointed as deputy. The next regular session of the legislature replaced full-time assessors in the smaller counties with the county clerk, acting ex officio.

The proceedings of the assessors conference, held biennially by the state tax commission, provide an excellent record of the problems faced by property tax administrators. The nature of the problems can be summarized by dividing them into three classes.

Assessor disagreement with the law. There were some instances in which the law was clear and easily applied, but was contrary to the assessors' opinions. This is illustrated by the discussion of the exemption of Masonic property. A tax commissioner explained that the law was clear and well settled, but the assessors found the idea of taxing such property distasteful. It is safe to assume that few such properties were put on the rolls.

Assessors unable to understand and apply commission instructions. The commission was composed of well-informed, full-time officials who devoted much time and thought to the problems of assessment. They attended national conferences and read the latest writings in the field. They understood the issues far better than did the county assessors or county clerks acting as assessors. Consequently, some commission statements were too abstract to be of use to the assessors. For example, the commission's definition of "value" was a good statement of appraisal theory as it then existed. It provided a framework for analyzing a particular case and, thoughtfully applied, would have resulted in a quality appraisal of most kinds of property, but the assessors paid little attention to it. They asked questions about the value of particular kinds of property, but made little effort to apply the commission's definition. One commissioner expressed irritation at this failure by bruskly advising an assessor to read the proceedings of the last conference.

The commissioners had no answer. There were a number of instances in which the commissioners had no answer to difficult questions. For example, they failed to give good answers to repeated questions about methods of valuing capital stock. In some cases the legislature was at fault. For example, when it abolished the county assessors' freedom to choose deputies and required them to appoint the township trustee, it provided no authority for hiring additional deputies in large townships. The commissioners counseled that the law be obeyed, urged them to work harder, and avoided expressing approval of the extra-legal actions that some counties had taken.

The Tax Commission made a vigorous effort to bring the property tax into conformity with the uniformity clause of the Kansas Constitution. Tax forms were prescribed, instruction manuals were issued to assessors, and every county assessor attended the first two biennial assessors' conferences. The commission was vigorous in its role as the State Board of Equalization and as the assessor of railroad and utility property. Members traveled widely, collected a large amount of data, and demanded and received a great deal of information from the railroad and utility corporations they assessed. They heard many taxpayer appeals and issued many equalization orders. They also made many recommendations to the legislature.

Often these recommendations were not adopted immediately, but some were eventually adopted by the legislature.

The commission published a great deal of material for the guidance of assessors and for the education of legislators and the general public. Publications included reports that contained details about state-assessed property and the proceedings of the State Board of Equalization. Reports to the legislature described developments in other states and suggested changes in Kansas laws. The 1916 assessors' manual, presented in a new topical format, was cited by a national authority on property taxation as the best that had ever been prepared.[44] The commission's file of sales data may have been the largest collection of such data in the United States. It was to provide the data for a path-breaking assessment/sales ratio study by a Kansas State College professor.[45]

The commission's biggest accomplishment was the reappraisal of 1908, but the resulting shifts in tax burdens weakened the already limited political appeal of tax reform. Actually, it is not clear that the idea ever had a great deal of appeal to the mass of voters. Vague promises to reduce taxes often appeared in political platforms or campaign oratory, but property tax *reform* was not an appealing political issue, even in the populist and progressive era. Perhaps the complexity of tax administration, and the certainty that the taxpayers who lose from reform efforts will be much more vocal than those who gain, makes it a politically dangerous issue for a party or political leader. Property tax reform may be considered a crusade for a few well-informed individuals, but the mass of people are not likely to enlist unless they believe they will receive tax reductions.

In spite of the problems, the property tax proved to be a good revenue producer. By 1913, Kansas governments levied property taxes in the amount of $27,732,000. Eighty-eight percent of this was levied by local governments and it amounted to an average of $15.73 per capita or to 5.7 percent of the income payments received by Kansas residents.[46]

9
Replacing the General Property Tax

It is tempting to conclude that the early years of the Tax Commission represented Kansas' last effort to make the general property tax work. In fact, such a conclusion is only partly true. The failures of the Tax Commission make it clear that there were inherent problems in implementing a general property tax so that all property is taxed and taxed uniformly. It is also clear that Kansans were reluctant to weaken local authority by accepting centralization or professionalization of property tax administration, even for the promise of more uniform taxation. They were also reluctant to supplement or replace the property tax with another broad-based tax.

The delay in accepting changes in the tax system was not because Kansas was isolated or unaware of possible alternatives. The members of the Tax Commission were leaders in the National Tax Association and the commission's reports contained lengthy summaries of current thought about the principles of taxation and often included accounts of tax reform in other states and nations. Professors in Kansas universities were active in studying tax questions and in assisting legislative commissions with their work.

When change finally came, it was triggered by a distressed economy and guided by a progressive governor.

TAXES AND EXPENDITURES IN 1913

In 1913 a U.S. Census report provided the first statewide view of local expenditures and nonproperty taxes. As shown in Table 9.1, the state received almost 65 percent of its revenues from property taxes. Most of the balance was received from nontax sources such as interest, rents, and earnings of general departments. Counties received 87.7 percent of their revenue from the property tax and 9.6 percent from interest, rents, and earnings. Cities received 57.8 percent from property taxes and 21.7

Table 9.1. Kansas State and Local Revenues, 1913 (in thousands)

	State	Counties	Cities over 2,500
General property taxes	$3,310	$6,525	$6,560
Special property taxes	170		
Poll taxes			69
Special assessments		25	2,462
Business taxes	352		29
Business licenses		9	179
Nonbusiness licenses		41	55
Fines, forgeits and escheats	10	62	81
Highway privileges		11	68
Interest and rents	552	187	105
Subventions and grants	77	40	186
Donations and gifts			24
Earnings of general departments	907	524	147
Earnings of public enterprises		8	1,388
Total	$5,379	$7,432	$11,353
Percent from property taxes	64.7	87.8	57.8

Source: United States Bureau of the Census, *Wealth, Debt and Taxation, 1913*
(Washington, D.C.: United States Government Printing Office, 1915), 36–37.

percent from special assessments. Receipts of city operated enterprises (e.g., utilities) provided substantial sums for the cities, but most of this was expended in operating the enterprises and was not available to finance general governmental services.

The magnitude of government revenue is pictured more clearly in Table 9.2, where the information is presented on a per capita basis. The state property tax amounted to $1.88 for each person in the state. County property tax revenue

Table 9.2. Kansas per Capita State and Local Taxes, 1913

	State	Counties	Cities (000)		
			Over 30	8–30	2.5–8
General property taxes	$1.88	$3.87	$13.64	$12.40	$11.29
Special property taxes	0.10	—	—	—	—
Poll taxes	—	—	—	0.13	0.31
Special assessments	—	0.01	6.23	4.44	3.01
Business taxes	0.20	—	0.07	0.06	0.03
Business licenses	—	0.01	0.44	0.34	0.26
Nonbusiness licenses	—	0.02	0.14	0.10	0.06
Fines, forfeits, and escheats	0.01	0.04	0.15	0.18	0.13
Highway privileges	—	0.01	0.17	0.03	0.20
Interest and rents	0.31	0.11	0.21	0.28	0.10
Subventions and grants	0.04	0.02	0.36	0.29	0.43
Donations and gifts	—	—	0.04	0.02	0.09
Earnings of general departments	0.51	0.31	0.21	0.29	0.36
Earnings of public enterprises	—	—	1.99	2.47	3.79
Total	$3.05	$4.40	$23.65	$21.03	$20.06

Source: United States Bureau of the Census, *Wealth, Debt and Taxation, 1913* (Washington, D.C.: United States Government Printing Office, 1915).

Table 9.3. Kansas State and Local Government Expenditure, 1913
(in thousands)

	State	Counties	Cities over 2,500
General government	$535	$2,465	$449
Protection of persons and property	281	306	823
Conservation of health and sanitation	40	50	250
Highways		607	678
Charities, hospitals, and corrections	1,581	604	32
Education (direct)	1,719	718	2,506
Education apportionment	458		
Libraries	5		87
Recreation	2		111
Miscellaneous and general	103	116	95
Public service enterprises		10	944
Interest	15	497	1,423
Outlays	471	1,329	4,934
Total	$5,211	$6,703	$12,332

Source: United States Bureau of the Census, *Wealth, Debt and Taxation, 1913*
(Washington, D.C.: United States Government Printing Office, 1915).

amounted to $3.87 per resident. In three cities with a population greater than 30,000, property tax revenue amounted to $13.64 for each resident. Smaller cities collected smaller amounts per capita.

Table 9.3 provides a snapshot of government expenditure in 1913. The state spent the largest sum for education. About $1.7 million was spent directly for that purpose, mostly for higher education. In addition, almost one-half million dollars was apportioned to units of local governments for school purposes. The next largest expenditure was for charities, hospitals, and correction facilities. Undoubtedly, most of that was for the operation of state institutions, since direct payments for welfare or medical purposes were rare at that time. The item labeled "outlays" was for permanent improvements or, in today's terminology, capital outlay.

Counties, which had much of the responsibility for administering state laws, spent the largest sum for general governmental purposes, followed by outlays, and then education. Forty percent of city expenditure was for outlays. This reflects the role of cities as providers of urban infrastructure, such as sidewalks, streets, and drainage. Much of this was financed by special assessments. The next-largest city expenditure was for schools.

The biggest weakness of the 1913 Census data, as a picture of the revenues and expenditure of Kansas state and local government, is that township and school district data are not included. Because school districts and townships had little access to nonproperty tax revenues, it would seem that the data void could be filled by looking at property tax statistics. Unfortunately, there are discrepancies between the collection figures reported by the Census Bureau and the tax levies. Taxes levied in 1912, for expenditure in 1913, were as follows:[1]

State	$ 3,296,000	Townships	3,584,000
Counties	6,502,000	Schools	9,292,000
Cities	4,981,000	Drainage and cemetery	77,000

These data show state property taxes levied in 1912 to be somewhat less than state property tax collections reported in 1913 (Table 9.1). The discrepancy is small and could be accounted for by the difference in timing of the reports or by collection of back taxes. However, the discrepancy between city tax levies, as reported in state sources, and the city revenue figures, as reported by the U.S. Census Bureau, is far too large to be accounted for in this way—especially when it is remembered that the Census figures include only cities of over 2,500 population. The most likely explanation is that levies of city school districts were reported as city taxes by the Census Bureau.

In any case, there is no doubt that education was the most expensive activity of government in 1913. Almost 40 percent of property tax levies were school district levies, and in addition, the state, counties, and cities reported substantial expenditures for this purpose.

THE ENGLUND REPORTS

Efforts to measure the quality of assessment in Kansas began before the turn of the century when the Kansas Board of Labor began to compare actual sales prices with assessed values. This activity was expanded by the Kansas Tax Commission after its organization in 1907. These data were important in studies of Kansas taxation by Eric Englund of Kansas State Agricultural College. First published as bulletins of the Agricultural Experiment Station in 1924 and 1925, they were accepted as a doctoral dissertation by Harvard University.[2]

Englund utilized data from 10,307 farm sales in fifteen counties and 10,231 city real estate sales from sixteen counties from the years 1913 to 1922. The sales had been reported to the Tax Commission by county assessors, who were in-

Table 9.4. Assessed Valuation as Percent of Sale Price, 1913–22

Size Group[1]	Farm[2]	City[3]	Size Group[1]	Farm[2]	City[3]
I	85.7	97.0	VI	65.3	74.5
II	76.7	89.0	VII	62.3	70.9
III	72.9	82.9	VIII	58.7	69.1
IV	70.0	80.5	All groups	65.6	73.3
V	66.4	76.5			

1. Size group I is composed of the parcels with the smallest sales price.
2. Farm data are from fifteen counties.
3. City data are from sixteen counties.
Source: Eric Englund, Assessment and Equalization of Farm and City Real Estate in Kansas (Manhattan, Kansas: Agricultural Experiment Station, Bulletin No. 232, July 1924), 14–15.

structed to report only bona fide sales. Analysis revealed that smaller parcels, as measured by sales price, were assessed at a higher percentage of sale price than were larger properties. City and rural sales ratios in each county were divided into eight groups and a weighted average of the ratios was computed by dividing the total assessed value of each group by the total sales price of the group. In every county smaller properties were assessed at higher ratios than large properties. Table 9.4 shows statewide averages.

Englund analyzed the data to determine whether the apparent overassessment of small properties was a statistical bias resulting from the undervaluation of improvements or from rising land values during the period. He concluded that neither was an adequate explanation and that, in fact, larger properties were undervalued.[3] Analysis also showed that the inequality among large and small properties had increased in the ten-year period being analyzed.

Englund analyzed inequities among individual parcels of property by computing the coefficient of dispersion from the arithmetic mean of the ratio of assessed valuation to the sales price of farm parcels for each of the ten years. These were averaged to produce a coefficient for each county. These coefficients are the mean percentages by which the assessment ratio (assessment to sales price) of individual ratios varies from the mean ratio. In simple language, coefficients are the average percentage by which properties are over- or under-assessed, when compared to the average property. The coefficients for the ten counties were:

Bourbon	18.8%	Leavenworth	19.0
Chase	19.0	Reno	16.8
Cherokee	25.8	Rooks	23.4
Comanche	28.5	Shawnee	21.4
Decatur	23.6	Average	22.5
Meade	27.7		

A similar procedure was followed for ten of the largest cities. The results were:

Hutchinson	16.5%	Topeka	19.7
Leavenworth	22.1	Winfield	17.5
Manhattan	19.5	Average	19.7
Fort Scott	22.9		

Englund's research was the most sophisticated statistical analysis of property assessment that had been conducted at the time, but there is some question as to the validity of the sales data. Apparently the county assessors were allowed to determine what sales were bona fide. If they systematically excluded those sales in those instances in which the sales prices and assessed values varied greatly, Englund's statistics would have understated the assessment inequities.

Englund repeated the often heard call for county assessors and pointed out that the problem of county-to-county differences in the level of assessment could be eliminated by discontinuing the property tax as a state revenue source. He recommended that the state get its revenue from a personal income tax, a gross production tax on oil and minerals at the point of production, and an excise tax on certain nonessentials, such as tobacco and commercialized entertainment.

ECONOMIC CHANGE AND ECONOMIC CRISES

Englund's approach to tax reform was not unique or original. Both the demand for improved administration and broadening of the revenue base were related to changes in society and the economy. Property in a specialized urban economy is more diverse, more mobile, and more difficult to value than property in a largely self-sufficient rural economy. The methodology for appraising real estate was being improved, but its application lagged. Finding and valuing many kinds of intangible personal property was rendered difficult by technical and jurisdictional problems. To compound the difficulty, demands for government services were rapidly increasing. As the society became more complex and richer, there were increased demands for education and for public infrastructure, such as roads and streets. The data from the 1913 Census show that expenditures for education accounted for a substantial part of state and local expenditures, but in the next few years highway expenditure became increasingly important. In 1920 the voters approved a "good roads amendment" that permitted the state to reimburse local governments for part of the cost of constructing highways. Englund, like so many other students of government before and since, observed that the fundamental reason for the increasing cost of government is that people demand more government services. He suggested that the reader could supply many examples, but mentioned a few:

Better schools. There had been a great improvement in Kansas schools. Well-constructed school buildings were common, teachers were required to be better prepared, and school attendance had risen rapidly.
Wide range of government services. Roads and highways were better, libraries were found in all cities and some small towns, and streets were paved and often well lighted. Police and fire protection was provided at public expense and the discovery of new facts and principles by experiment stations and other research institutions had greatly increased the productive power of agriculture and industry.
Development of public health service. Improvements in public health resulted from government attention to water supply, sanitary sewerage disposal, milk supply, and methods of handling food. In addition, there was a certain amount of free medical and dental inspection in the public schools and the number of school and public health nurses was increasing. Practical results of these measures included decreasing death rates from tuberculosis, typhoid fever, and other communicable diseases, and a lengthening of the human life span.[4]

The tax consequences of the increased demand for government expenditures are reflected in tax levy data for the years 1895 through 1936. In 1900 total property tax levies in Kansas amounted to about $13.5 million. By 1921 levies had increased more than fivefold, although population increased by only 24 percent. The rise in property tax levies was interrupted in 1922 by the agricultural depression but resumed its rise, at a slower pace, until interrupted again by the nationwide depression of the 1930s. These developments are illustrated in Figure 9.1

Looking back, it is clear that a long period of change in the economy created the need and demand for changes in the administration of the property tax and in the tax structure. Nationally, scholars and policy-makers wrote and spoke about the need for change. Kansas tax commissioners and other Kansas leaders recognized and recommended changes, but it took the economic crises of the early 1920s and 1930s to bring about the drastic revision in revenue structure.

One aspect of these crises is illustrated by Figure 9.2, which shows Kansas property tax levies as a percentage of personal income payments in the state. The drop in the percentage that began in 1915 resulted from the rapid rise in incomes, especially farm incomes during World War I. Taxes were rising rapidly in that period, but incomes were rising even faster resulting in a lighter overall state and local tax burden. A reversal began in 1920. Farm prices fell drastically and income payments received by Kansas residents followed. Property taxes levied as a percent of income payments rose almost continuously until they reached the astonishing total of 12.6 percent of income payments in 1932.

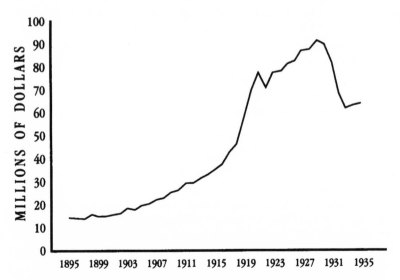

Figure 9.1. Kansas property tax levies, 1895–1935. *Source:* Kansas Legislative Council, Research Department, *A Summary History of Kansas Finance 1861–1937.* (Topeka: Publication No. 60, October, 1937), 25–27.

Table 9.5. Taxes Levied on Farm Real Estate in Kansas, 1910–23 (in thousands)

Year	State	County	Township	School District	Drainage	Total
1910	$1,426	$2,736	$2,112	$3,373	$59	$9,706
1911	1,626	3,114	2,339	3,572	53	10,704
1912	1,632	3,199	2,287	3,708	88	10,914
1913	1,640	3,340	2,375	3,795	111	11,261
1914	1,685	3,699	2,474	3,911	113	11,882
1915	1,752	4,049	2,845	3,919	140	12,705
1916	1,866	4,217	2,910	5,324	111	14,428
1917	2,083	5,089	2,946	4,386	139	14,643
1918	1,853	5,388	3,668	4,972	146	16,027
1919	2,804	7,076	3,596	5,985	143	19,604
1920	2,618	8,104	4,144	8,412	175	23,453
1921	4,163	8,837	4,521	9,582	164	27,267
1922	2,886	7,826	3,979	9,405	163	24,259
1923	4,043	7,981	4,190	9,602	179	25,995
Increase	183.5%	191.7%	98.4%	184.7%	203.4%	167.8%

Source: Eric Englund, *The Trend of Real Estate Taxation in Kansas from 1910 to 1923* (Manhattan, Kansas: Agricultural Experiment Station Bulletin No. 235, September, 1925), 10.

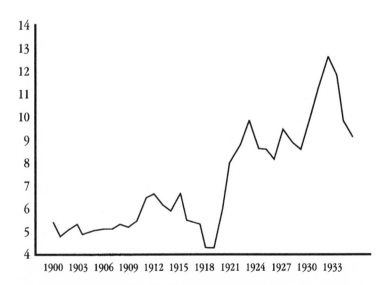

Figure 9.2. Kansas property tax levies as percent of personal income, 1900–1935. *Sources:* Kansas Legislative Council, Research Department. *A Summary History of Kansas Finance 1861–1937* (Topeka: Publication No. 60, October, 1937), 25–27; Paul W. Zickefoose, *Kansas Income Payments, 1900–1951* (Lawrence: The University of Kansas, School of Business, Bureau of Business Research, 1955), 75.

Table 9.6. Taxes Levied on City Real Estate in Kansas, 1910–23
(in thousands)

Year	State	County	City	City Schools	Total
1910	$447	$911	$2,401	$2,083	$5,842
1911	528	1,065	2,979	2,329	6,901
1912	532	1,107	2,828	2,485	6,952
1913	535	1,158	3,009	2,667	7,369
1914	537	1,229	3,194	2,943	7,903
1915	569	1,378	3,449	3,105	8,501
1916	625	1,452	3,616	2,521	8,214
1917	711	1,808	3,751	4,227	10,497
1918	605	1,856	3,416	4,854	10,731
1919	878	2,229	4,731	5,485	13,323
1920	702	2,148	5,335	7,432	15,617
1921	1,177	2,703	5,982	8,209	18,071
1922	922	2,635	6,356	8,708	18,621
1923	1,331	2,840	7,024	9,873	21,068
Increase	197.8%	211.7%	192.5%	374.0%	260.6%

Source: Eric Englund, *The Trend of Real Estate Taxation in Kansas from 1910 to 1923*
(Manhattan, Kansas: Agricultural Experiment Station Bulletin No. 235, September,
1925), 35.

Table 9.5 shows taxes levied on farm real estate during the period 1910 to
1923 by the various types of government. In the thirteen year period, farm real estate taxes increased by 167.8 percent. Increases for the various types of government
were relatively uniform except that township taxes increased at a slower rate than
did taxes for other types of government. The state, counties, and school districts all
took a larger percentage in 1923 than in 1910. The abrupt increase in the state's
share in 1923 resulted from a levy to begin repayment of veterans' bonus bonds.

Table 9.6 shows similar data for city real estate. The total tax levies on city
real estate had increased by 260.6 percent as compared with 167.8 percent on farm
real estate. The levies for city schools increased by 374 percent in the same period.

Table 9.7 displays the result of Englund's calculations of taxes as a percent of
the selling price of real estate. It shows that taxes on rural real estate almost doubled

Table 9.7. Taxes as Percent of Selling Price, 1910–23

Year	Farm	City	Year	Farm	City
1910	0.53	1.07	1918	0.69	1.49
1911	0.56	1.19	1919	0.70	1.79
1912	0.55	1.17	1920	0.75	1.95
1913	0.56	1.28	1921	0.91	2.11
1914	0.59	1.34	1922	0.90	2.23
1915	0.63	1.48	1923	1.01	2.29
1916	0.70	1.30	Increase	90.6%	114.0%
1917	0.66	1.55			

Source: Eric Englund, *The Trend of Real Estate Taxation in Kansas from 1910 to 1923*
(Manhattan, Kansas: Agricultural Experiment Station Bulletin No. 235, September, 1925) 17, 45.

Table 9.8. Taxes Levied on Farm Real Estate, by Purpose, 1916–23 (in thousands)

Year	Administration	Education	Roads and Bridges	Interest	Sinking Fund	Drainage	Miscel-laneous	Total
1916	$3,259	$6,612	$2,969	$324	$436	$111	$716	$14,427
1917	3,380	5,775	3,727	263	451	139	908	14,643
1918	3,495	6,306	4,517	317	437	146	809	16,027
1919	3,784	7,912	5,473	260	426	143	1,605	19,603
1920	4,020	10,344	6,466	326	444	175	1,678	23,453
1921	4,368	12,451	6,848	515	631	164	2,290	27,267
1922	3,506	11,997	5,785	476	569	163	1,763	24,259
1923	3,470	12,220	5,941	481	573	179	3,131	25,995
Increase	6.5%	84.8%	100.1%	48.5%	31.4%	61.3%	337.3%	80.2%

Source: Eric Englund, *The Trend of Real Estate Taxation in Kansas from 1910 to 1923* (Manhattan, Kansas: Agricultural Experiment Station Bulletin, No. 235, September 1925), 32.

as a percentage of selling price. Taxes on city real estate more than doubled. For most years, taxes on city real estate were more than twice taxes on rural real estate.

Data showing the purposes for which property taxes were levied, shown in Tables 9.8 and 9.9, give some indication of the changes in the functions of state and local governments. Taxes on farm real estate increased by 80 percent in the eight-year period from 1916 to 1923, but the increase in taxes levied for general administration rose only 6.5 percent. Taxes levied for road and bridge purposes doubled, taxes for education increased by 84 percent, and taxes for miscellaneous purposes more than tripled. Taxes on urban real estate increased considerably faster than taxes on farm real estate. Taxes for administration increased 22.6 percent, but that increase was dwarfed by a 264.5 percent increase in taxes for education, a 319 percent increase for miscellaneous items, and a 107.6 percent increase in taxes for roads, bridges, and streets. Clearly, government in Kansas was moving from a time in which most tax revenue was spent for maintaining the basic administrative func-

Table 9.9. Taxes Levied on City Real Estate, By Purpose, 1916–23 (in thousands)

Year	Administration	Education	Roads, Bridges, Streets	Interest	Sinking Fund	Miscellaneous	Total
1916	$2,190	$2,951	$868	$781	$671	$753	$8,214
1917	2,263	4,702	970	690	807	1,065	10,497
1918	2,126	5,289	1,021	715	651	929	10,731
1919	2,772	6,078	1,433	796	692	1,552	13,323
1920	2,817	7,934	1,507	792	888	1,680	15,618
1921	2,640	9,035	1,787	941	1,151	2,518	18,072
1922	2,606	9,549	1,662	1,072	1,208	2,525	18,622
1923	2,685	10,755	1,802	1,288	1,383	3,155	21,068
Increase	22.6%	264.5%	107.6%	64.9%	106.1%	319.0%	156.5%

Source: Eric Englund, *The Trend of Real Estate Taxation in Kansas from 1910 to 1923* (Manhattan, Kansas: Agricultural Experiment Station Bulletin No. 235, September 1925), 52.

tions to one in which governments provided services, especially school and transportation facilities. The change was more rapid in urban areas, but it was also occurring in rural areas.

Englund presented a number of what he calls "mitigating factors" in the higher levels of taxation of city real estate. Englund's discussion of the level and fairness of the tax burden on rural and urban dwellers was not entirely without bias, but it was an early attempt to analyze one of the most difficult and persistent controversies in Kansas politics. Conflict between rural and urban interests over taxation has been intense in many American states, but it probably has been most intense in Kansas.

CLASSIFICATION OF INTANGIBLE PROPERTY

The first report of the Kansas Tax Commission to the legislature recommended that the Kansas constitution be amended to remove the uniformity clause and add the words "the legislature shall have power to establish and maintain an equitable system for raising state and local revenue, and may classify the subjects of taxation so far as differences justify the same, in order to secure a just return from each."[5]

It was five years before the proposed amendment was submitted to a popular vote. Just before the 1914 election, the commission released a sixteen-page pamphlet arguing in favor of voter approval. Several pages of the publication were devoted to reprinting letters from nationally known authorities. Among those writing in support of the amendment were Professor Charles Bullock of Harvard; Lawson Purdy, president of the Department of Taxes and Assessments of the borough of Manhattan, New York; Oscar Leser, member of the Maryland State Tax Commission; and Professor Thomas S. Adams, member of the Wisconsin Tax Commission. There were quotations regarding the inequities of the present system, particularly those resulting from the inability to collect the tax on intangibles. The pamphlet included a reprint of a newspaper interview with Professor Bullock who had visited Topeka at the invitation of the Tax Commission.

The proposal failed by a narrow margin. In 1920 the voters rejected a proposed amendment that contained similar wording and, in addition, specifically authorized graduated income, franchise, privilege, and occupation taxes.

The first two proposals were generally described by their supporters as classification amendments, and proponents placed great emphasis on the advantages of permitting the legislature to classify property. Emphasis was placed on the advantages of being able to subject intangible properties to a lower rate of taxation or to a tax not based on value. It was argued that this would produce more revenue than was being obtained from intangibles under the poorly administered general property tax. However, the proposals were "wide open" amendments that gave the legislature power to classify every kind of property for taxation and to impose nonproperty taxes.

A third attempt to secure a classification amendment was far less ambitious. The pertinent part of the amendment adopted in 1924 read: "The legislature shall provide for a uniform and equal rate of assessment and taxation, except that mineral products, money, mortgages, notes and other evidences of debt may be classified and taxed uniformly as to class as the legislature shall provide." This wording gave the legislature power to classify specified kinds of intangible property and mineral property. It did not permit classification of any other kind of real estate and gave the legislature no additional powers to levy nonproperty taxes. The 1925 legislature implemented the new provision by adopting a mortgage registration fee and a tax on moneys and credits. The proceeds were to be credited one-sixth to the state general fund, one-sixth to the county general fund, one-third to the township or city general fund, and one-third to the school district general fund. Money was defined to include gold and silver coin, U.S. treasury notes, and bank notes. Credits were defined to include notes, mortgages, foreign stocks, bonds, annuities, royalties, contracts, copyrights, claims secured by deeds, and every liquidated claim for money or other valuable thing except mortgages, on which the registration fee had been paid.[6]

In 1929 the state supreme court held the money and credit tax unconstitutional because it violated federal law forbidding a state to tax national banks at a rate higher than imposed on moneyed capital in competition with national banks.[7] A new law was enacted in 1931.

Kansas' early experience with the intangibles tax was not encouraging to those who saw it as a major property tax reform. Table 9.10 shows the assessed values of intangibles and collections from this source for the four years before and after enactment of the new law. Intangible assessments, declining before the new law was passed, increased sharply, but revenue dropped precipitously and, after four years, was still less than half as much as they were under the old law.

Table 9.10. Intangible Tax Assessments and Revenue, 1921–28 (in thousands)

Year	Assessments	Revenue	Year	Assessments	Revenue
1921	$176,846	$3,536	1925	340,144	852
1922	148,315	2,888	1926	331,704	833
1923	141,061	2,979	1927	346,495	1,150
1924	120,063	2,566	1928	288,679	1,088

Source: Kansas Tax Code Commission. *Report to the Governor.* (Topeka: State Printer, December 1, 1929), 168. Data for 1925 and after included both the money and credit tax and the mortgage registration fee.

PROLOGUE TO CHANGE

In 1928 Kansas Governor Ben S. Paulen called a special session of the legislature as a result of a ruling by the U.S. Bureau of Public Roads and the Secretary of the Interior that threatened Kansas highway aid. The federal highway aid law provided that federal aid could be granted to states only if a state highway commission had direct control over roads on which federal aid was expended. For the preceding three years, a special provision had permitted Kansas to receive aid without meeting this requirement, but the new appropriation bill did not contain such a provision. Secretary of Agriculture William Jardine, a Kansan, met with state officers in Topeka to discuss the matter and the governor reported to the legislature that unless Kansas modified its constitutional provisions against works of internal improvement, it would lose more than $2 million a year.[8]

The special session approved an amendment excepting highway construction and maintenance from the provision that the state could not engage in works of internal improvement.[9] The proposed amendment was approved, by more than a 4:1 margin, at the November 8 election. This amendment, unlike the earlier "good roads" amendment, permitted the state, itself, to construct or maintain highways.

In 1928 tax revision became a major political question. The platform of both parties gave prominence to the subject.[10] The legislative message of newly elected Kansas governor Clyde M. Reed to the 1929 legislature began by reviewing the economic situation. Reed dwelled on the importance of agriculture in Kansas. Over-production in the war and postwar years had created an imbalance between the agriculture and industrial sectors of the economy. He pointed out that many states had responded by modernizing their tax systems to place greater emphasis on indirect taxes, but Kansas continued to depend upon the tax on general property. As a result, the property tax in Kansas had reached prohibitive levels.[11]

The 1929 legislature did not enact comprehensive tax reform, but submitted a proposed constitutional amendment allowing the state to impose a graduated income tax and provided for a comprehensive study of the tax system. The income tax amendment was defeated at the November 1930 election, but the commission appointed to study the tax code made the most comprehensive tax study since 1901.

THE TAX CODE COMMISSION

The Tax Code Commission was made up of five members appointed by the Governor. As required by the legislation establishing it, one member was a state senator and two were state representatives.

The differences and similarities between the 1901 report and the 1929 report are interesting indications of the changing attitude toward taxation and the distribution of governmental responsibilities. The 1901 report was devoted almost entirely to the property tax. The 1929 report, by contrast, examined many potential tax sources as well as administrative and distributive matters and made recommendations affecting broad areas of state-local fiscal relations.

Both commissions drew heavily on the experiences in other states and foreign countries. The 1929 commission made reference to the proceedings and discussion of the National Tax Association, to conferences with tax officials from several states, and to discussions with members of the Kansas Tax Commission. Assistance was obtained from Professor Jens Jensen, of the University of Kansas, and Professor Harold Howe, of Kansas State College. Dr. Eric Englund, then of the Bureau of Agricultural Economics of the U.S. Department of Agriculture, and personnel from the U.S. Internal Revenue Service were consulted. Local input was received at a number of hearings around the state.

The 1929 report was organized into fourteen chapters. Ten dealt with a particular tax source or the taxation of a particular occupation or business. There was no chapter title containing the words "property tax," but the chapter on administration largely dealt with property tax administration. Evidence of poor assessment was cited, and the usual recommendations for larger assessment districts and for increased state supervision were repeated. One variation was the recommendation for a board of three county assessors. The chapter also included discussion of the problem of tax delinquency, especially of personal property taxes, and proposed that the state be given powers to prescribe a uniform system of accounts for local governments and to require an audit of local accounts. The commission also recommended that local governments be required to publish all budgets and bond proposals. Any ten local taxpayers would have the right to appeal a budget or bond proposal to the State Tax Commission.[12]

The Income Tax

Chapter 1 dealt with the income tax. Its successful use in Europe and in several American states was noted. Attention was called to the fact that several states had unsuccessful income taxes on the books for many years and added that no state had used the tax successfully until Wisconsin centralized administration at the state level in 1911. Data concerning the revenue yield of state income taxes were presented and there was a discussion of administrative costs. The incidence of both the individual and corporate income tax was discussed as were the advantages of income as a base for taxing business.

Among the advantages of the income tax, the report listed its merit as an index of ability-to-pay and its ability to reach income not taxed under the property tax. The commission asked whether the enactment of an income tax would simply mean more money to spend. It answered that it was the responsibility of the state, the legislature, the administrative officers, and all tax levying bodies to make sure that higher spending does not result and added, "If none of these agencies can be trusted, then the state is in a bad way."[13] Perhaps the commissioners did have some doubt, however. The first item in the summary of recommendations was: "That no new source of revenue be provided unless the legislature creates proper checks upon the expenditure of public money as suggested in this report, or by some other method which in the judgment of the legislature is equally effective."[14]

The commission recommended a graduated personal income tax and a flat rate corporation tax, both without exemptions. The rate on the personal income tax was to be 1½ percent on the first $1,000 of income. The proposed rates rose as income increased, with all income of more than $10,000 being taxed at 5 percent.

The Severance Tax

The commission pointed out the growing importance of mineral production in Kansas and the growing belief that the natural resources of the state are, to some extent at least, a heritage of the people. Kansas law provided for the assessment of oil and gas wells on an ad valorem basis, but the commission discovered that assessors were actually valuing oil properties by applying a certain sum per barrel of average daily production in a period immediately preceding the assessment rendition date. The commission stated that it found no warrant in the law for such a procedure and suggested this method was the result of assessors lacking the technical training necessary to evaluate properties in accordance with the methods prescribed by law.[15]

After noting the wide variation in the ways other states taxed mineral interests and examining the issues involved, the commission concluded that the imposition of a tax on the privilege of extracting oil and gas would return to the state, the creator and guarantor of property rights, a definite and just share of the income from these ventures. The commission estimated that a 2 percent tax in lieu of the tax on the value of minerals produced would yield $1.4 million. One-third of that amount was to be returned to school districts and county governments where produced.

Sales Taxation

The Tax Code Commission made a detailed analysis of sales taxation.[16] Reports were sought from foreign countries having some form of sales taxation, and authorities from American states having some form of sales taxation offered advice.

The commission report mentioned several forms of sales taxation, but devoted the most attention to the gross sales or turnover tax. This form of taxation is usually levied at a low rate, but is imposed on every sale, at every stage of production and distribution. In 1929 it was used in several foreign countries and the state of West Virginia had experimented with its use. Although the tax was said to be simple to administer and to yield considerable revenue, the commission concluded it would produce grave inequalities among various types of businesses.

In discussing the shifting and incidence of the gross sales tax, the commission dismissed as erroneous the common assertion that the sales tax is shifted to the final consumer. They quoted a publication of the National Industrial Conference Board concluding that a turnover tax would generally raise prices to the consumer, but there would be differences in the incidence depending on the nature of the good, the circumstances of its production, the stage of the business cycle, and the period of time being considered.

The commission report briefly discussed the possibility of a tax limited to retail and wholesale sales, or to retail sales only. Major problems of the retail sales tax included discrimination against enterprises having a high rate of turnover, the problems of separating sales of commodities from the sales of services, and determining whether a sale was retail or wholesale. In the end, the report concluded no form of sales taxation offered a satisfactory solution to the taxation problems of Kansas. The idea of "uniform taxation of all sales," or "equal taxation of everybody," were said to have great popular appeal, but to be impossible to apply.

Bank Taxation

The taxation of banks was a controversial subject in the United States long before Kansas became a state. On the frontier, banks epitomized the intangible wealth that often escaped taxation under the general property tax system. The Jacksonian-populist mistrust of banks and other financial institutions focused special attention on bank taxation. In many states, constitutional provisions singled out bank capital as a form of intangible property that should be taxed. The situation was further complicated by the federal government's responsibility for the banking and currency system. The U.S. Constitution assigns the money power to the federal government and early Supreme Court decisions declared nationally chartered banks to be instrumentalities of the federal government not subject to state taxation without federal consent.

Congress, wanting to protect national banks from hostile state action but aware of the unfairness of exempting national banks from all taxation, passed legislation in 1864 and 1868 authorizing state taxation of national banks, subject to restrictions. Kansas, like most other states, had long taken advantage of the provisions allowing states to tax real estate as other real estate is taxed and to tax the shares of national bank stock to the shareholders.

In 1919 the U.S. Supreme Court reversed previous decisions that shares of stock in state banks were the only moneyed capital in competition with national banks.[17] Unfortunately, neither this decision nor a series of later decisions provided a comprehensive definition of moneyed capital. In 1923 and 1926 changes in Section 5219 of the federal law provided additional options for the taxation of national banks,[18] but the Kansas commission concluded that none of the available options were consistent with the Kansas constitution. It recommended an attempt to secure a change in federal policy.

The commissioners also concluded from their analysis of bank taxation that it was absurd to use the property tax to raise revenue from corporations, when more than one-third have no earnings in a given year. They saw this as supporting the commission recommendation that personal and corporate income taxes be enacted.

School Finance

In a chapter entitled, "Allocation of New Revenues," the commission discussed educational organization and finance.[19] The school organization question had been studied by the School Code Commission, but a proposed school code based on its recommendations had been withdrawn during the 1929 legislative session because there was no means of financing the proposal. The commission pointed out that the school tax was, by far, the largest element in state and local taxation and then detailed the chaotic conditions that existed in the organization of school districts. Rural high schools were first authorized in 1915 and expenditure for rural high schools rose from $157,000 in 1916 to $3,801,000 in 1927. In the eagerness to provide high school education for rural youth, many small high school districts were organized. School districts overlapped to such an extent that property could be assessed for four separate school taxes.

Data gathered in 1927 revealed there were 856 districts with an enrollment of seven or fewer pupils, and 216 districts did not maintain a school. Data based on average daily attendance was even more striking. There were 1,357 schools with an average daily attendance of less than seven pupils. Predictably, there were wide variations in tax levies.

The State School Code Commission had proposed that expenditure per pupil, in all districts, be brought up to the then current state average expenditure per teacher by imposing a county property tax and distributing $8 million raised by the state. The Tax Code Commission rejected the idea of a state-wide property tax levy for school purposes but recommended revenue from nonproperty taxes be devoted to that purpose. In support of its belief in greater state responsibility and the need to give the legislature greater authority, the Tax Code Commission recommended the existing revenue article be replaced with a single sentence reading, "The legislature shall provide by law for assessment and taxation."

Except in its analysis of school finance, the commission gave little attention to government organization but, in fact, it was proposing new financing mechanisms that would ultimately affect the structure of government. Abandoning the property tax as the source of most tax revenue in favor of state-collected taxes was certain to impact the relationships between state and local government. Perhaps those who successfully resisted tax reform recognized this, although it was rarely articulated.

BALANCING THE TAX SYSTEM

The election of 1930 was an exciting one in Kansas. The country was mired in depression, and John R. Brinkley, the goat gland doctor, made a strong bid as a write-in candidate for governor. Brinkley had come to Kansas in 1916 and soon attracted a national following by performing "goat gland" transplants, advertised by his own powerful radio station to restore masculine virility. Attacks on him by the medical societies and federal agencies attracted a large number of sympathizers and provided the support needed to launch a campaign for governor on a platform broad enough to attract support from every shade of discontent. The Republican party was somewhat divided and the race was close. Harry Woodring, a Democrat, was declared the winner, although it is possible that an honest count would have given the office to Brinkley.[20]

In his message to the 1931 legislature, Governor Woodring reported the steady increase in tax burden combined with the economic depression had made taxes the paramount problem. He advocated economy, stating that the power to issue bonds had been so grossly abused by local government that sinking fund and interest payments made up 25 percent of city expenditures. He recommended that no unit of local government be permitted to incur general obligation debt without a vote of the people and made the usual plea for improved administration of the property tax. He also suggested that the income tax amendment, which had been defeated in December, be resubmitted.

The 1931 legislature passed little important tax legislation, but did resubmit the income tax amendment and submitted a tax limitation amendment. That amendment provided that property located in a city should be taxed at no more than 2 percent of its true value and that no property located in a rural area should be taxed at more than 1.5 percent of its true value. The legislature was to prescribe the manner in which taxes were to be prorated among the several taxing units. Emergency levies exceeding the limit could be voted by the electors for a period not exceeding two years. Alf Landon, the Republican candidate for governor, campaigned against the tax limitation amendment and for the income tax amendment.[21]

In November 1932, the income tax amendment was passed by a vote of 389,145 to 283,148, but the tax limitation amendment was defeated. The defeat of the limitation amendment seems surprising in view of the extremely high property tax burdens in the depression period. It is possible that some voters were reluctant to subject school districts and other local governments to the legislative control that would result from giving the legislature power to "ration" taxes among the various local governments. Perhaps, many accepted Landon's argument that tax limits were desirable but should not be frozen into the constitution.

In the 1932 election, Franklin Roosevelt carried Kansas and was elected president, but Alf Landon, the Republican candidate for governor, narrowly defeated Governor Woodring. In his message to the legislature, Landon reviewed the economic problems facing Kansas and the nation. He stated that the relationship between industries, trades, and professions was out of balance and that agriculture did not enjoy a proportionate share of the national income. He recommended a comprehensive economic program that included government reorganization, economy, and changes in the tax system. He asked for an income tax and a proportionate reduction in the property tax. He stated, "Today we are still spending tax moneys on the basis of 1929 incomes. We are collecting taxes on the basis of a tax plan belonging primarily to 1861."[22]

Specifically, Landon proposed that county commissioners should be given full power over the expenditures and salaries of the various county offices. He recommended that the legislature review the salaries of elected county officers and that all fees go to the public treasury rather than to officers. He proposed strengthening the law passed in 1931 requiring local governments to adopt budgets by requiring them to be complete, properly itemized financial plans. He also requested legislation setting up a uniform auditing and accounting system for all governments.

The legislature responded promptly to many of the governor's requests. On March 24, 1933, he signed an income tax law. Rates were graduated from 1 percent on taxable income up to $2,000, to 4 percent on income over $7,000. Single individuals were allowed a personal exemption of $750. A married couple, living together, received an exemption of $1,500 plus $200 for each child. Corporation income was taxed at a 2 percent rate. The proceeds of the tax were to be paid into the state general fund and were to be used to reduce the property tax levy for the state general fund and the soldiers' compensation (bonus) fund.[23] On the day the governor signed the income tax law, he also signed the cash basis law prohibiting local governments from expending any money not actually in the treasury.[24] Legislation was passed abolishing the fee method of compensating county officers and employees and setting new, generally lower, salaries for county officers and employees.[25] There was also a comprehensive tax limit law that limited the mill rate of various local government funds.[26] Another action of great historic interest, but of little fiscal importance, was the repeal of the poll tax.[27]

As New Deal legislation began to be passed in Washington, Landon found it necessary to call a special session of the Kansas legislature to get state laws in harmony with federal laws. Legislation was passed permitting counties to levy taxes for relief purposes, and laws were changed to permit state and local government to take advantage of federal work relief programs.[28]

In 1934 Landon was the only Republican governor elected in the United States. In 1936 he called a special session of the legislature that submitted two constitutional amendments to the voters. These allowed Kansas to participate in the federal old age assistance program[29] and the unemployment compensation program.[30] Both passed overwhelmingly.

Governor Alf Landon was the Republican candidate for president of the United States in 1936. He was defeated in the Democratic landslide that also saw Walter Huxman, a Democrat, elected as governor of Kansas.

The most important tax legislation passed by the 1937 legislature was the sales tax. Governor Huxman regarded the sales tax as a tax on the poor but reluctantly recommended a $.01 sales tax and a gross production tax on oil and gas. The legislature rejected the oil tax and imposed a 2 percent sales tax. From the proceeds, $200,000 was to be allocated to the crippled children's commission,

$2,400,000 for social welfare, and the remainder was to be distributed to counties and their local taxing units. The local units were required to reduce the property tax levy by 75 percent of the amount of sales tax money received.

SUMMARY AND CONCLUSIONS

In the years after its creation in 1907, the Kansas Tax Commission had made a valiant effort to make the general property tax work by professionalizing and centralizing administration. Perhaps success in this effort would have revitalized the property tax and strengthened local governments as makers of government policy. On the other hand, there were strong counterforces. Property and property rights were becoming more complex. Economic activity was becoming more mobile and interrelated. These changes made the inherently difficult problem of finding, valuing, and taxing property even more difficult.

In any case, the Tax Commission's efforts were of limited success and Kansans spent another twenty-five years complaining about the burden of the property tax, deploring its poor administration, and refusing to take the steps that might have improved the situation. Complaints, especially from farmers and their representatives, intensified with the severe agricultural depression following World War I. Even this brought only a few changes.

The 1929 legislature debated the sales tax and established the Tax Code Commission. This commission faced the problem squarely and analyzed new tax sources being used or considered in other states and nations. It concluded Kansas should enact an income tax and a severance tax on oil and gas and distribute the revenue to local school districts.

In the light of past history, it would have been reasonable to predict that transition to the system of taxation recommended by the Tax Code Commission might require many years or decades, but an unprecedented series of economic, political, and climatic events accelerated the process. The farm depression became a general nationwide depression and years of drought added to the woes in the nation's midsection.

Kansas, under the leadership of a progressive governor, Alfred Landon, moved quickly to put its own house in order. The state imposed new tax limits, eliminated the anarchistic fee system of compensating local officials, reduced government salaries, required local governments to improve their planning and budget procedures, and imposed standardized accounting and auditing procedures. An income tax was imposed with the express purpose of reducing the state property tax.

In order to obtain the benefits of the federal programs, Kansas changed its constitution and laws to enlarge the power of state government, either to take on new governmental functions or to take a greater role in supervising functions previously performed at the local level.

The adoption of the sales tax in 1937 broadened the state tax base still further and put Kansas on the road to a balanced tax system—one that would place roughly equal dependence on property, income, and sales taxation.

The idea that a uniform property tax would be the major source of state and local government revenue was dead.

10
Kansas Taxation Since 1930

Since the 1930s, Kansas government finance has been characterized by the increasing importance of nonproperty taxation and the centralization of finance at the state level. In that period, the property tax continued to be an important and controversial source of local government revenue. Developments in property taxation and school finance since the mid-1980s raised controversy to a new height and posed important questions for the future of the property tax and for autonomous local government in Kansas.

KANSAS FINANCIAL TRENDS SINCE THE 1930s

In 1930, 82 percent of all state and local tax revenue came from the property tax, slightly over 8 percent came from motor fuels taxation, and about 10 percent came from all other tax sources combined. Ten years later, the property tax produced slightly less than 63 percent of the revenue, the sales tax produced about 10 percent, and the income tax 2 percent of all state and local tax revenues. In the years that followed, the property tax continued to decline in relative importance, but in 1990 it still produced 38.2 percent of the total state and local tax revenue. The sales tax was the second largest tax for many years, but a rapid growth in income tax collections in the 1970s made the income tax the second largest tax revenue. Trends for the major taxes are shown in Table 10.1.

The diversification of the state and local tax system has been accompanied by the centralizing of government functions and finance. Figure 10.1 shows that local tax revenues have declined from 76.3 percent of total state and local revenues in 1930 to 42.9 percent in 1990. The trend was temporarily reversed during the 1950s and again in the 1980s, but the overall downward trend is strong. The availability of revenues was not the only factor contributing to increasing centralization of fi-

Table 10.1. Kansas State and Local Tax Revenues, 1930–90 (as percent of total taxes)

	1930	1940	1950	1960	1970	1980	1990
Property[1]	82.02	62.98	52.28	56.75	53.21	39.38	38.20
Income		2.04	4.95	6.73	10.57	21.42	22.55
Sales		9.94	15.76	15.34	15.54	19.75	21.87
Unemployment compensation		4.85	2.51	2.21	1.77	3.86	3.49
Motor fuels	8.18	9.92	11.00	8.26	8.81	5.24	4.61
All other	9.80	10.27	13.50	10.71	10.10	10.35	9.28
Total	100.00	100.00	100.00	100.00	100.00	100.00	100.00

1. Includes motor carrier property and (for 1990) motor vehicle property.
Source: Kansas Legislative Research Department, *Tax Facts,* Fifth ed., 1983 and 1992 Supplement, Table VII.

nance. Economic and social change created pressure for centralizing many government services. Federal grants often required the state to assume responsibility for expenditure of the grant funds, and mandates made the state accountable for matters previously left to local government.

Figure 10.1 does not tell the whole story of state-local fiscal relationships. Accompanying the centralization of tax collections was also an increase in the amount of state-collected tax revenues distributed to local government. In 1930 the state returned $3.5 million to local governments, mostly from highway user taxes. In 1970, $209.7 million was returned to local governments, with 59.6 percent of state grants used for education. In 1990, $1.2 billion was returned to local governments. Of that amount, 81.9 percent was for education. The amount distributed to local governments in 1990 was 43.4 percent of state taxes collected.[1] The large amount of state

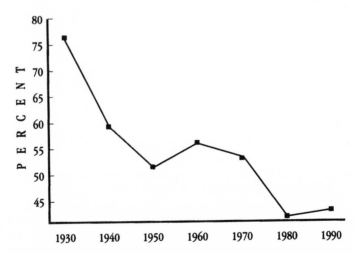

Figure 10.1. Local taxes as percent of state and local taxes. *Source:* Kansas Legislative Research Department, *Tax Facts,* Fifth ed., 1983 and 1992 Supplement, Tables II and V.

funds distributed to local governments, especially school districts, creates another complex set of administrative relationships between state and local governments.

In its 1929 report, the Kansas Tax Code Commission rather gingerly addressed the fear that broadening the tax system to include nonproperty taxes would increase government spending. The answer was a rather cautious "probably not." It is difficult to know whether or not the commission was right, but Figure 10.2 suggests it may have been. The figure shows state taxes, local taxes, and total state and local taxes as a percentage of Kansas personal income at ten-year intervals since 1930. State taxes now take a higher proportion of income than they did in 1930, but local taxes take a smaller share. Although there has been much criticism of government growth, state and local taxes as a percentage of Kansas personal income increased only moderately between 1930 and 1990. In 1930, taxes were 10.8 percent of income. In 1990, they were 11.9 percent, which is well below the peak of 14.5 reached in 1940.

THE ROAD TO CLASSIFICATION AND REAPPRAISAL

The reform efforts that surrounded the local property tax from the end of World War II to the mid-1980s followed the pattern established earlier. Commissions or legislative committees studied the problems and made recommendations for improved administration. Usually some of the recommendations were adopted, resulting in a political backlash that prompted legislative or administrative retreat.

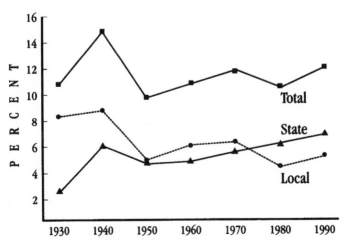

Figure 10.2. Kansas state and local taxes as percent of personal income. *Source:* Kansas Legislative Research Department, *Tax Facts,* Fifth ed., 1983 and 1992 Supplement, Table IX.

Attempted Reform in the 1950s

In the 1950s, concern with the poor quality of property tax assessment was so widespread that Kansans conducted an elaborate "grassroots" study of the property tax.[2] A coalition composed of several statewide groups representing agriculture, business, and government asked the 1953 legislature to establish a study commission. The legislature, with the support of the governor, responded by creating a commission consisting of four legislative leaders and eighteen citizens. The state commission held hearings throughout the state and developed a manual to aid county committees in organizing and conducting research. County committees were organized in 104 of the 105 counties. The county committees were asked to develop "target charts" that depicted the results of the state assessment ratio studies in the county and were furnished with copies of the National Association of Assessing Officers' manual, Assessment Principles.[3]

Ninety-nine county committees made individual reports and the state commission formulated them into its final report. The report stated that the statutory requirement for assessing all tangible property at its true value in money was violated in every county. The report included a list of twelve ways in which assessments were unequal. Some of these were: among counties, among state assessed properties, and between state assessed property and locally assessed property.

Eleven causes of inequality were spelled out. All had to do with assessment districts that were too small, assessors who were untrained or underpaid, and a lack of central supervision. Recommendations centered around proposals to professionalize assessment, provide additional state assistance, and create a state property valuation department.[4] The author of one article dealing with the work of the commission expressed the opinion that even the adoption of those recommendations would not result in obtaining adequately trained assessors because the recommended salaries were too low and the specific job qualifications were not outlined.[5]

The 1957 legislature enacted much of the legislation recommended by the commission.[6] It established a Department of Revenue to administer the state income tax, sales tax, and other state taxes. Within the Department of Revenue was a Division of Property Valuation headed by a director. All duties of the Commission of Revenue and Taxation relating to property taxation were assigned to the division or to the Board of Tax Appeals. The division was given the responsibility of devising and prescribing uniform assessment forms, records, maps, and other tools for assessing real estate. It was to devise and prescribe personal property assessment manuals and otherwise to assist county officials to obtain uniform assessment. The division was to provide assistance in the assessment of specialized properties and to compute assessment ratios.

The State Board of Tax Appeals was to be composed of three members serving on a part-time basis. The board was the appeal board for state-assessed property and heard appeals from decisions of the local boards of review and equalization. It was given the authority, on its own motion, to equalize between classes of property in any county and to authorize local governments to make tax levies in excess of those provided in the statutes. The board was permitted to authorize local governments to issue emergency warrants and to rule on applications for refund of protested taxes.

The 1959 legislature enacted a lengthy bill dealing with the organization of assessment at the local level.[7] It provided that cities of the first or second class were to compose separate assessment districts. The county assessor or clerk acting as assessor was to appoint needed deputies. Townships outside first or second class cities could be subdivided into assessment districts, but the elected township trustee had to be appointed as the assessor in one of the districts. The county assessors were to supervise deputy assessors and had the power to revise assessments made by them. The county assessors could appoint advisory committees to assist in the assessment process.

A 1961 law gave the Board of Tax Appeals power to order a reappraisal of a county or part of a county.[8] The 1963 legislature reduced the level of assessment from 100 to 30 percent of justifiable value and provided that any assessing official, including members of the county boards of equalization, who willfully failed to assess at 30 percent of justifiable value was guilty of a misdemeanor and was subject to a $500 fine or ninety days in jail.[9] The change to 30 percent assessment had no effect on how taxes levied were distributed among taxpayers, but it was believed there would be less opposition to reappraisal because assessments would be raised less.

Subsequent to the passage of these acts, the Kansas supreme court held that uniformity of assessment was more important than the level of assessment. The court said, "Where it is impossible to secure both actual value assessment and uniformity in assessment, the constitutional and statutory requirement of uniformity must prevail."[10]

Reappraisal in the 1960s

Lawrence Leonard, writing in the late 1950s, reported that no assessment in the previous 100 years had attained even approximate equality between state and locally assessed properties, among classes of properties, or among individual properties. The normal situation, he reported, had been inequality and regressivity. Leonard added that the use of available techniques of review and equalization had done little to correct inequalities in the original assessments and, in fact, had often resulted in greater inequalities. He speculated about the reasons for the failure of reform and concluded that one of the important factors was the widespread feeling that the property tax was such an integral part of the American democratic way of life that any major reorganization of the tax was seen as "undemocratic." This belief results in strong and usually successful resistance to reform.[11] Leonard's words proved to be prophetic. It took eleven years between 1959 and 1970 for all counties in Kansas to be certified as having completed the reappraisal ordered by the legislature and there is little evidence that it was done well. Many counties utilized outside reappraisal firms who often failed to develop and leave in place any system for correcting and maintaining their work. Generally, the entire process was regarded as an intrusion on local responsibility.

In a thesis written when the reappraisal process was about one-half finished, a student examined the records in fifty-five counties in which reappraisal was finished. She said, in part:

> The phrase "taxpayer revolt" has been used in connection with the reappraisal program. The court cases presented here substantiate that phraseology. . . . The court cases also point out that county clerk-assessors are failing to record the results of reappraisal. Again, conjecture would center around the fact that county clerks are elected officials and not likely to institute programs that are extremely unpopular with the majority of the voting public. There is also evidence in the court cases that County Boards of Equalization are not allowing reappraisal values to be entered on the records or are arbitrarily reducing the values.[12]

Another study reported similar results—or lack of results. After a detailed examination of the results of reappraisal in Douglas and Sedgwick counties, Robert Foster reported that equity had not been served. He believed that the poor results were caused by failure to professionalize assessment, to revise assessment procedures, or to establish a training program that would influence results for a long period of time.[13]

Quantifying Assessment Inequality

It is not clear that the quality of assessment at the end of the 1960s was worse than it had been 100 years before, but the documentation of the inequalities was better. Kansas has conducted annual assessment-sales ratio studies since 1949.[14] Legislation in that year required the register of deeds in each county to provide the State Commission of Revenue and Taxation with data on each parcel sold since 1933. For years, the reports were rather simple. The 1962 report, for example, was only fifteen pages long. The conveyance price was used, if available, to compute the ratio of assessment to sales price. Otherwise, the sales price was estimated on the basis of the amount of revenue stamps and the mortgage assumed. After the ratio of assessment to sales price was computed for each property, the median ratio for urban and rural real estate in each county was weighted to create a median for each county and the state. Frequency distributions showing the distribution of ratios for rural and urban real estate in each county were published. Coefficients of dispersion were not computed.[15]

In the 1966 report, the statistical analysis was expanded to include computation of the quartile deviation and the standard error. The quartile deviation was divided by the median and the result was labeled the "coefficient of dispersion."[16] Although this was an advance in statistical sophistication, the statistical methodology was inferior to that used by Eric Englund in the 1920s.

The biggest weakness of the ratio studies was not the statistical analysis but the gathering and editing of data. The 1965 legislature authorized the Director of Property Valuation to obtain additional information from the county register of deeds and to utilize questionnaires to grantors, grantees, and other contracting parties.[17] After July 1, 1967, a certificate of value was required from the purchaser and special field checks were made periodically to determine the validity of sales, but doubts about the quality of data remained.

In 1969, the legislature authorized and directed the Director of Property Valuation to order a county to reappraise any classification or subclassification of property for which the coefficient of deviation was greater than twenty. The effective date of this provision was January 1, 1972. The 1972 legislature changed the effective date to January 1, 1974. The 1974 legislature changed it to 1976, and the 1976 legislature changed it to 1978. The 1978 legislature again postponed the effective date for two years,[18] but the provision was rendered moot by another act of the 1978 legislature prohibiting any county from implementing reappraisal until all 105 counties had completed reappraisal.[19]

Beginning in 1973, the county assessment ratios (weighted medians) were used to adjust the assessed value of each school district for the purpose of determining the amount of state school aid a district was to receive.[20] This, of course, increased the importance of the study, because the school aid formula provided less state aid to districts with higher property valuations per pupil.

Even if allowance is made for possible weaknesses in the choice of sales to be included in the assessment-sales ratio study, it is clear that the quality of assessment was incredibly bad. The statewide average coefficient of deviation (COD) in 1984 was 52.31. This number can be made more meaningful by looking at the frequency distribution of assessment-sales ratios for a county that had a COD very close to the state average. Butler County had a COD of 52.33, almost exactly the statewide average. The median ratio was 7.30. For all taxes levied in Butler County to have been assessed equally, all parcels should have been assessed at the median level of 7.30 percent of sales price but, as shown in Table 10.2, very few ratios were close to that number. If it is assumed that the average ratio in the "under 2 percent bracket" was 1 percent, then there were thirty-two parcels that were paying only one-seventh of the proper tax. A perfect reappraisal would have resulted in a 600 percent tax increase for those parcels. Similar reasoning suggests that 102 parcels would have had tax increases of 150 percent. There would have been little change in the taxes on those parcels in the 6 to 8 percent bracket, but there would have been major decreases for properties in the higher brackets. Those parcels in the 16 to 18 percent brackets would have had taxes cut by more than half. Some of those in the over 18 percent bracket would have had their taxes cut

Table 10.2. Sales Ratios, Butler County, 1984 (number of parcels)

Ratio (%)	Rural	Urban	All Property
Under 2	21	11	32
2–4	63	39	102
4–6	90	77	167
6–8	104	167	271
8–10	57	222	279
10–12	26	90	116
12–14	16	30	46
14–16	6	13	19
16–18	5	8	13
Over 18	28	26	54
Total	416	683	1,099
Coefficient of deviation			52.33
Median ratio (%)	6.54	8.37	7.30[1]

[1] Aggregate county ratio.

Source: Kansas Department of Revenue, Division of Property Valuation, *Real Estate Assessment/Sales Ratio Study, 1984.*

much more because it is an open-ended bracket. In fact, ten parcels were assessed at more than 48 percent of sales price. These parcels were being taxed at more than seven times the proper amount.

Use-Value Assessment of Agricultural Land

In 1972 the Kansas Citizens' Tax Review Commission made a number of recommendations dealing with tax structure and school finance. The citizens' commission pointed out that Kansas depended more heavily on the property tax than many states and recommended restructuring of the revenue system to place less emphasis on property taxation. The commission also called for the property tax to be administered by professional, non-political personnel, supervised and partly paid by the state.[21]

At about the same time, much attention began to focus upon the taxation of agricultural property. The Cooperative Extension Service of Kansas State University published a number of research studies and conducted a series of seminars throughout the state. One publication, *Financing State and Local Government in Kansas,* was a compilation of statistics regarding taxation at all levels. It was used at eighty seminars, attended by over 3,000 people, and over 10,000 copies were distributed.[22]

One of the most startling sets of statistics in the Kansas State University publication was the set comparing the yield of the property tax with other taxes. Replacing the property tax with the sales tax would have required a state-wide tax rate of 10 percent. This would have been in addition to the 3 percent already levied for state purposes. To replace the property tax with an income tax would have required a flat rate of 17.2 percent on Kansas taxable income.[23] Imposing local sales or income taxes to replace the property tax would have resulted in widely varying rates. One county would have needed a 51.7 percent sales tax rate and another would have needed a 52.7 percent income tax rate to replace the property taxes raised in the county.[24] These data illustrated the fiscal importance of the property tax, made it clear that the property tax was likely to be an important element in Kansas finance for many years to come, and called attention to the wide geographic variation in fiscal resources in Kansas. Obviously, the geographic distribution of the property tax base was very different from the distribution of the sales and income tax base.

Several subsequent editions of *Financing State and Local Government in Kansas* were prepared and distributed and, in response to the interest in use-value assessment of agricultural land, Kansas State University published several reports on that subject.[25] The use-value concept was first applied in eastern states in an attempt to reduce the premature development of land on the urban fringe. Use-value appraisal is based on the property's potential ability to earn income in agricultural use. Unlike market-value appraisal, use-value appraisal ignores the value that the land might have for other uses, such as residential or industrial development. By the time serious discussion of the concept began in Kansas, some form of use-value assessment had been adopted in approximately forty states.

Fringe development was not a major problem in most Kansas counties, but it was important in a few. More important was the strong feeling among farmers that Kansas farmland was selling above its use value because of the popularity of land as an inflation hedge. In fact, the increase in land prices had been extremely rapid. The average value of farmland and improvements in Kansas tripled in the fifteen years from 1959 to 1974. In 1959 the average value was $100 per acre. In the next ten years the average value rose by 59 percent, and in the next five it rose by 89 percent, to reach $301 per acre.[26] Because little of the land had been reassessed, most farm land was appraised for tax purposes far below market value. Many believed that taxation based on "inflated" market values would be unfair and would greatly burden one of Kansas's major industries.

Farm interests were successful in selling this viewpoint and the 1975 session of the Kansas Legislature approved a constitutional amendment permitting the valuation, assessment, and taxation of agricultural land on the basis of its use value. In November 1976, Kansas voters approved the amendment by a vote of 433,347 to 343,259. With this vote Kansas took another step away from constitutional uniformity. For the first time, the constitution did not require all tangible property to be uniformly assessed on the basis of value.

The 1977 legislature attempted to implement the amendment. Bills provided that soil classification data, crop yield data, farm price data, and production cost data were to be used to calculate the expected income from agricultural land. The productivity of land for each land class in each county for eight preceding years was to be determined by the Director of Property Valuation using information from state and federal crop and livestock reporting services, the soil conservation service, and other sources. Commodity prices and rangeland rental rates and expenses were to be based on the eight preceding years. Except in the case of range land, the normal landlord's share was to be considered as income to the land. The net rental income normally received from range land was considered income to the land. In all cases, the income was to be capitalized using as a capitalization rate the rate of interest on Federal Land Bank loans for the preceding five years plus .75 percent.[27]

The capitalization rate to be used was a critical issue. In market-value appraisal the proper capitalization rate is the rate currently being demanded and obtained by those investing in the kind of property being appraised. In the mid 1970s, this was a very low rate because many investors were buying land as an inflation hedge and were willing to accept low current returns. In order to protect landowners from appraisals based on inflationary values, a higher discount rate was used.

The interdependence of agricultural and urban assessment practices quickly came to the attention of the interim committee set up to study use-value appraisal. Professor B. L. Flinchbaugh of Kansas State University made county-by-county estimates of the effect of implementing use-value under varying assumptions. He estimated the impact of implementing use-value by means of several different capitalization rates and assuming that other real property was not reassessed. Not surprisingly, the results varied from county to county, but it was clear that if use-value was implemented without reappraisal of other property, the percentage of tax falling on agricultural land would increase. If other property was reappraised, there would be a shift from agricultural land to other real property. The study also showed there would be shifts among the various kinds of agricultural land, particularly to irrigated land.[28]

Obviously, the matter was more complicated than many supporters of use-value had assumed. Rural interests now realized that implementing use-value without reappraisal might not be to their benefit. They also discovered that not all agricultural land owners had the same interests. As a result, attempts to implement use-value assessment stalled. The final report of the committee gave a clue to the reason when it stated that, except at the first meeting, the subject of reappraising nonagricultural, real property was discussed at every meeting of the committee.[29]

In 1978, a special committee on taxation recommended a bill that mandated statewide property reappraisal, but stipulated that the new values were not to be used until approved by the legislature. In 1979, a bill based on this recommendation passed the Senate but not the House.

While the legislature was debating statewide reappraisal, one county took action on its own. Atchison County undertook a complete reappraisal, but taxpayers in school districts extending into other counties protested that increasing assessed values of their property without increasing the value of property in the other counties would place an unfair school tax burden on Atchison County taxpayers. The 1978 legislature responded to this complaint by enacting legislation that forbade any county from applying reappraised values until it was certified that all 105 counties had been reappraised.[30] This statute had the effect of suspending the uniform and equal provision of the Kansas Constitution.

Taxing Agricultural Personal Property

Clearly, there were strong pressures to maintain the status quo, but a series of events unfolded that made this impossible. One event had it origins in the brief farm prosperity of the 1970s. As a result of high prices of farm products, the price of used farm machinery rose rapidly. Representatives of Kansas farmers complained that farm machinery was being taxed according to the inflated prices reported in farm machinery "bluebooks," while business machinery was being appraised at depreciated costs.

A number of counties defied state orders to use the appraisal manuals furnished to them. In 1980, the Director of Property Valuation sent legal notices to Russell, Rooks, Nemaha, and Lincoln counties and a letter to Washington County asking that the guide be followed.[31] A few days later a crowd of more than 500 persons, described in a newspaper headline as "angry," attended a meeting with the Director of Property Taxation in Holton.[32] This was only one of several such meetings around the state.

On three occasions, the legislature responded to the farmers' complaints. In 1978, a bill was passed requiring a one-year, 15 percent reduction in the value of farm machinery as established in the Kansas Appraisal Guide, published by the Division of Property Valuation. In 1979, the law was extended for one year and the reduction was increased to 20 percent.[33] This law was declared to be an unconstitutional violation of the uniform and equal provision of the Kansas Constitution.[34] The 1981 legislature then passed a law prescribing a depreciation schedule to be used in assessing farm machinery.[35] It also was held to be unconstitutional.[36]

The Kansas Division of Property Valuation attempted to correct the alleged inequality between farm and business machinery assessment by bringing about an increase in the assessments of business machinery. Local appraisers were instructed to utilize trending factors that took into account both depreciation and inflation. This led to large increases in assessments of certain types of machinery that generated complaints, particularly from the owners of small manufacturing businesses in Sedgwick County. These taxpayers pointed out that machinery assessed in this way was greatly overtaxed in relation to real estate, which was appraised at values far below market. Individual members of the Kansas Small Business Trust filed complaints with the Kansas Board of Tax Appeals. The complainants presented evidence that their own and other residential properties were assessed at less than the legal 30 percent of market value and asked the board to order a reappraisal of three counties. The board found against the manufacturers, ruling that the relief requested was not in the best interest of the people of Kansas and stated that statewide reappraisal was the answer.[37]

In response to the Board of Tax Appeals ruling, suits were filed in Sedgwick and Rice counties asking the court to order all real estate reassessed to conform with the constitutional uniformity provision. The Kansas Small Business Trust sent the governor a letter threatening to pursue the suit until the legislature ordered statewide reappraisal. Representatives of the Small Business Trust and other business interests also testified before legislative committees asking that personal property, such as inventories and machinery, be exempt from taxation.

REAPPRAISAL AND CLASSIFICATION

As the decade of the 1980s began, it was clear to careful observers that another attempt to reappraise real property was inevitable. The assessment-sales ratio studies, although imperfect, provided ample evidence that the constitution was being flagrantly violated. The statutes stated that the assessment-sales ratio study alone was not sufficient evidence of assessment inequalities. This made it difficult for a taxpayer to prove the inequalities that everyone knew existed, but it was widely believed that sooner or later some individual or group would win a court order to reappraise.

Crafting a Reappraisal Bill

Those most familiar with the situation were anxious to avoid the experiences of the 1950s and 1960s when reappraisal was on a county-by-county basis and lasted over a decade, resulting in little or no improvement. Legislative leaders and tax officials understood that local and state officials had to work together to reappraise property and to establish a system that would maintain and update the values. At the same time, elected officials were haunted by stories of the political fallout that resulted from the earlier effort to reappraise. Stories circulated in Topeka to the effect that almost all legislators and many county officials were defeated in the first election after reappraisal in the 1960s. One attempt to determine the truth of those stories found turnover of county commissioners was little affected by the earlier reappraisal, but it was impossible to study the effect on legislative elections because of court ordered reapportionment of legislative seats.[38] The fear of political Armageddon was not relieved by a look at the assessment-sales ratio data. These data revealed very large variations in the assessment of individual properties but also showed large differences in the level of taxation of different classes of property. The largest increase in assessed values would be on farm and residential property. In other words, a large majority of the voters would be adversely affected. Taxes would be shifted from state-assessed (utility) property and business property to homeowners and farmers—not a pleasant prospect for Kansas politicians.

The legislature spent a great deal of time and effort developing a reappraisal bill. In his message to the legislature in 1979, Governor John Carlin warned that reappraisal would result in a drastic shift of tax to homeowners and farmers. He reiterated his support for use-value assessment of farmland, but indicated he would oppose any measure that would begin the reappraisal process or result in reappraisal.[39]

The following year, Governor Carlin indicated that he would support reappraisal if homeowners and farmers were protected.[40] In subsequent messages he referred to the likelihood of court-ordered reappraisal and the large tax increases that would result. He stated that rural real estate taxes would increase at an average of 82 percent and urban real estate taxes would increase at an average of 37 percent. At the same time, taxes paid by state assessed utilities would decrease by 57 percent.[41]

The governor was correct in regard to the direction and general magnitude of the shift, but it is difficult to say whether the numbers were correct because shifts in assessed values and shifts in taxes are not the same. This is a problem that plagues efforts to explain property taxes to the general public and resulted in untold confusion throughout the classification-reappraisal process. Property taxes in Kansas, with a few minor exceptions, were levied as a dollar amount, and the tax rate was computed by dividing this amount by the assessed value of the property in the taxing district. Reappraisal could result in an increase in total taxes only if the jurisdictions raised the dollar amounts of their levies. The amount of tax shifts from one class of property to another would depend upon the composition of the tax base in the overlapping jurisdiction taxing the property. Because of the large number of taxing jurisdictions and the overlapping boundaries, computing the effect of reappraisal on *taxes* was a complicated matter. As a result, most of the data produced during the debates were based on assessed values rather than taxes.

In the 1985 legislative session the deadlock was broken. Two developments seem to have played important roles in the breakthrough. One was a political compromise, the other was a development in assessment technology that affected the reappraisal bill. The political development was the organization in 1984 of a series of meetings of representatives of special interest groups. The coalition, which never had a name or formal organization, included representatives of the main interest groups concerned with taxation. Among those attending were representatives of public utilities, oil and gas producers, manufacturers, real estate interests, and farm interests. After a number of meetings and the examination of a number of computer printouts showing the effect of various proposals, the coalition agreed that use-value assessment should be adopted, all real estate should be reappraised, and a classification amendment should be submitted to the voters. The amendment was to be drafted so that the tax burden on the principal classes of property would be roughly maintained. To do this agricultural land would be appraised according to use-value. Improvements to agricultural land and urban residential property would be assessed at a lower percentage of market value. Commercial and industrial real estate, oil and gas, and utility property were to continue to be assessed at 30 percent. Farm machinery, merchants' and manufacturers' inventory, and livestock were to be exempt, and commercial and industrial machinery were to be assessed on the basis of depreciated value. It was believed that the exemption of inventories and the reduction in machinery taxes would largely offset the higher assessments on commercial and industrial real estate. The exemption of business personal property would eliminate administrative problems, bring Kansas into closer conformity with other states, and contribute to economic development.[42] These general principles were to be influential in the 1985 legislative deliberations, although there was much debate over details.

The Reappraisal Bill

The legislative committees attempting to draft reappraisal bills did their work carefully. They were aware of the developments in mass appraisal methodology and realized that a considerable amount of statewide standardization and supervision would be necessary to take full advantage of it. The use-value assessment bills drafted earlier contemplated a considerable amount of centralization of the assessment of farm land since the soil capability classifications and the data regarding productivity, farm product prices, and farm expenses had to be collected and analyzed by state or federal agencies.

Early drafts of the bills included provisions for state assistance to counties and for considerable statewide supervision of the assessment process. Although it was generally conceded that the assessment process needed to be standardized and supervised, many were uneasy about it. Proposals for a statewide computer system, with the possibility of state access to all the appraisal-related records of a county, were especially troubling. At this time, microcomputers were still new and it was argued that a computer mainframe located in Topeka would be the most efficient method of providing county appraisers with the necessary computer power. The apprehensions that this created were only slightly eased by the suggestion that several regional computer centers could be created.

However, both mass appraisal methodology and technology were changing rapidly. In March 1985 the author of this volume offered the following testimony to House and Senate tax committees:

> I spent the last two weeks in Chicago attending an intensive course on mass reappraisal of property. This course was sponsored by the International Association of Assessing Officers, the professional and educational organization of assessors. Among the eighteen participants were two persons from the Kansas Property Valuation Department and the deputy assessor from Sedgwick County. . . . Much of the time was devoted to the newest developments in computer assisted appraisal. . . . New developments include:
>
> 1. Computer software that makes it possible to assess sizeable jurisdictions using IBM compatible micro-computers. This has been developed by the non-profit Lincoln Institute and the International Association of Assessing Officers. This is, or will be, available free to qualified users and is being fur-

ther developed by IAAO for free distribution to members. Commercial firms are also developing the software for sale or use in their own reappraisals.

2. This software is very flexible. It permits the appraiser to choose from several methodologies (cost, several kinds of multiple regression, feedback and comparable sales). It also permits the local assessor to feed his/her own knowledge of the local situation into the process. In other words it is computer *assisted* appraisal—not computer appraisal.

3. Much emphasis has been placed on using models that can be understood by appraisers and taxpayers and that follow common sense notions of what affects value.

4. Appraisers do not have to be statisticians or computer experts to use this software. However, it will take time and experience to use it well. Thus, there will be many cost advantages if there is some statewide standardization of computer software and methods. This will permit a great deal of "learning from your neighbor" and facilitate Division of Property Valuation assistance to local appraisers.[43]

The Deadlock Broken

Finally, in the closing hours of the 1985 legislative session, the pieces for a compromise came together. The legislature passed Senate Bill 164, providing that reappraisal should be completed in all counties by January 1, 1989. The Division of Property Valuation was to make a determination of the use-value of various classes of agricultural land in each county and county appraisers were to apply the values to determine the appraisal of agricultural land. The Secretary of Revenue was to provide for the development of a computer system for processing appraisal data. The state was to bear part of the costs and the State Division of Property Valuation was to assist counties in carrying out reappraisal or in contracting with appraisal firms.[44]

Appraisers were to submit quarterly reports to the Director of Property Valuation, who was to monitor progress toward reappraisal. The director was to notify the Board of Tax Appeals if any county was not in substantial compliance and the board, after holding a hearing, could authorize the director to take over the appraisal process in the county. County boards of equalization were forbidden to issue any change order uniformly applicable to all property in the county or to any class or area in the county without approval of the Board of Tax Appeals.[45]

Both houses of the legislature also passed, with the required two-thirds vote, House Concurrent Resolution 5018 submitting a classification amendment to the vote of the people at the November 1986 election. It established the following classifications:

Property Class	*Appraised Value*
Real Estate	
Residential (urban, rural, including multifamily)	12%

Agricultural land (use-value)	30
Vacant Lots	12
All other (includes, commercial, industrial and utility)	30
Personal Property	
Mobile homes	12
Mineral leaseholds, public utility, motor homes, and others	30
Commercial and industrial machinery (cost less depreciation)	20
Farm machinery, merchants' and manufacturers' inventories, livestock	Exempt

Although many computer runs showing the expected shifts in assessed values were made, there were many uncertainties. It was generally assumed that use-value appraisal of agricultural land would result in assessment at about 8 percent of market value, but this was only an estimate. It was also difficult to estimate the effect of the new method of appraising commercial and industrial machinery. Legislators knew that the shift in assessed values would not correspond exactly to the shift in taxes, but it was generally assumed that the classification system would greatly moderate the class-to-class shifts.

Table 10.3 summarizes the last computer run before passage of the reappraisal-classification package.

Table 10.3. Estimated Effects of Reappraisal and Classification (shifts in assessed value as a percent of tax base)

Class	Assessed Value 1984 (1)	Assessed Value After Reappraisal (2)	Assessed Value After Class (3)	Increase from Reappraisal and Class (4)
Rural real estate	19.0	39.2	25.4	33.7
Urban real estate	29.0	40.7	43.3	49.3
Residential	18.7	26.6	20.8	11.2
Multifamily	1.8	2.3	1.8	0.0
Commercial	7.1	8.8	17.3	143.7
Industrial	0.9	1.1	1.9	111.1
Vacant lots	0.4	1.9	1.5	275.0
State Assessed	20.1	7.8	14.7	−26.9
Rural personal (except oil and gas)	5.7	1.7	0.6	−89.5
Machinery and equipment	1.5	0.6	0.6	−60.0
Merchants inventory	0.4	0.2	0.0	−100.0
Manufacturers inventory	1.1	0.4	0.0	−100.0
Livestock	1.3	0.5	0.0	−100.0
Other subclasses	1.4	0.0	0.0	−100.0
Oil and gas	16.1	6.3	12.3	−23.5
Urban personal	10.1	3.1	1.5	−85.1
Machinery and equipment	4.0	1.5	1.5	−62.5
Merchants inventory	2.7	1.1	0.0	−100.0
Manufacturers inventory	1.2	0.5	0.0	−100.0
Other subclasses	2.2	0.0	0.0	−100.0

Source: Computer printout from Kansas State Department of Education, Division of Financial Services and Kansas Legislative Research Department, April 23, 1985.

Data in Table 10.3 are expressed as percentages of total assessed value. For example, rural real estate made up 19 percent of the total tax base in 1984. If all property were to be reappraised at the legally required 30 percent, rural real estate would have made up 39.2 percent. In other words, reappraisal without classification would have more than doubled the appraised value of rural real estate as a percentage of all assessed value. Whether or not taxes on farm real estate would have doubled depended on the distribution of such real estate in the various taxing jurisdictions. Implementation of both the classification and reappraisal proposal would have increased the valuation of rural real estate to 25.4 percent of the total assessed value—an increase of 33.7 percent over the existing situation. These data show that reappraisal and classification would result in very large increases in the percentage of the tax base made up of commercial and industrial real estate. Much of the increase would be offset by decreases in assessment of business personal property.

The classification proposal was ratified at the November 1986 election by a vote of 534,799 to 253,123. This, together with the reappraisal act passed in 1985, set in motion the most comprehensive attempt to reform property tax administration in Kansas history.

THE REAPPRAISAL PROCESS

Reappraisal was a project of enormous size and complexity. As the reappraisal coordinator reported a few months before the scheduled completion date:

> Three and a half years is not much time to hire a state oversight staff of forty experienced appraisers and cartographers; orient and develop a comprehensive training program for hundreds of project supervisors and technical personnel hired by the counties, map 80,000 square miles of land; locate, measure and list 5 to 6 million improvements; install or upgrade a computer system in every county; and appraise 1.5 million parcels of property. Meeting the deadline is made even more imperative by the fact that a recent Constitutional Amendment implements a property assessment classification system on that same January 1, 1989 date, whether reappraisal is completed or not.[46]

To carry out this task the state contracted with a number of firms to produce aerial photographs. Negatives were supplied to the counties who themselves or through private companies produced cadastral maps according to state specifications. The state reappraisal bureau worked with a Computer Assisted Mass Appraisal (CAMA) consultant to produce a 1,200-page reappraisal manual and to assist counties in obtaining adequate computer facilities. The state hired a CAMA consultant to prepare a systems requirements definition outlining options and recommendations concerning software and hardware needs. The state undertook an

extensive educational campaign, which included workshops for appraisal personnel, consultants, and public officials. Topics ranged from basic instruction on project management or office layout to advanced topics in computer modeling. The
state also established a telephone information system in an effort to respond
quickly to problems at the county level.[47]

Political Backlash and the Response

The first tax bills computed after reappraisal were mailed in December 1989. The
outcry was immediate and loud. Large changes in the taxes levied on individual
properties should not have been a surprise to those who had followed the situation.
The purpose of reappraisal was to eliminate the inequalities of the kind shown in
Table 10.2, and public officials and others had repeatedly stressed that large
changes would occur. This, of course, did not lessen the impact or the protest from
property owners whose taxes had increased. Those whose taxes had decreased said
little.

More surprising than the shift within classes was the shift of tax burdens
among subclasses of taxpayers. Many estimates had assumed that the elimination of
inventory taxation and reduction in the amount of business machinery taxes would
approximately offset the increase in taxes on business real estate. Few observers
had anticipated the massive shifts within the business community. The reduction in
inventory and machinery taxes was of great benefit to manufacturing or merchan-
dising concerns that had large amounts of business personal property. In individual
cases, these reductions greatly exceeded the increase in real estate taxes. On the
other hand, there were many owners of office and apartment buildings who received much larger real estate tax bills but got no benefit from the personal property
tax changes. A major "sore spot" resulted from the large increase in taxes on vacant
lots. Vacant lots were given a favorable classification of 12 percent in the classification amendment. Because many lots had previously been given only token assessments, reappraisal resulted in large tax increases. Developers, caught by surprise,
argued that vacant lots were their "inventory" and should be tax exempt.

There were regional differences in the shifts. Johnson County, in the Kansas
City metropolitan area, was most severely affected by increased taxes on commercial and industrial real estate, while Sedgwick County was the site of the greatest
protest about taxes on vacant lots. There were also area-related differentials in the
impact on governmental bodies. For example, there were a few school districts in
which a high percentage of valuation had been made up of business personal property. In these districts classification resulted in large increases in real estate taxes.

Protest meetings were held, letters to the editor brimmed with indignation,
many taxpayers paid their taxes under protest, and a number of people saw the occasion as an opportunity to further or launch a political career. In the elections of
1990, former governor John Carlin, who had been constitutionally barred from
running for reelection in 1986, was defeated in the primary election by State Trea-

surer Joan Finney, who then defeated incumbent governor Mike Hayden, who had been speaker of the House of Representatives when reappraisal and classification were passed. Many observers attributed both defeats to a backlash against the property tax.

At the local level, many of the appointed county appraisers lost their jobs, although some were hired by other counties. The large number of tax protests overloaded the appeal process and the legislature compounded the problem by adding additional levels of appeal to the process.

The 1992 legislature reacted to the controversy by submitting another classification amendment and by passing a new school finance act. The proposed classification amendment made relatively small changes in the system adopted earlier. The assessed value of residential real property was reduced from 12 percent of appraised value to 11.5 percent. A new classification was created for property owned by not-for-profit corporations to be assessed at 12 percent. The assessed value of utility, real estate, and personal property was raised from 30 percent to 33 percent of appraised value. Industrial and commercial property assessments were reduced from 30 to 25 percent of appraised value and the assessed value of commercial and industrial machinery was raised from 20 to 25 percent of depreciated value.[48] There was little public discussion of the amendment before the 1992 election, but it passed by a vote of 473,415 to 421,813.

SCHOOL FINANCE AND ASSESSMENT ADMINISTRATION

In 1991 the district court of Shawnee County handed down a far-reaching school finance decision. After reviewing the states' constitutional duty to provide equal educational opportunity to every child, Judge Terry Bullock asked if it meant that 100 percent state financing is required for public schools? The judge then answered his own question with a simple "yes." He went on to state:

> The reasons are two: (a) that is what the constitution says; and (b) that is what we have always had—for so-called local school districts are legally only political subdivisions of the state, exercising such of the state's taxing authority as the legislature delegates to them in partial fulfillment of the *legislature's* obligation to finance the educational interests of the state. Thus money raised by school districts through "local" taxation is still state money. It just hasn't been thought of that way. [Emphasis in the original.][49]

The sentiments expressed by Judge Bullock are in line with Dillon's Rule, which emphasizes that local governments are "creatures of the state." This rule of statutory construction has been modified by home rule provisions in many states and has, itself, been subject to various interpretations by the courts. Judge Bullock did not flinch from the implications of a strict interpretation as applied to school districts in Kansas.[50] His decision, if upheld and implemented, would have enormous ramifications for government structure in Kansas.

The 1992 Kansas legislature responded to Judge Bullock's demand that the legislature provide equal educational opportunity for all children by enacting a centralized system of school finance. The system included a ceiling on per-pupil spending and required all districts to impose a 32-mill property tax levy. Any amounts above the spending ceiling for each district were to be remitted to the state for distribution to "deficit" districts. Although technically levied by the school districts, the levy was, in effect, a state property tax levy. The action restored the property tax to its original position as a major source of finance for state government and simultaneously expanded the responsibilities of state government to include a much greater role in financing elementary and secondary education.[51]

The implementation of the uniform statewide levy resulted in very large geographic shifts in property tax levies. The thinly populated but mineral rich counties in southwest Kansas and high-income Johnson County experienced large increases in tax levies and decreases in the amount they were permitted to spend on public education. This brought forth a new round of protests, including the widely publicized threats from several southwestern counties to secede from the state.

Obviously, the existence of a uniform statewide school finance levy made uniformity of assessment even more important. On June 30, 1992, Judge Bullock, in response to a suit brought by Attorney General Robert T. Stephen, issued another sweeping order, this one addressing property tax administration. The judge found the new school finance levy to be a statewide property tax levy and ruled that the constitution requires a uniform and equal basis of valuation and rate of taxation on property subject to taxation within a jurisdiction. He declared that the Director of Property Valuation to have general supervision over the administration of the assessment and property tax laws of the state and "*over all county, city and township officials* involved in the process to the end that all property of every kind and character, including real estate, is assessed (appraised) at its actual and full cash market value" (K.S.A. 1991 Supp. 74-1404). (emphasis added)."[52]

The court entered a consent decree requiring the Department of Revenue, Secretary of Revenue, and the Director of Valuation to perform their statutory duties to ensure to the fullest extent possible that appraisal be at fair market value. Specifically, the defendants were ordered to compel county appraisers, county commissioners, and all others whose duty it is to value and assess property according to the laws of the state. The Department of Revenue was required to devote all necessary resources to develop a valid ratio study to be completed by February 28, 1993. The department was told to continue and expand county audits of appraisal systems, to test the computer-assisted mass appraisal system, and to correct deficiencies as they were discovered. The Department of Revenue was also ordered to establish minimum standards of education for county appraisal personnel and to withdraw and review all directives regarding property tax appraisal before codifying and reissuing them. The department was to determine the adequacy of resources available to support the counties in carrying out their duties and to develop and present to the legislature plans for ongoing educational programs in connection with both the state universities and junior colleges. The court retained jurisdiction and indicated that a conference would be held in early February 1993 to review progress.

In remarks accompanying an additional order in July 1993, Judge Bullock summarized the situation that had faced the court. There were some 1.4 million parcels of real estate in Kansas. The constitution and the statutes required that they be appraised (not assessed) at fair market value—defined as the price the parcel would bring at an arm's length sale. He pointed out that possible remedies included enjoining the collection and spending of all real estate taxes until constitutional appraisals were in place or ordering another statewide reappraisal at a cost of $120 million. The first option would have had the effect of bringing city governments, county governments, and public schools to a standstill. The second would have placed local government in limbo for four to six years until reappraisal was completed.

Rather than accept either of these unpalatable alternatives, the attorney general and officials of the Department of Revenue had assisted in the development of the 1992 consent degree. The judge praised the officials for their efforts and thanked the Kansas supreme court for a decision confirming the authority of the Director of Property Valuation to carry out the steps outlined in the 1992 plan.[53]

The 1993 order spelled out assessment standards and set a timetable for achieving them. The order requires that by January 1, 1998, every county is to meet specific standards. The median ratio for the residential property class and the commercial and industrial property class must be within 10 percent of the statutory standard (95 percent confidence level). The coefficients of dispersion for these classes must be less than 20 percent. The regressivity measure is to be within the .98 to 1.03 range.[54] These were to be measured by the official 1998 appraisal-sales ratio study as required by the statutes.

The new order reiterated a number of the requirements imposed or agreed to in the 1992 orders and spelled out some additional ones. Included were requirements for improving commercial and industrial appraisal by developing a capitalization rate study, a statewide cost index study, a statewide land valuations study, and a statewide income and expense study. A sales data base, organized by type of commercial property, was also to be developed.

The order plainly states that the director of Property Valuation has authority over boards of county commissioners, county appraisers, and other officers involved with the appraisal, assessment, and collection of property taxes. It states that the Director has agreed to suspend or terminate the employment of county appraisers for cause, pursue mandamus actions, assume control of county appraisal operations, withhold funds appropriated to assist county appraisal, and take any other actions deemed appropriate to achieve the objectives of the order.

The court's 1992 and 1993 orders were bold assertions of its authority and competence to command quality administration of the property tax. Underlying this assertion were the assumptions that uniform assessment is possible and that ratio studies could be good measures of the quality of assessment. In fact, neither assumption is beyond doubt.

The Division of Property Valuation has attacked the problem with considerable vigor, but both political and technical problems have hampered achievement of quality appraisal. County appraisers are caught between the state's demands and the complaints of local property owners. County commissioners often make the county appraisers the scapegoats and turnover among appraisers has been high. Many counties, especially the smaller ones, complain that CAMA appraisal methods cannot be applied because of insufficient sales data and that the ratio studies used to measure performance suffer from the same problems. In response to this, the Director of Property Valuation modified the methods of determining compliance to place greater emphasis upon an audit of procedures. The 1993 court order, however, depends entirely on statistical measures to determine compliance.

The nature and difficulty of the problems faced by the Director of Property Valuation is indicated by the questions he has placed before the ratio study technical advisory committee. That committee, composed of professors from Kansas universities, meets regularly to advise on technical problems relating to the ratio study.

A number of questions have been related to the editing of the sales sample. Property transfers recorded in the county courthouses include many transfers that do not represent valid, arm's length sales. Some are to correct mistakes in titles, some are transfers between relatives or related corporate interests, some are bankruptcy-related transfers, and some are sales made under threat of condemnation. According to Kansas statutes, many transfers of this type are exempt from the requirement that a sales validation questionnaire be filed. For other sales, the questionnaire provides additional information, which the director uses to determine whether or not the sale is valid. Often there are borderline cases and the director is responsible for developing rules and seeing that they are consistently applied. Unfortunately, even with careful editing there are often a few extremely high and extremely low ratios. These may result from a clerical error or incorrect information in the questionnaire, or it may be that either the buyer or seller was badly informed and made a very bad or very good deal. Sometimes additional research can determine the problem, but at other times no reasonable explanation can be discovered. To leave such ratios in the sample unfairly penalizes the appraiser whose work is being judged. Eliminating too many sales would eliminate evidence of bad appraisal and overstate the quality of assessment in the county. The International Association of Assessing Officers guidelines permit the "trimming" of a certain percentage of outliers, but this arbitrary percentage seemed inadequate for some situations and the advisory committee approved the use of a rule that seemed better suited to the situation.

Many other questions dealing with the size and representativeness of the sample have been considered by the advisory committee. Unfortunately, the number of sales of some classes of property in some counties is very small. This creates problems both for the original assessment and for the ratio studies used to measure the quality of the assessment. The standard statistical tests for adequate sample size assume a "normal" bell-shaped curve. Actually the distribution of sales ratios is never normal. No ratio can be less than zero, but there is no upper limit to its size. Division of Property Valuation revenue personnel have been exploring the statistical literature for procedures that might be useful.

In the larger counties, the number of valid sales of certain classes of property are far greater than is needed and procedures have been developed that will save money and produce more reliable results. This involves not only determining the size of sample to be used, but also its representiveness. Property sold in a given time period is often not representative of taxable property. For example, in the residential class, newly constructed houses will be over represented. This can be corrected by developing a stratified sampling technique. Under authority granted by the 1993 legislature, the director, with the advice of the advisory committee, has developed procedures for sampling the sale of certain classes of property in the larger counties.

One bizarre incident involving statistical procedures resulted from a ruling by the Board of Tax Appeals. In response to an appeal brought by a county, it ruled that the literal wording of the statute required that all sales for which a validation questionnaire is required, not just those determined to be valid by the director, be included in the 1993 study. This meant that sales that were clearly not at market value had to be included. The result was absurd. Coefficients of dispersion for many classes of property were in the thousands. For example, in one county a commercial building appraised at $5.6 million had a recorded sales price of $100. The coefficient of dispersion for commercial and industrial property in that county was 87,762.6.

SUMMARY AND CONCLUSIONS

Clearly CAMA has not overcome the inherent problems of determining the value of property. In the hands of skilled appraisers it can be of great assistance, but the technical nature of the decisions that have to be made makes it difficult to explain to taxpayers. It also opens new avenues for attorneys, representing either taxpayers or local governments, and assisted by well paid, expert witnesses to challenge appraisals or the ratio study on technical grounds.

The eventual outcome of reappraisal, classification, and the revision in school finance is not clear, but the potential for change is enormous. This "reform" effort differs from earlier ones in two important respects. One is the existence of computer-driven mass appraisal technology. Kansas was the first state to require local officials to utilize uniform CAMA methodology. Its success or failure may influence assessment administration throughout the world. The second difference is Shawnee County court's insistence that education and uniform appraisal are the state's responsibility. Rarely has an American court stated these doctrines so boldly or so boldly faced up to the implications. Unless reversed by a higher court, they are likely to have an enormous impact on property tax administration and school finance in Kansas and, perhaps, elsewhere.

On the other side are the forces that have defeated tax reform in the past. One is the inherent difficulty of the assessment process. Even with CAMA, mass appraisal is not an exact science. Another is the opposition that will be encouraged by centralizing so much power at the state level. Centralization of a function so vital as school finance, tax assessment, and tax levy goes against deeply held American values. Whatever its legal validity, Judge Bullock's assertion that local money is state money is not a universally held political value. Equally important, however, are the political forces generated by all those who lose from so radical a change. Those whose property was previously underassessed (relatively) and those in areas impacted unfavorably by a statewide levy are much more active politically than those who gain. In any case, Kansas, which has rarely been at the forefront in the reform of property tax administration, may provide technical and political tests of modern mass appraisal techniques.

11
Property Taxation in the United States Today

A well-known student of the property tax recently wrote that the property tax as found in most states "resembles a structure designed by a mad architect, erected on a shaky foundation by an incompetent builder, and made worse by the well-intentioned repair work of hordes of amateur tinkerers."[1] In fact, the tax was not designed by an architect, and the repair work is not the result of amateur tinkers, but is the outcome of years of political conflict.

The universal truth about taxation is that people want government without paying for it. The history of taxation is the story of a struggle among individuals and groups intent upon achieving that goal for themselves or for their groups. If that judgment appears unduly harsh, it is because debates over tax policy are usually carried on in somewhat more polite terms. Naked self-interest is usually masked by reasoned analysis of the equity or economic effects of a particular tax system. Compromises are common because few want to risk a breakdown in the constitutional order or the termination of valued government services.

The novel thing about the property tax is that the idea of uniform taxation of all wealth muted the rhetoric and, for a time, served as a guide to distribution of the tax burden. It was an exciting idea, but inherent administrative difficulties and conflict between administrative efficiency and local democracy soon became apparent. Special interest groups seized the opportunity to advance their interests at the administrative, statutory, or constitutional level. Out of the resulting political conflict grew the variety of odd-shaped tax structures that called forth the mad architect analogy.

This book has emphasized the history of a single state so that the evolution of the tax could be examined in some detail. Understanding the administrative and political details in one state can contribute to one's understanding of the property tax systems in other states, even though the timing of the process and the shape of the resulting structures may differ.

THE PROPERTY TAX BASE

Currently, property taxes differ from the idealized general property tax in several ways. Departures from uniformity involve many different combinations of the following:

- Statutory or de facto classification
- Preferential treatment of agricultural land
- Relief for low income or elderly persons
- Tax limits or freezes
- Economic development incentives

All involve permanent or temporary modifications to the tax base.

Classification

Classification means that property is divided into two or more classes and that differential rates of assessment (sometimes rates of taxation) are applied to each class. Uniformity within classes is still required.

The earliest proponents of classification proposed to place intangible property in a separate class. It was to be taxed at a lower rate or to be subject to taxation by a method other than ad valorem. Others proposed exempting intangibles from the property tax. Both courses have been followed. According to one tabulation, twenty-one states tax some kinds of intangible property, but only nine include intangibles as part of general property. In eight of the nine, intangibles are taxed at an effective rate lower than most other classes.[2]

More than 78 percent of the total revenue collected from intangible taxation is state revenue, and two states, Florida and Connecticut, collect 69 percent of that. The states receiving more than 1 percent of state and local tax revenue from intangible taxes are Connecticut, Florida, Kentucky, New Hampshire, and Tennessee. Of these, only Kentucky has a broad-based income tax.

The wide variety of intangible tax bases makes it difficult to generalize about them. Often several types of taxable intangible property are named in the statutes. Examples include equities, bank deposits, mortgages, cash value of insurance policies, copyrights, and patents. Typically, value is the base, but in some states the tax is based on income from the property. It appears that current intangible taxes are often remnants of some past situation or are as closely related to income taxation as to the property tax. An example of the former is the tax on computer software in the state of Washington. There the statute provided that intangible property was taxable unless specifically exempted. In 1989 a court ruled that software, previously considered tangible property, was intangible property. Since the exemption statute had been written before the existence of computers, it did not contain an exemption for software, which became taxable as intangible property. Examples of the relationship of intangible taxation to the income taxes are found in Connecticut, Florida, New Hampshire, and Tennessee, which have no broad-based income tax but do tax income from some kinds of intangible property. Undoubtedly, this represents an attempt to tax income from property that escapes ad valorem taxation. It is of historic interest that Ohio, which set a pattern in 1851 by carefully specifying in its constitution that all classes of intangibles were to be taxed, changed in the 1980s to an intangible tax applying only to dealers in intangibles.[3]

Classification or exemption of tangible personal property is also widespread. Personal property is often difficult to locate and can be even more difficult to assess than real estate. Except for a few kinds of property, such as motor vehicles, there is no system of registration or licensing that assessors can use to locate personal property. The mapping and land registration system that eases administration of real estate taxation does not exist for most kinds of personal property. This leaves the personal property tax administrator the choice of depending on self-listing by property owners or actively seeking to locate the various kinds of personal property. Self listing was first tried early in the history of the property tax and failed woefully, even when accompanied by severe penalties.

There are a variety of methods that assessors can use to locate tangible personal property. Some kinds of property can be located through registration or license lists. Lists of businesses can be obtained through the telephone book or other business lists. Industry standards can be used to determine the probable presence of certain kinds of machinery or equipment. Used equipment price guides or public records of sales are useful in determining the value of property. Assessor-initiated searches are expensive procedures that yield uneven results and result in an immense amount of taxpayer resentment. Most states now tie the taxation of motor vehicles to the vehicle registration process. Payment of the property tax may be a prerequisite for registration, or the registration fee may be in lieu of property taxes.

Nine states exempt all tangible personal property. Many exempt certain kinds of tangible personal property. Only two states attempt to tax household goods. Sixteen states tax business inventories, but even in these states certain kinds of inventories may be exempted by local authorities. Most of the states that tax personal property have some kind of exemption for goods-in-transit or free port arrangements, which permit companies to store and, perhaps, repackage goods within the state without paying personal property taxes. Several states that have exempted inventories tax depreciable business assets, such as furniture, machinery, and equipment.[4]

The exemption of many kinds of tangible and intangible personal property has reduced the revenue from personal property taxation but, as in many aspects of property taxation, there is great variation from state to state. In 1986, locally assessed personal property made up only 10.1 percent of the property tax base in the United States.[5] It made up 41.7 percent, however, of the base in West Virginia. Personal property made up 29.6 percent of the base in Kansas prior to the effective date of the classification amendment. At the other extreme are the nine states that exempt all personal property.[6]

According to one tabulation, twenty-one states have more than one class of real estate.[7] The number of classes varies from two to thirty-four, although the situations in some states, such as Minnesota, have become so complex that it is difficult to specify the number of classes. The differential between the high class and the low class is usually less than 3:1, although it reaches a high of 27.5:1 in Minnesota. In a few states the tax share of the various classes of property is fixed and assessment ratios fluctuate to maintain that share.[8] In Illinois, any county with a population of more than 200,000 may classify property, but only Cook County does so. In California, Proposition 13 provided that real estate assessment may not rise more than the rate of inflation or 2 percent per year, whichever is less, until the property changes hands. This is a kind of assessment freeze, which, in effect, creates a classification system based on the date of sale of the property. Nine other states have some kind of limit on the amount by which an individual assessment may increase within a given time period. In some states these limits apply only to specified types of property or in certain geographic locations.[9]

The rates at which the various classes are taxed reflect the political power of groups of property owners. Generally, commercial and industrial property is assessed or taxed at a higher rate than residential or agricultural property, but there are often provisions whereby some industries or firms are given tax reductions as an economic development incentive. In states with a classification system, utility property is assessed higher than residential or farm property, but federal legislation requires that railroad property be taxed no higher than other commercial and industrial property.

If the classification system is statutory, debate over the system occurs at every legislative session and classifications change frequently. If the system is specified in the constitution, annual changes are generally limited to those resulting from legislative definition of terms or from court decisions.

Preferential Assessment of Agricultural Land

Almost every state has adopted some form of use-value assessment of agricultural land. These laws were intended to prevent the premature development of urban fringe land and to protect farmers from assessments based on speculative values. The laws vary considerably, but value is typically determined by capitalizing the income that could be expected from the land in agricultural use. Often the capitalization rate is set high enough that even land far from urban areas is appraised well below the market value. These laws have also led to valuable urban land being "farmed" right up to the day construction starts. In some states there are provisions for levying back taxes when land is sold for development.

Use-value assessment of agricultural land has accelerated the trend toward centralization of administration. Often a state agency is responsible for providing the information about soil classes, productivity, income data, and expense data that is used in calculating agricultural use value.

Incentives for Economic Development

There have been many studies of the effect of taxes and tax incentives on economic growth and the location of businesses. There has been far less study of the reverse question, "What is the impact of the politics of industrial location upon tax structure?"

There are basically three approaches to providing tax incentives. One is to implement a tax policy believed to be conducive to economic growth and development but not targeted to particular industries or firms.

Another approach is to provide statutory exemptions or tax reductions that favor certain types of business activity. For example, exemption of manufacturing inventory or machinery may be granted as a way of encouraging manufacturing activities. A variation of this approach is to grant automatic exemptions to firms that engage in certain activities, such as creating new jobs or constructing or renovating buildings in specified redevelopment areas. Critics of this approach say that many firms are rewarded for actions they would have taken anyway.

A third approach is to negotiate tax breaks with individual firms. Often the negotiation is carried on by local authorities and may be part of a package that includes financing assistance and the provision of infrastructure or ongoing government services. At its best, this approach attains results at less sacrifice of public revenue than broad-gauged exemptions. Wisely done, benefits are provided only to firms that would not have located in the community anyway and to those that will be of economic benefit to the community. On the other hand, negotiating tax burdens departs from the idea of uniform tax statutes administered by neutral administrators and opens the door for mistakes in judgment or political favoritism. Existing firms may resent that new competitors receive benefits not available to them.

Statutory exemptions or reduced taxation of the property of certain industries were common in the colonial period, but uniformity clauses in state constitutions made concessions to particular industries, as well as concessions to particular firms, unconstitutional. This, of course, did not prevent assessors and other local officials from favoring firms considered to be of economic importance to the community. Understandably, these cases are not well documented. With the repeal of uniformity clauses, statutory concessions for particular industries returned. Today there are numerous examples. In Arkansas all capital invested in cotton mills is exempt from property taxation for seven years. Alabama provides a ten-year exemption to the manufacturers of aluminum, aluminum products, and calcium cyanamide. Hawaii exempts pulp and paper mills from real property taxation.

The current trend is toward comprehensive economic development programs that include low-cost financing, employee training programs, infrastructure development, and tax incentives. The intent is to target the incentives, including tax incentives, to particular firms. Many state and local governments have active development agencies that work with individual firms to develop and implement packages of incentives.

Some thirty states have programs permitting exemption of real estate to encourage economic development, the redevelopment of blighted areas, or the preservation of historic areas. There is great variety in the kinds of property eligible, the conditions attached, and the amount of relief provided. Sometimes the property constructed, added to, or reconstructed must be in a specific development or redevelopment area. The boundaries of areas may be specified in state statutes or may be designated by local authorities.[10]

Often the exemptions are for a limited time period, or the exemption may phase out over a number of years. For example, in Iowa cities and counties may grant newly constructed, industrial real estate a partial exemption that begins at 75 percent in the first year and declines by fifteen percentage points per year. In urban revitalization districts the exemption may be a total exemption for three years or one that declines over ten years.

In most instances, local governments have a major voice in the granting of property tax exemptions. Often it is the local government that decides whether or not property tax exemptions are to be granted, and in a number of states they have the authority to negotiate "in lieu" payments in exchange for property tax exemptions. Often the exemption affects the revenue of all governments taxing the property, but in some states the exemption is more limited. For example, in Mississippi the local governing authority, with state approval, may grant exemption from all nonschool taxes.

Sometimes the development incentive involves a change in expenditure pattern or responsibility for services. Tax increment financing involves the sale of bonds to clear and redevelop the infrastructure in a blighted area. The tax revenues received by the governments that tax the area are frozen and the increase in revenues resulting from new development is earmarked to repay the bonds. Some states offer firms relief from certain taxes in return for providing their own services. For example, in Louisiana a majority of landowners may form a special industrial area. Industries in such an area are free from taxation by special service districts if they do not use the services of that district. The industry must provide its own utilities, road maintenance, police, and fire protection.

States have responded to environmental problems with a variety of tax relief provisions. Often these take the form of exempting pollution control facilities from property taxation. Some have encouraged the development of alternative energy facilities by exempting facilities for producing alternative fuels, solar power, and the like. These environmental related exemptions are usually small with little effect on revenue.

Circuit Breakers and Homestead Exemptions

One of the most frequently encountered criticisms of the property tax is that it is regressive and places an undue burden on homeowners. The impact upon low-income people or upon elderly people who want to continue to live in the family home is of special concern.

In times of rapid real estate inflation, the taxation of unrealized capital gains produces problems, even for the more affluent. This was a major factor in the success of Proposition 13 in California. Rapid increases in the value of residential real estate and good property tax administration combined to place heavy and unexpected burdens even on middle- and upper-class homeowners.

In the depressed 1930s when many homeowners and farmers were losing their homes to tax sales, a few states enacted exemptions for owner-occupied residences or farms. These homestead exemptions removed the tax from a certain amount of property valuation, but there was no limit on the total value of eligible property or the income of the recipient. Critics of homestead exemptions argued that they gave benefits to the wealthy as well as the needy, they discriminated against renters, and the burden fell unevenly upon local governments. Local governments whose tax base included many low-valued, owner-occupied houses were especially hard hit.

In the post–World War II period, a variation of homestead exemptions, with the curious name "circuit breaker," spread rapidly among the states. The name arose from an analogy to a electrical circuit breaker that interrupts the flow of electricity when the load becomes too heavy. Circuit breakers differed from homestead exemptions in that they were targeted to low income, handicapped, or elderly individuals, and the cost was paid by the state rather than the local government. Sometimes renters were included. Usually, the taxpayer was required to pay the tax and receive a refund or income tax credit based on the amount of tax paid and income received.

Today every state and the District of Columbia has some form of homestead exemption or circuit breaker. Many states have both. There is great variety in the criteria for eligibility and the size of the exemption or credit. For example, Florida has an extensive and long-established homestead exemption program. The first $25,000 of assessed value of owner-occupied homes and all of the assessed value of disabled veterans' property is exempted for taxation. There are more than 3.1 million beneficiaries, and the revenue lost to local governments is about $1.6 billion. Michigan has a circuit breaker program for homeowners and renters with an $82,650 income ceiling. There are over 1.5 million beneficiaries receiving an average benefit rebate or income tax credit of $503.68. Michigan also provides a total homestead exemption to disabled veterans. West Virginia provides a state financed circuit breaker for elderly homeowners and renters with incomes of less than $5,000 and a homestead exemption of the first $20,000 of assessed value of elderly and disabled owner-occupants.[11]

In some cases there are several property tax relief programs. In California there is a circuit breaker for blind, disabled, and elderly homeowners and renters with incomes of less than $13,200. There are 196,000 beneficiaries receiving an average benefit of $92.12. California also provides a homestead exemption on the first $7,000 of the full cash value of owner-occupied residences with full state reimbursement to local governments. There are almost 4.8 million recipients of this exemption. In addition, Proposition 13 limits the annual increase in assessed value of property that does not change hands to 2 percent or the rate of inflation, whichever is smaller.

In Minnesota there is a state-reimbursed homestead exemption for all homeowners, a state-financed circuit breaker for homeowners and renters, and a separate credit for homeowners with a tax increase of more than 10 percent over the previous year. In addition, Minnesota's complicated classification system provides a lower rate of assessment for residential property.

A few states have enacted tax deferral programs for elderly homeowners. Property taxes can be deferred until death. In the meantime the accumulated taxes become a lien upon the property. For the most part, these programs have not been very popular. Apparently many elderly people resist the idea of mortgaging their homes to pay the taxes, even though it will not become payable until after their death.

ADMINISTRATION OF THE PROPERTY TAX

Assessment is the weakest part of property tax administration. In the early history of ad valorem taxation it was assumed that the local, elected assessor would be familiar with the value of his neighbors' property. As the economy became more complex and property more specialized, the unreality of that assumption became apparent and attention turned to the development of more systematic methods. Appraisers and economists turned to the task of applying the abstract principles of economics to the concrete question of appraisal.

By about 1910 the famous "three approaches" to value had been developed and were being taught to assessors and private appraisers. The *comparative sales* approach is based on the idea of comparing the property to be assessed (subject property) with similar, recently sold properties (comparison properties). The sales prices of the comparison properties are adjusted up or down to allow for differences between the comparison properties and the subject property. If the adjusted prices differ, the appraiser must use judgment and knowledge of the market to assign a value to the subject property.

The *income* approach is based on the idea of capitalizing the expected stream of income to convert annual values to capital values. Because it is the property value, not the management or the income, that is being valued, it is important that the income stream be the income that could be expected for the property under average management, not the actual income. The capitalized rate is the rate that investors in similar property are receiving.

The *cost* approach is based on the principal of substitution. A rational purchaser would not pay more for an existing building than the cost of constructing a new building of equal utility. The value of an existing building is the cost of replacing it with a building of similar utility minus the depreciation resulting from physical deterioration or obsolescence (not accounting depreciation). To this value must be added independently determined land values. The cost approach is popular with many assessors because cost manuals purchased from commercial sources or provided by a state agency provide a relatively simple, systematic method of valuing property that can be used to convince property owners that all property is assessed by the "same method." However, unless the manuals are constantly and accurately updated to reflect local conditions, the values produced may differ considerably from market value.

In an economist's theoretically perfect market, all three methods would yield the same result. In practice they do not. In fact, it may be impossible to obtain the information needed for some of the approaches. The appraiser must choose the most appropriate methods and "correlate" the values obtained in several ways using his or her own judgment and knowledge of the market.

The three approaches are still the bases of appraisal methodology, but the entire field has been revolutionized by developments in computer technology and mapping techniques. Computers permit the appraiser to collect larger amounts of data and to analyze larger amounts of information. In the precomputer era, sales comparisons often involved only three to five properties and a small number of property characteristics. With computers, multiregression and other kinds of sales comparison approaches make it possible to use hundreds of comparison properties and to consider a large number of property characteristics.

A modern mass appraisal system consists of a data management system, a sales analysis system, a valuation system, and an administrative system.[12] The data management system is used to collect, organize, and store information about property and its ownership. It may include a digitalized, cadastral mapping system, which may be shared with other departments.

The sales analysis system facilitates the screening and processing of sales data. This includes routines for identifying and eliminating invalid sales and analyzing valid sales so that sales ratios can be computed. Sales ratios are used in the appraisal process to evaluate the quality of assessment.

The valuation system includes several variations of the sales comparison approach, such as multiple regression, adaptive estimation procedures (feedback), and automated sales comparison. It also includes programs useful in the cost approach, such as cost equations, schedules, and programs to derive depreciation schedules from market data. The income approach is facilitated by programs for developing and applying income multipliers and overall rates and for deriving capitalization rates from market data.

The administrative system is concerned with such tasks as preparation of assessment notices and tax bills. It should also facilitate the production of information needed for tax appeals and may provide information useful to other governmental functions, such as planning and budgeting.

A computer-assisted mass appraisal (CAMA) system has the potential for greatly improving the quality of assessment, but it also offers challenges and dangers. Developing CAMA systems requires a high degree of statistical and computer skills as well as a knowledge of the theory and practice of appraisal. Rarely will all these skills be found in the same person. Successful use of CAMA requires a well functioning organization, including highly trained specialists with carefully defined responsibilities. Much of the work can be delegated to clerical workers, but they must be carefully supervised and the organization must avoid overreliance on machine-generated answers. Knowledgeable appraisers must make the final judgment and be able and willing to explain the process in understandable terms.

CAMA is essentially a statistical procedure and, like all statistical processes, it requires adequate amounts of accurate data. The purpose of appraisal is to determine market price and all three approaches depend on market data. The sales comparison approach requires adequately sized samples of valid or arm's length sales. The income approach requires information about rents, operating expenses, and knowledge of the capital markets in the area. The cost approach requires data about construction costs as well as information about the impact of obsolescence and physical depreciation on market values.

There are several circumstances that may inhibit the collection of such data. In some areas there are simply not enough sales of certain types of property. There is often opposition to making such information available. During the Kansas reappraisal, for example, some trade groups advised their members not to provide appraisal authorities with information such as rents or operating costs. Legislatures are often reluctant to require information that may be considered private or of a proprietary nature.

There are aspects of statistical procedures that present problems or make it difficult to secure public acceptance of the new appraisal methods. Early use of multiple regression analysis, for example, revealed several problems. One is the difficulty of explaining the process. Correlations among independent variables may result in coefficients that are counter-intuitive. Assessors soon learned that attempting to explain the impact of the various variables as they appear in the estimating equation could lead to serious misunderstanding. In one case the coefficient of the term representing the presence of a swimming pool was negative. This could put an appraiser in the position of explaining to a taxpayer that a neighbor's house was assessed lower because it had a swimming pool. It was also discovered that even well fitting regression equations sometimes result in rapid year-to-year changes in the values of particular properties. Using different statistical models in different neighborhoods sometimes results in differences in the calculated values of similar properties separated by the neighborhood boundary. Statistical procedures for smoothing such differences can be developed, but it requires a considerable degree of statistical skill and constant vigilance to locate and correct these and other problems.

In some cases, there simply is not enough information for CAMA to work. Perhaps, in fact, there are cases where the entire idea of market price makes little sense. What, for example, is the value of a vacant building that housed a now defunct department store in a small, declining town? Perhaps some enterprising local citizen or a refugee from a large city will buy it and convert it to another use. Equally likely, the owner will eventually have to pay the cost of demolishing it. It seems unreasonable to expect the appraiser to predict which will happen.

Assessment Organization

The development of computer models to assist in the appraisal process has not eliminated conflicts over property tax administration. On one side are those who believe assessors should be highly trained professional appraisers isolated from political influence and armed with the latest technology. On the other side are those who favor locally elected assessors who understand local conditions, respond to political considerations, and realize that formulas or computers do not always produce "correct" answers.

The arguments are much the same as they were a century ago and it is difficult to discern how much assessment organization and practice has changed as a result of a century of arguments. The International Association of Assessing Officers conducted an elaborate survey in an attempt to describe the assessment administration in the United States and Canada.[13] The survey reveals that there are 15,837 primary assessing units in the United States. The number ranges from one in Maryland, where the state performs the assessment function, to 2,713 in Minnesota. In Delaware and Hawaii assessment is entirely a local function. In all other states the responsibility for assessment is shared between the state and its local units. Counties have the primary responsibility for assessment in nineteen states. In eight states municipalities or townships have the prime responsibility. In seventeen states the state is responsible for valuing certain types of property, usually public utility property, with counties and municipalities responsible for the rest.

Local assessors are elected in twenty-two states and appointed by county or municipal officers in fourteen states. In the others they may be elected or appointed. Most assessors serve for a definite term with four years being the most popular length of service. In most states the cost of assessing is borne by the responsible government, although a few states have some kind of cost sharing arrangement.

Twenty states have laws requiring the certification of assessors and fifteen require that staff appraisers be certified. Seventeen states have no specific educational requirement for staff appraisers, twenty require high school graduation, and thirteen require graduation from a two- or four-year college. Administration of the certification laws are usually the responsibility of a state agency, but there are a few instances of local or shared administration.

The state's responsibility for property taxation is assigned to the state revenue or taxation department in twenty-nine states and to the tax commission in eight states. There are independent boards of equalization in four states. The heads of the state agencies are usually appointed, but in a few states have civil service status. The resources available to the state agencies differ greatly. The median number of employees is forty-one. In New York an appropriation of almost $32 million supports 520 employees. In Maryland, where the state has complete responsibility for assessment, there are 731 employees.

It is not easy to describe the extent of state supervision of local assessment, but the International Association of Assessing Officers survey gives some clues. According to that survey a state agency in forty-one states is involved in supervising or training local assessors. In thirty-nine states the state agency publishes an assessment manual. In twenty-four states assessors are required to follow an assessment manual. In some states they may use the state-published manual or choose another manual. Fifteen states monitor the computer systems used by local assessors.

In thirty-six states there is state equalization of local assessment. In twenty-eight states the state is involved in intergovernmental appeals of assessment. In about half of the states a nonjudicial or quasi judicial state board hears appeals from individual assessments. In other states appeals from local assessment decisions go to the ordinary courts.

Unfortunately, the survey provides little help in judging the effectiveness of state assistance and supervision. It is not possible to tell what powers the state agencies have to enforce their orders and how often such powers are used. On paper it seems that many state government agencies have about the same powers and duties that the Kansas Tax Commission had in 1907. Perhaps the major difference is that the Kansas Tax Commission provided the local assessors with forms and manuals. Today state agencies in a number of states assist local officials in acquiring computer programs.

More important than the structure and form of assessment organization is the overall quality of the result. That is not easy to determine. For several years the U. S. Census Department conducted ratio studies in several states, but budget limitations have curtailed that activity. Computers and advances in statistical techniques make it possible for states to do detailed analyses of assessment quality, but financial and political obstacles often stand in the way. Because of varying quality and differences in methods, it is also difficult to cumulate or compare the results from state to state.

In the IAAO survey of assessment practices, only twenty states answered the question regarding statewide coefficients of dispersion. The median reported by the twenty states was 18.7 percent. The mean was 20.7 percent. The minimum reported was 6.5 percent by Massachusetts. Only one other state had a COD of less than ten. Because of the wide differences in the quality of the ratio studies, these numbers may have little meaning. Answers to questions about the technical aspects of ratio studies revealed that the respondents in eight states were not familiar with the IAAO standards for conducting such studies; only eleven states attempted to measure sample reliability. Only seventeen states required a minimum sample size of twenty or more. Thirteen states accepted a sample size of nine or less, and twelve states reported that the answer to the question was not available. Many states do not require that sales prices be recorded or reported. There is a great deal of variety in adjustments to sales price because of such factors as financing arrangements, inclusion of personal property, time since sale, closing costs, realtor fees, and similar items.

Even if the ratio studies were well conducted, it would be difficult to report the results in a consistent fashion. The quality of assessment within a state may vary greatly from region to region and from one property type to another. There is no standard method for combining the CODs of different local jurisdictions and of different classes into a statewide total.

It does seems safe to say that few states are close to achieving uniform assessment. The property tax survives not because it results in equal taxation of property, but because it remains the only tax capable of producing the revenue needed to provide revenue to the various semiautonomous local governments that play such a large role in providing services to American communities.

PROPERTY TAX REVENUES

The property tax may appear to have been designed by a mad architect, erected by an incompetent builder, and repaired by amateur tinkerers, but it is historically more accurate to say that it was formed by an evolutionary process occurring in the political and economic environment of the states and communities of America. From the American Revolution to sometime near the end of the nineteenth century, the environment favored evolution toward uniformity. Complete uniformity was never achieved, but the legally defined base was broad and major departures from uniformity were de facto rather than statutory or constitutional. Most resulted from lack of administrative capacity or local defiance of state policy.

As the uniform tax base was modified in response to political and economic forces, the revenue role of the property tax also changed. The balancing of the need for a stable constitutional order tax against the unpopularity of taxation has had different results in different places and, especially, at different levels of government. After one final effort to impose a property tax during the Civil War, the federal government temporarily turned to the income tax. After the ratification of the Sixteenth Amendment in 1913 the income tax became the major source of federal revenue and there was no further talk of a federal property tax.

By the beginning of the twentieth century, state governments had already diversified their tax systems away from dependence on the property tax. As shown in Figure 11.1, states received only 52 percent of their tax revenue and 45 percent of their general revenue from the property tax in 1902. Both percentages declined rapidly until 1942. In the post–World War II period the decline has continued, and today the property tax is an insignificant source of revenue for most states.

As shown in Figure 11.2, the local government situation is different. In the depression year of 1932 local governments received 97 percent of their tax revenue and 85 percent of their general revenue from property taxation. Since then, amid talk about tax revolts and the unpopularity of the property tax, the role of the property tax at the local level has declined. However, it still makes up more than three-fourths of the tax revenue of local governments. Because of the rise in fees, charges, and earnings from various sources, the property tax accounts for slightly less than half of local governments' "own source" revenue. These data do not include revenue from state and federal grants.

Combining data for all types of local governments hides many differences. Figure 11.3 shows the major tax revenues for the five types of local government in the United States. These reveal that cities have been most successful in developing

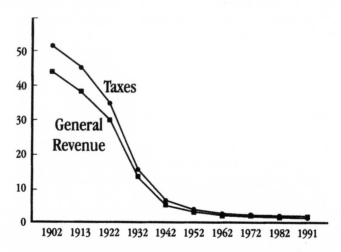

Figure 11.1. State property taxes as percent of state taxes and state revenue. *Source:* U.S. Bureau of the Census, *Historical Statistics of State and Local Finances, 1902–1953* (Washington, D.C.: U.S. Government Printing Office, 1955), and U.S. Bureau of the Census, *Government Finances* (Washington, D.C.: U.S. Government Printing Office, various years).

other forms of taxation. They receive more than 27 percent of their tax revenue from sales taxes and more than 13 percent from income taxes, but the property tax still provides over half of their tax revenue. The success of cities in diversifying revenue sources represents both economic and administrative considerations. Cities, especially larger ones, are apt to encompass a more diversified economy and are more apt to have the administrative capacity to administer nonproperty taxes.

Special districts raise about 27 percent of their tax revenue from sales taxation.[14] These districts are usually limited to providing single kinds of service, such as hospitals, fire protection, transportation, or drainage. Some receive a bulk of their revenue from fees and charges, but the high percentage received from sales taxes probably reflects taxes levied for special transportation, water, or sewerage districts that overlie metropolitan areas. Many of these are collected by the state government on behalf of the special districts. The property tax provides 69.5 percent of special district tax revenue.

Counties, like cities, are more apt to have a diversified economic base and to have substantial administrative capacity. There are many rural counties, however, that have a limited ability to collect taxes based on commercial activity. Counties are also less apt to have been granted home rule powers that permit revenue diversification. For these reasons, counties are still heavily dependent on property taxation. Almost three-fourths of their tax revenue comes from the property tax.

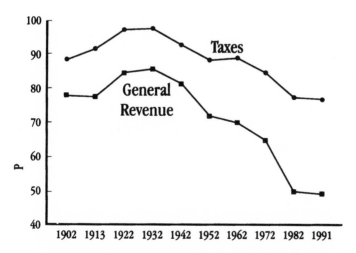

Figure 11.2. Local property taxes as percent of local taxes and local revenue. *Source:* U.S. Bureau of the Census, *Historical Statistics of State and Local Finances, 1902–1953* (Washington, D.C.: U.S. Government Printing Office, 1955), and U.S. Bureau of the Census, *Government Finances* (Washington, D.C.: U.S. Government Printing Office, various years).

COUNTY TAX REVENUE

CITY TAX REVENUE

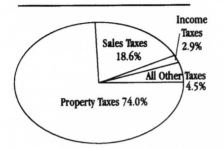

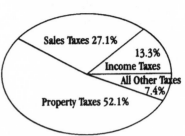

SCHOOL TAX REVENUE

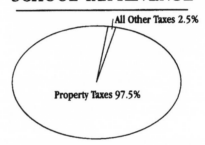

TOWNSHIP TAX REVENUE

SPECIAL DISTRICT REVENUE

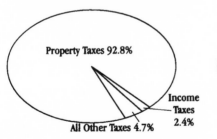

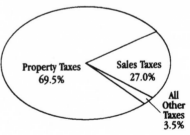

Figure 11.3. Local tax sources, by type of local government. *Source:* Advisory Commission on Intergovernmental Relations, *Significant Features of Fiscal Federalism, 1993,* Vol. 2 (Washington, D.C., 1993), 76–77.

School districts and townships are most heavily dependent on property taxes. Townships receive almost 93 percent of their tax revenue from the property tax. More than 97 percent of school district tax revenue comes from the property tax. For practical purposes, it is correct to say that school districts are financed entirely by property taxes and grants or other revenue received from state and federal government.

Much of the decline in the importance of the property tax as a source of local finance comes not from wide use of nonproperty taxes, but from the increased importance of federal and state grants. Table 11.1 is a comparison of the growth in local government own-source revenue with the growth in state payments to local governments since 1965. Between 1965 and 1991, total state payments to local governments rose by 1,216 percent. Payments for educational purposes rose by a slightly higher 1,290 percent. In comparison, local government own-source revenue rose by 950 percent and property tax revenue by 641 percent. Clearly, property tax revenue is growing less rapidly than the total own-source revenues of local government, but state payments to local governments are growing much faster than local government own-source revenue.

There is substantial regional variation in the use of the property tax by local governments. Table 11.2 shows the property tax as a percentage of local tax revenue by region for selected years since 1965. In 1965, 98.9 percent of local tax revenue in the New England states came from the property tax. There was virtually no change during the next twenty-five years. The 1991 percentage was 98.2. The mideastern states received the smallest percentage of tax revenue from the property tax in 1965, and they still held that position in 1991. Even so, local governments in those states received more than two-thirds of their tax revenue from the property tax. The largest decline in the relative importance of the property tax occurred in the Rocky Mountain and Far West states. Alaska is excluded from these calculations because of its unusual economic and tax base.

Table 11.1. Local Government Own Source Revenue and State Payments (in millions)

	State Payments		Own Source Revenue	
Year	Total	School	Total	Property Tax
1965	$14,174	$8,351	$32,326	$21,817
1970	28,893	17,085	51,392	32,963
1975	51,004	31,110	84,353	50,040
1980	82,758	52,688	130,027	65,607
1985	119,608	74,937	216,063	99,772
1990	175,028	109,438	321,599	149,765
1991	186,469	116,109	339,890	161,706
Increase	1,216%	1,290%	950%	641%

Source: Advisory Commission on Intergovernmental Relations, *Significant Features of Fiscal Federalism, 1993,* Vol. 2 (Washington, D.C., 1993).

Table 11.2. Local Property Taxes as Percent of Local Tax Revenue

	1965	1970	1975	1980	1985	1990	1991
United States	86.9	84.9	81.6	75.9	74.2	74.5	75.3
New England	98.9	99.2	99.2	99.1	98.4	98.0	98.2
Mideast	77.2	74.7	71.4	66.6	64.6	66.7	68.2
Great Lakes	92.4	90.4	87.3	83.4	82.6	81.1	82.5
Plains	93.6	93.3	89.6	86.1	83.6	82.9	82.9
Southeast	83.0	78.5	74.6	70.5	68.8	70.2	71.1
Southwest	92.2	85.8	84.1	80.3	78.5	78.7	78.3
Rocky Mountains	92.3	90.4	83.1	78.4	76.2	76.4	74.7
Far West[1]	87.9	88.5	85.6	70.4	69.4	70.0	70.8

[1]Alaska excluded from Far West totals.
Source: Advisory Commission on Intergovernmental Relations, *Significant Features of Fiscal Federalism, 1993,* Vol. 2 (Washington, D.C., 1993), 130.

Another indication of the variation in the importance of the property tax is provided by Table 11.3, which shows the property tax on a per capita basis and as a percentage of personal income in every state. In New Hampshire, which does not have a sales or a broad-based income tax, 1991 property tax collections averaged $1,342 per person and were equal to 6.3 percent of personal income of state residents. Not surprisingly, the New Hampshire state government collects only 29.5

Table 11.3. Property Taxes, by State, 1991

	Per Capita	% of Income		Per Capita	% of Income
New Hampshire	$1,342	6.3	South Dakota	$ 579	3.8
New Jersey	1,258	5.0	Indiana	571	3.4
Alaska	1,213	6.0	Pennsylvania	562	3.0
Connecticut	1,138	4.5	Ohio	541	3.1
New York	1,101	5.0	Montana	524	3.6
Vermont	925	5.3	Georgia	506	3.0
Wyoming	912	5.6	North Dakota	505	3.3
Michigan	898	4.9	Nevada	456	2.4
Rhode Island	879	4.7	Hawaii	430	2.1
Oregon	877	5.3	Idaho	426	2.9
Massachusetts	830	3.7	South Carolina	423	2.9
Maine	797	4.7	Utah	416	3.0
Wisconsin	797	4.6	North Carolina	382	2.4
Illinois	786	3.9	Missouri	377	2.2
Nebraska	744	4.3	Mississippi	344	2.7
Minnesota	718	3.9	Tennessee	329	2.1
Kansas	691	3.9	Delaware	311	1.5
Colorado	690	3.8	Kentucky	277	1.9
Florida	688	3.8	Louisiana	275	1.9
Iowa	686	4.1	West Virginia	272	2.0
Texas	679	4.2	Oklahoma	250	1.7
Arizona	662	4.2	Arkansas	244	1.8
California	639	3.2	New Mexico	222	1.6
Virginia	639	3.3	Alabama	171	1.2
Washington	626	3.4	United States	666	3.6
Maryland	617	2.8			

Source: Advisory Comission on Intergovernmental Relations, *Significant Features of Fiscal Federalism, 1993,* Vol. 2 (Washington, D.C., 1993), 196.

percent of state and local tax revenue. By contrast, in Alabama property tax collections were $171 per capita, and the state government collected 70.7 percent of state and local tax revenue. Other states with a high degree of revenue centralization included Maryland, where the state government's share is 82.4 percent, Hawaii with 81.1 percent, and West Virginia, where the state's share is 79.1 percent. There is an indisputable, but not perfect, correlation between the level of property taxation and the degree of fiscal decentralization.

SUMMARY AND CONCLUSIONS

The property tax today is far from the uniform tax that was envisioned by those who wrote the constitutional uniformity provisions and statutes in the nineteenth century. The property tax base varies greatly from state to state because of a variety of departures from uniformity that have been justified on the grounds that they make the tax easier to administer, less burdensome to low income or elderly people, or that they promote environmental policy, urban redevelopment, economic growth, or historic preservation.

Undoubtedly, many of the claims are true, but the particular form that these provisions take has been shaped by the political forces in the state or community. These forces resulted in a tax that is not necessarily uniform, but which is politically tolerable and produces enough revenue to be the major own-source revenue of thousands of local governments in the United States.

In spite of the differences in the property tax base from state to state, there are many similarities. Real estate now makes up the bulk of the tax base in most states. It is largely a local tax, although Kansas has recently returned to a state property tax as a major source of school finance.

The results of the political evolution of the property tax are indicated by the way business property is treated. In those states with a legal classification system, business property is assessed or taxed higher in relation to value than residential or farm property. Within the business class, utility property is usually assessed or taxed higher than other business property.[15] Clearly this reflects the reality of electoral and legislative politics. Every home and every farm is represented by one or more voters. Utility companies are far less represented in the electorate and voters are little impressed by the argument that utility taxes are passed on in a regressive fashion. Offsetting the higher taxes on business property, for some firms, are a variety of special exemptions granted in the name of economic development. Mobile business firms that create high-paying jobs have a powerful political weapon that has enabled them to obtain tax relief in the form of development or job creation concessions. This weapon has been used aggressively and many firms have been able to secure low property taxes and other concessions.

12
Past As Prologue

Federalism and the general property tax are, arguably, American innovations, but often the connection between the two is overlooked. This was not always so. The founders of the United States were well aware of the relationship between taxes and government structure. Alexander Hamilton and his federalist followers hoped to use tax and debt policy to strengthen the federal government at the expense of the states. They also believed in a professional administrative corps that would provide impartial, quality administration. The Jeffersonians, the Jacksonians, and their populist heirs fought to ensure that the powers of taxing and spending would be retained at the local level. Many of them were willing to sacrifice administrative quality in order to keep the government responsive to public demand and to maximize participation in the governmental process.

During much of the nineteenth century it seemed that the advocates of local responsibility had the best of the argument. Most of the nonmilitary responsibilities of government were assigned to local governments. Statutes were written at the state level, but much of the responsibility for financing and administering them fell upon counties and their subdivisions. In more densely populated areas, citizens could incorporate municipalities to provide additional services to its citizens. During this period, most of the tax revenue of state and local governments came from property taxes. Uniformity clauses were written into many state constitutions and were included in the statutes of others. The property tax became a widely accepted symbol of uniformity that muted arguments over tax structure.

As the level of taxation and the complexity of the economic system increased, the utility of uniformity as a symbol decreased. Complaints about tax administration rose, and there was concern about the forms of property that were escaping taxation. Reformers weighed in on the side of centralization and professionalization, but local resistance was strong. Ironically, extra-legal local adaptations to the tax may have contributed to its survival by making it more acceptable politically.

In the twentieth century, states turned away from property taxation as a means of financing state functions. Income and sales taxation proved to be practical sources of revenue when administered at the state level. This enabled states to take over many of the functions formerly carried on by local governments and reduced the states' concern with the administration of the property tax. Many local governments followed the path of least resistance. Assessors copied the previous assessment rolls, with occasional adjustments to reflect changes in the property or complaints of particular property owners. In the long run, the levels of assessment strongly reflected the political power of particular groups. Individual assessments often betrayed the owner's political savvy and aggressiveness in appealing assessments on his or her property. Quiet periods were interrupted by taxpayer revolts of one kind or another. Sometimes taxpayer suits resulted in court-ordered reappraisal, but more commonly, legislative bodies reacted by enacting some kind of reform measure. Some were aimed at improving administration and some resulted in changes in the tax base. In many states classified tax systems were established and certain kinds of property were exempted. Relief provisions to alleviate the burden on low-income or elderly taxpayers and a great variety of changes intended to promote economic growth and development were enacted.

During these years, a wide variety of property tax limitations were passed. Some of the earlier ones were limits on the mill or percentage rates that could be levied for a particular fund. These limits were often bypassed by the creation of new funds or the establishment of special districts that could tax the same property. Sometimes tax freezes limited the amount that could be levied by a unit of government to a percentage of the amount levied in a base year. Such freezes usually allowed increases based on values from new construction or other additions to the tax base. There were often exemptions for debt service costs and mandatory payments, such as pension fund or Social Security taxes. Other exemptions were added as unusual situations came to light. Often the result was a complex statute that greatly complicated administration and was of limited effectiveness. At times, the purported ceiling became a floor as local governments found it advisable to levy the maximum tax to prevent a possible reduction in their future levy authority.

In a number of instances, most notably in California's Proposition 13 and Massachusetts' Proposition 2½, overall limits were imposed. This requires that the state "ration" the total tax authority among the various local governments that have jurisdiction to tax a given parcel of property. The state legislature, or some body established by them, determines the tax authority, and therefore the size and scope of services that can be provided by the various levels of local government. Since the passage of Proposition 13 in California, the press has given a great deal of attention to the various tax referenda and tax limitation measures that have been considered or passed in other states. The entire movement has been labeled as a tax revolt and some are predicting the end of the property tax. Certainly a great deal of attention has been focused on the matter and politicians at every level have used the tax issue as a major element in their campaigns. On the other hand, it is

easy to lose perspective. In the first place, property tax revolts or reform movements are not new. The periodic attempts at reform of the Kansas property tax
were paralleled by events in many other states. One big difference today is that
news of developments in one state reaches the general public through the mass
media and ideas may spread more rapidly. Earlier in the century, information about
developments in other states spread among the political and academic elite
through scholarly publications and meetings of organizations such as the National
Tax Association. It is also true that in the period since 1978 a number of tax limitation measures have been voted down and most of those that have passed are far
less restrictive than the well-publicized ones in California and Massachusetts.

The modifications in the tax base and the various limits imposed on property
tax levies permitted a much-modified property tax to survive and to remain the
major revenue source for local government, but the general property tax is no
longer part of anyone's dream of equality. Today the tax is not an equal tax upon
all wealth, but a tax whose burden depends upon a variety of fortuitous circumstances, the taxpayer's personal financial condition, and skill in negotiating with
the assessor or the economic development authorities.

The history of the property tax teaches us that public policy-making is a complex process. Constitutional and statutory provisions are only a part of it. If provisions cannot be administered by means that are considered acceptable to most of
those who make up the body politic the policy will fail. The entire process may
bring about unintended consequences, such as a change in relationships between
the levels of government or other changes in the constitutional order. Unfortunately, some of these consequences may be irreversible.

ISSUES FOR THE FUTURE

It is not possible to predict the future of the property tax, but the historic record
gives some clues to the direction of its evolution and, combined with rational
analysis, can tell us something about the consequences of possible future developments. It is, therefore, appropriate to describe some possible developments and
suggest some of the consequences of each.

Improved Administration

The Hamiltonians of the day can still make a strong case for their position in favor
of expert, centralized administration of the property tax. The arguments are much
the same as those that have been advanced by administrative reforms throughout
the history of this country. Advances in our understanding of how markets work
and the availability of computer-assisted assessment methodology have altered the
situation. We now have a greater than ever capacity to appraise property and to
evaluate the quality of the result, but doing so still requires professionalization and

centralization of administration. CAMA demands a well-organized team, composed of statisticians, computer experts, and real estate market experts. They need access to unbiased market data—not only sales prices but also information about construction costs, building operating expenses, and financial data. To make such an operation feasible, the assessment area must be large enough for the management team to direct the work of less specialized personnel. All personnel must be insulated from political pressures that would cause them to depart from their assigned task of arriving at market value. The appeal process must be carefully designed to ensure that all property owners have opportunities to present their cases before trained, nonpolitical, appeal boards. Such a system could provide reasonably good, up-to-date assessment of most parcels of property. It should be possible, for example, to achieve a coefficient of dispersion of less than 10 percent in most urban residential areas. A somewhat higher COD might be expected in mixed or changing neighborhoods, for older commercial property, and in other more heterogenous properties.

Even with the ideal administrative machinery in place, there would still be problems with assessment. There are unusual types of property, or properties that are unique within the market area, to which the concept of market value has little meaning. Disputes over values of such property would be difficult to resolve.

Charges that such a centralized, professionalized system of property tax assessment violates the cherished principles of local autonomy might be answered by pointing out that centralizing the purely administrative act of assessment of property removes the grounds for one of the frequent criticisms of the property tax. If true, this would help preserve local governments' more important power to determine local government policy by controlling local budgets and the revenue raised to fund them.

Improved administration of the property tax will not stop criticism. It is a "lump sum" tax that is highly visible and often inconvenient to pay. It falls heavily on unrealized capital values, burdens shelter, and may be unrelated to the ability of the owner's current income. A number of measures to deal with these criticisms have been taken and others are possible. Circuit breakers, homestead exemptions, preferential treatment of farm land, and tax deferral for elderly homeowners are some examples. Unfortunately, every such provision creates administrative complexity and fuels demands for additional relief for those near the cutoff point.

Politically and legally, the policy of improved assessment has its weaknesses. The highly technical procedures involved in CAMA are not easy to explain, and local officials will continue to resist ceding of their authority to state-level technicians. Taxpayers, real estate interests, and trade groups oppose measures needed to provide the assessment officials with necessary market information and there are strong pressures to maintain a politically responsive appeals process. State legislators and executives find it difficult to resist these pressures.

Court-ordered and monitored assessment improvements, as exemplified by the recent decision in Kansas, are possibilities, but the success of such efforts is not yet certain. Courts are blunt instruments for monitoring a complex administrative process. The technical and statistical questions involved are complex, and expert witnesses will always be able to cast doubt upon the procedures used. Court cases do not deal with statistical averages but with real taxpayers. Judges may find it difficult to uphold procedures that produce satisfactory coefficients of dispersion but treat the taxpayer at the bar unfairly.

Administration has been made more complex by the proliferation of relief provisions and economic incentives. The tax is no longer an impersonal, in rem tax, but is a tax that depends upon the age or financial condition of the taxpayers eligible for one of the relief provisions and upon the business practices of corporations that have been granted economic development exemptions. In the future, those who want to improve the administration of the property tax will need to give more attention to the problems of tax evasion and avoidance made possible by these provisions. Undoubtedly, this will lead to further centralization of administration.

Abandon the Property Tax

There are those who advocate abandoning the property tax. The income tax is a better measure of ability to pay. The sales tax is convenient to pay and administrative costs are low. Unfortunately, those arguments ignore the intergovernmental aspects of government finance. There are no taxes capable of financing our current system of local governments that can be locally levied and administered, except the property tax. The Kansas State University studies, cited earlier in this book, found that sales or income rates of over 50 percent would be required in some Kansas county areas to replace the property tax. Among the 84,855 governments in the United States, there are many that have little or no sales tax base and some that have little income tax base. Many do not have the administrative capacity to collect nonproperty taxes.

If the property tax was eliminated and the current governmental structure maintained, it might be possible to expand the "piggy back" or tax supplement arrangement whereby local governments levy taxes and the state collects and returns the tax to the levying government. These arrangements solve the problem of lack of local administrative capacity at the cost of some loss of local autonomy. They do nothing to solve the problem of variations in tax base.

One solution would be to radically restructure local governments into regional governments encompassing a diversified economic base. In most states it would be possible to identify regions that have per capita income, sales, and property tax bases adequate to support local government. Often these are centered around a sizable urban area, or in some cases, contain several such areas. Such regions are large enough to support an administrative structure capable of administering sales taxes, income taxes, and a variety of fees and charges that could be used to support the regional government.

Although one could make a case for such a restructuring, the probability of it occurring is close to zero. Except for school district consolidation, very few governmental consolidations have occurred in the entire history of the United States. There have been attempts to consolidate counties, townships, and especially municipalities in metropolitan areas, but only a few have succeeded.[1] Those few metropolitan consolidations that have occurred have usually involved unusual circumstances, and some are more accurately described as local federations than as consolidations.

Given these circumstances, it appears that elimination of the property tax would require that the state assume responsibility for many of the functions and services now provided by local governments or that a massive system of grants-in-aid be developed to return state-collected revenue to local governments. Developing a grant system for the total support of multipurpose local governments presents substantial difficulties. Local governments carry out a wide variety of functions under widely varying conditions. In some localities special districts carry out functions, such as parks, sewerage, or transportation, that are the responsibility of multipurpose governments, such as cities and counties, in other locations. It would be difficult to develop measures of need or the cost of providing the wide variety of services provided by multipurpose governments. Many existing formulas are related to property tax levies or the property tax base (assessments). Present tax levies can serve as an indication of local demand for governmental services, and the tax base is a measure of local tax capacity. If the property tax was abandoned, both of these measures would be lost. Initially, the distribution of state funds could be based on past spending, but this would soon be out of date.

Local governments financed from state funds would have little incentive to operate economically and would lobby hard to maintain or increase their share of revenue. Legislators would be judged on their success in obtaining favorable treatment for local governments in their districts. Inevitably, the state would be forced to increase its control over local government spending. Local governments entirely dependent upon state grants will, in the long run, have little autonomy.[2]

Abandon School Property Taxes

Far more likely than the abandonment of all property taxes is the abandonment of the property tax for the support of schools. There are several reasons why this course is more feasible than is abandoning the property tax for the support of general local governments.

One is that school districts are single-function governments. They are organized for the purpose of providing a single service to a defined population—schooling for children in a defined age group. Although the formulas for granting state aid to school districts have been the subject of bitter political conflict in some states, the task is far easier than determining appropriate formulas for general purpose governments. Need is reasonably well represented by the number of children to be educated, and the cost of providing this education can be calculated with some degree of accuracy.

Another thing that may make this course of action appropriate is that the constitutions of many states direct the state to provide equal education for all children. There is much case law regarding the meaning of these provisions, and the courts of many states have directed that the state provide equalization aid to poorer school districts. Many states already have extensive systems of grants in place, and some already provide a considerable portion of the cost of education.

There is a long history of school consolidation in this country. Although there have been many hard-fought political battles over the issue, it is clear that many Americans will accept consolidation of school districts if they believe that a better quality of education will result. There is already a great deal of state control of local education. Curriculum, textbook selection, teacher qualifications, length of school year, and many other such matters are already decided at the state level in many states. Assumption of state responsibility for financing public school would be far less traumatic than would state assumption of responsibility for functions now performed by city or county governments.

Abandoning the property tax for school purposes would provide major property tax relief. In the fiscal year 1991 over 41 percent of the property taxes collected in the United States were collected by school districts.[3] Additional sums were collected for educational purposes by cities and counties that are responsible for elementary and secondary education.

State assumption of responsibility for financing elementary and secondary education would continue trends already in progress. State and federal grants make up an increasing share of revenues for educational purposes. State assumption of education finance in Kansas, described in Chapter 10, was accompanied by a statewide property tax levy for education, but resulted in an overall decrease in school property taxes. Sales and income tax rates were increased. Even more recently, Michigan imposed a statewide educational property tax that varies by type of property. The net result was a significant reduction in the property tax for homeowners and a slight reduction in the average tax paid on business property.[4]

Muddle Through

The rational model of decision-making assumes that the decision-makers agree on an objective, analyze the various ways of achieving that objective, and make a decision based on the analysis. Important and complicated political decisions are not made that way, and the future of the property tax is such a decision. The property tax will continue to evolve in response to conditions and political interests in a particular place. The legislature, the courts, and local authorities will continue to make decisions on matters brought before them. Some will have limited, local impact. Others will be major decisions, such as the adoption of constitutional classification in Kansas, Proposition 13 in California, or adoption of a classified, statewide educational tax in Michigan.

In all probability the cumulative effects of these decisions will be to continue the long-term trend toward less uniformity and less dependence on the property tax. One can hope that improved statistical procedures and the storage and computing power of computers will result in improved assessment, and thus in greater uniformity, within whatever classes the legislature or the constitution require.

Because of the tendency of a political system to transform itself in response to high levels of system stress, it is reasonable to believe that the changes that occur will contribute to the short-term stability of the political system. Unfortunately, changes often bring with them unintended consequences that may produce system stress at some time in the future. For example, the adoption of a classification system, especially if it is statutory rather than constitutional, is apt to lead to continuing debate as interest groups endeavor to secure more favorable classification. It is unlikely that these debates will lead to abandoning classification. More likely, they will result in additional property classes and additional preferences that may, in the long run, increase complexity and foster more dissatisfaction with the system.

Perhaps even more important than the details of the revenue system is the impact that revenue decisions have on the structure of government. One of the major political issues of the day has to do with the scope and scale of governmental organizations. Federalism was invented as a way of allowing state governments to retain elements of sovereignty while delegating certain functions, such as foreign affairs and the regulation of commerce among the states, to a central or federal government. States, in turn, delegated much of the day-to-day operation of government to counties or towns. The logic of the arrangement was clear. Some governmental tasks can appropriately be carried on at the local or state level. Others require a government with authority over a wider geographic area. Just how to define these tasks and to avoid conflict between the levels of government was not always so clear. These issues have been the subject of controversy in America ever since the Constitution was adopted.

In a sense, the American experience was a rehearsal for a world-wide struggle. At a time when cheap, rapid transportation has made the world more interdependent and impersonal, even national governments find their jurisdiction too small to deal with problems such as maintaining national security, promoting fair trade, or protecting the environment. At the same time, rapid change and the impersonality of the modern world have led to a renewed emphasis on tribal, ethnic, linguistic, and local identity. In Eastern Europe, in the Balkans, in Africa, and elsewhere, people struggle to establish nations strong enough to deal with modern problems while still protecting diversity and local self-government. In the United Nations, world and regional trade organizations, the European Union, Canada, and Kansas, the issues are similar. How can the responsibility for governing be divided so as to promote common objectives without creating an over-centralized, repressive governing structure?

A FINAL WORD

It may seem strange to conclude an account of the property tax, which began in the American colonies and included detailed accounts of administering the property tax in nineteenth-century Kansas with a discussion of international problems of the late twentieth century. However, if there is one lesson that seems clear from the material presented, it is that government finance has many ramifications. Among the most important is the relationship between finance and the structure and functioning of government. The writers of the U.S. Constitution recognized it, the federalists and the anti-federalists recognized it, and those in charge of the finances of the United Nations recognize it.

American taxpayers may not know or may have forgotten the importance of these relationships. Attacking the property tax may seem to be an easy way to vent frustrations about problems that seem beyond individual control. Unfortunately, such attacks may have long-term consequences that will make government more remote and even less responsive. One must hope that in the political battles for short-term advantages, the protagonists will not forget that acts that change the tax system may change the structure of government in ways that could be detrimental to both uniformity and equality.

NOTES

INTRODUCTION

1. Howard Jarvis and Robert Pack, *I'm Mad as Hell: The Exclusive Story of the Tax Revolt and Its Leader* (New York: Times Books, 1979).

2. Clarence Y. H. Lo, *Small Property versus Big Government: Social Origins of the Property Tax Revolt* (Berkeley: University of California Press, 1990), 144.

3. Ibid., 171.

1. GENERAL PROPERTY TAX

1. E. R. A. Seligman, *Essays in Taxation,* 5th ed. (New York: Macmillan Company, 1905), 61.

2. "Regime or constitutional order" refers to the broad set of rules for political conduct that serve as practical guides to acceptable political behavior. This may include written constitutions, such as those of American national or state governments, and informal specification of the rules of political behavior. It is similar to the concept of "political system" as the term is used by David Easton. Dall W. Forsythe, *Taxation and Political Change in the Young Nation, 1781–1833* (New York: Columbia University Press, 1977), 2–5; David Easton, *A Systems Analysis of Political Life* (New York: John Wiley & Sons, 1965), 190–93.

3. J. David Greenstone and Paul Peterson, *Race and Authority in Urban Politics* (New York: Russell Sage Foundation, 1973), esp. Ch 4.

4. Easton, *Systems Analysis,* 190.

5. Adam Smith, *An Inquiry into the Nature and Causes of the Wealth of Nations,* ed. E. Cannan (New York: Modern Library edition, Random House, 1937), 777–79.

6. Leonard D. White, *Trends in Public Administration* (New York: McGraw-Hill Book Company, 1933), 143.

2. REVOLUTION AND REFORM

1. Major studies of British taxation include: Edwin Cannan, *History of Local Rates in England,* 2d ed. (London: P. S. King and Son, 1912); and Stephen Dowell, *A History of Taxation and Taxes in England: From the Earliest Times to the Present Day,* 3d ed., 4 vols., Reprints of Economic Classics (New York: Augustus M. Kelley Bookseller, 1965, originally published by Longman Green, 1884).

2. Cannan, *Local Rates in England,* 22.

3. Ibid.

4. Robert A. Becker, *Revolution, Reform, and the Politics of American Taxation, 1763–1783* (Baton Rouge: Louisiana State University Press, 1980), 8.

5. Unless another source is cited, the descriptions of Colonial and Revolutionary War taxes in this chapter are drawn from ibid.

6. George S. Howard, *An Introduction to the Local Constitutional History of the United States* (Baltimore: Johns Hopkins University, 1889), 343.

7. Ibid.

8. Becker, *Revolution, Reform, and the Politics,* 11.

9. Ibid., 42.

10. Wayne Andrews, ed., *Concise Dictionary of American History* (New York: Charles Scribner's Sons, 1962), 809–10.

11. Quoted in Becker, *Revolution, Reform, and the Politics,* 97–98.

12. Ibid., 6.

13. Andrews, ed., *Concise Dictionary,* 893, 906–7.

14. Thomas P. Slaughter, "The Tax Man Cometh: Ideological Opposition to Internal Taxes, 1760–1790," *William and Mary Quarterly* 41:4, Third Series, (October 1984), 575.

15. Slaughter, "The Tax Man Cometh," 572.

16. Andrews, ed., *Concise Dictionary,* 820–25.

17. H. James Henderson, "Taxation and Political Culture," *William and Mary Quarterly* 47:1, Third Series, (January 1990), 92, 105.

18. Becker, *Revolution, Reform, and the Politics,* 169–170.

19. Joseph Dorfman, *The Economic Mind in American Civilization, 1606–1865,* vol. 1 (New York: Viking Press, 1946).

3. FEDERAL FINANCE, 1775–1836

1. Wayne Andrews, ed., *Concise Dictionary of American History* (New York: Charles Scribner's Sons, 1962), 823.

2. Dall W. Forsythe, *Taxation and Political Change in the Young Nation, 1781–1833* (New York: Columbia University Press, 1977), 14–15.

3. Joseph Dorfman, *The Economic Mind in American Civilization, 1606-1865,* vol. 1 (New York: Viking Press, 1946), 219.

4. E. James Ferguson, *The Power of the Purse: A History of American Public Finance, 1776–1790* (Chapel Hill: published for the Institute of Early American History and Culture at Williamsburg, Va., by the University of North Carolina Press, 1961), 125–45.

5. The rest of this section is drawn from Forsythe, *Taxation and Political Change,* 17–23.

6. Andrews, ed., *Concise Dictionary,* 865–66.

7. Gordon S. Wood, *The Creation of the American Republic, 1776–1787* (Chapel Hill: published for the Institute of Early American History and Culture at Williamsburg, Va., by the University of North Carolina Press, 1969), 471–75.

8. *The Federalist Papers,* No. 32.

9. James MacGregor Burns, *The Vineyard of Liberty* (New York: Alfred A. Knopf, Inc., 1981), 63.

10. Thomas P. Slaughter, "The Tax Man Cometh: Ideological Opposition to Internal Taxes, 1760–1790," *William and Mary Quarterly* 41:4, Third Series, (October 1984), 566-67.

11. Forsythe, *Taxation and Political Change,* 25–26.

12. For a more complete development of this thesis see Wood, *Creation of the American Republic,* 471–518.

13. Burns, *Vineyard of Liberty,* 84.

14. Henry Carter Adams, *Taxation in the United States, 1789–1816* (New York: Burt Franklin, 1970, originally published 1884), 6–7.

15. Leonard D. White, *The Federalists: A Study in Administrative History* (New York: Macmillan Company, 1948), 515.

16. White, *The Federalists,* 464.

17. Davis Rich Dewey, *Financial History of the United States,* 12th ed. (New York: Longmans, Green and Co., 1939), 35.

18. B. U. Ratchford, *American State Debts* (Durham, North Carolina: Duke University Press, 1941), 31.

19. Burns, *Vineyard of Liberty,* 84–85.

20. Forsythe, *Taxation and Political Change,* 27.

21. Burns, *Vineyard of Liberty,* 86.

22. Unless another source is cited, the description of the Whiskey Rebellion is drawn from: Leland D. Baldwin, *Whiskey Rebels: The Story of Frontier Uprising* (Pittsburgh: University of Pittsburgh Press, 1939).

23. Forsythe, *Taxation and Political Change,* 43–46.

24. Ibid., 47–51.

25. Unless otherwise noted, the description of the first federal property tax is based on Adams, *Taxation in the United States,* 52–68.

26. Gallatin was a native of Geneva. He was educated as an aristocrat, but was influenced by followers of Rousseau and the Physiocrats. He came to America as a young man and served for a while in the American army. He opposed the Constitution because of its leaning toward monarchy and he played a role in the Whiskey Rebellion.

27. Oklahoma imposed a progressive land tax in 1913, but because of a legal technicality, no attempt was made to enforce it. Simeon Elbridge Leland, *The Classified Property Tax in the United States* (Boston and New York: Houghton Mifflin Company, 1928), 362–63.

28. Forsythe, *Taxation and Political Change,* 54.

29. Ibid.

30. In fact, that turned out to be true until the adoption of the Sixteenth (Income Tax) Amendment in 1913.

4. CONSTITUTIONALIZING UNIFORMITY: THE NINETEENTH CENTURY

1. Charles Sellers, *The Market Revolution: Jacksonian America, 1815-1846* (New York: Oxford University Press, 1991), 31–33. According to Sellers, the word "democrat" did not appear in the English or French languages until 1789.

2. Ibid., 31–32.

3. B. U. Ratchford, *American State Debts* (Durham, North Carolina: Duke University Press, 1941), 68–75.

4. Ibid., 77–79.

5. Ibid., 82–83.

6. Ibid., 92–93.

7. Ibid., 96.

8. H. S. Hanna, *A Financial History of Maryland, 1789–1849* (Baltimore: Johns Hopkins University Press, 1907), 104.

9. Thomas K. Worthington, *Historical Sketch of the Finances of Pennsylvania* (Baltimore: Publications of the American Economic Association II, 1888), 38.

10. Ratchford, *American State Debts,* 99.

11. U.S. Congress. House. *Report No. 296,* 27th Cong., 3d sess., 1843.

12. Ratchford, *American State Debts,* 114–15.

13. Ibid., 105–21.

14. Peter Wallenstein, "More Unequally Taxed than any People in the Civilized World': The Origins of Georgia's Ad Valorem Tax System," *Georgia Historical Quarterly* 49:4, (Winter 1985), 461.

15. Ibid., 460.

16. Don C. Sowers, *The Financial History of New York State: From 1789 to 1912* (New York: AMS Press, 1969), 114–16. First edition published in 1914.

17. Ibid., 116–20.

18. James Ring Adams, *Secrets of the Tax Revolt* (New York: Harcourt Brace Jovanovich, 1984), 402.

19. Ernest Ludlow Bogart, *Financial History of Ohio,* vol. 1, nos. 1 and 2 (Urbana: University of Illinois Studies in Social Science, 1912), 10.

20. Robert Murray Haig, *A History of the General Property Tax in Illinois,* vol. 3 (Urbana: University of Illinois Studies in the Social Sciences, 1914), 16–17.

21. Ibid., 18–19.

22. The description of Ohio taxation is based on: Bogart, *Financial History.*

23. Ibid., 198.

24. Haig, *Property Tax in Illinois,* 37–38.

25. *Illinois Constitution,* 1818, Art. 8, Sec. 20.

26. B. P. Poore, *Federal and State Constitutions* (Washington: Government Printing Office, 1877), cited in Haig, *Property Tax in Illinois,* 39.

27. Haig, *Property Tax in Illinois,* 39, 42.

28. Ibid., 79.

29. *Missouri Constitution, 1820,* Art. 13, Sec. 19.

30. *Constitution of Ohio,* 1851, Art. 12.

31. Wade J. Newhouse, *Constitutional Uniformity and Equality in State Taxation,* 2d ed., 2 vols. (Buffalo: William S. Hein & Company, 1984), reprints many of the important constitutional provisions and was a prime source of information for Table 4.3. This was supplemented by consulting annotated constitutions and court reports when necessary.

32. William L. Matthews, "The Function of Constitutional Provisions Requiring Uniformity in Taxation," *Kentucky Law Journal* 38:1 (November 1949), 35–37.

33. Sumner Benson, "A History of the General Property Tax," George C. S. Benson, et al., *The American Property Tax: Its History, Administration and Economic Impact* (California: Claremont College Printing Service, 1965), 31.

34. Leonard D. White, *The Jacksonians: A Study in Administrative History: 1829–1861* (New York: Macmillan Company, 1954), 551.

35. Arthur W. Schlesinger, Jr., *The Age of Jackson* (Boston: Little, Brown and Company, 1945), 134.

36. Robert J. Walker, *Report from the Secretary of the Treasury on the State of Finances, etc., 1845.* Reprinted in F. W. Taussig, *State Papers and Speeches on the Tariff* (Clifton, N.J.: Augustus M. Kelley, 1972), 231–32.

37. Lawrence Frederick Kohl, *The Politics of Individualism: Parties and the American Character in the Jacksonian Era* (New York: Oxford University Press, 1989), 51–52.

38. Ibid., 25–26.

39. Benson, "A History," 35.

40. Ibid., 33–35.

41. Ibid., 32.

42. Ibid., 33.

43. Ibid., 33.

44. Ibid., 34.

5. WRITING A UNIFORMITY CLAUSE: THE CASE OF KANSAS

1. The Kansas territorial laws are described more fully in Glenn W. Fisher, "Property Taxation in the Kansas Territory," *Kansas History; A Journal of the Western Plains* 11:3, (Autumn 1988), 185–200.

2. This period of Kansas history has been described many times. Accounts of the territorial and early statehood years in general histories of the state include: Robert W. Richmond, *Kansas: A Land of Contrasts,* 2d ed. (St. Louis: Forum Press, 1980), 61–96; and William Frank Zornow, Kansas: *A History of the Jayhawk State* (Norman: University of Oklahoma Press, 1957), 43–117.

3. U.S. Congress, *An Act to Organize the Territories of Nebraska and Kansas,* 33d Cong., 1st sess., Sec. 32, 1854.

4. Zornow, *Kansas: A History,* 31–54.

5. U.S. Congress, *An Act to Organize the Territories of Nebraska and Kansas,* 33d Cong., 1st sess., Secs. 30, 33, 1854.

6. Ibid., Sec. 24.

7. Richmond, *Kansas: A Land of Contrasts,* 66.

8. "Message of A. H. Reeder, Governor, to the Honorable Council and House of Representatives of the Territory of Kansas," Territory of Kansas, *Journal of the Council,* (3 July, 1855), 18.

9. Territory of Kansas, Laws of the First Session (1855), Ch. 151.

10. Richmond, *Kansas: A Land of Contrasts,* 66–68.

11. The comparison is with the *Revised Statutes of Missouri* (1845). This was the latest compilation of Missouri laws at the time.

12. One of the meanings of the word poll is "a listing of individuals for voting or tax purposes." Poll taxes may or may not be related to qualifications for voting.

13. Territory of Kansas, *Laws of the First Session* (1855), Art. 4, Sec. 2.

14. Ibid., Ch. 138.

15. Ibid., Ch. 66, Sec. 11.

16. Ibid., Ch. 138, Secs. 11, 19, and 20.

17. William E. Connelley, *A Standard History of Kansas and Kansans* (New York and Chicago: Lewis Publishing Company, 1918), 448.

18. Territory of Kansas, *Journal of the House* (1855), 213.

19. Ibid.

20. John C. Marlin, "The Hoogland Examination: The United States v. John Brown, Jr. et. al." *Kansas Historical Quarterly* 7, (May 1938), 133–53.

21. Territory of Kansas, *Laws and Resolutions of the Fourth Session* (1858), Ch. 66.

22. Comparisons are with *The Revised Statutes of the State of Wisconsin,* 1849.

23. Territory of Kansas, *Laws and Resolutions of the Fourth Session* (1858), Ch. 66, Sec. 4.

24. Ibid., Sec. 71.

25. Ibid., Ch. 61.

26. Territory of Kansas, *Laws of 1860,* Ch. 114, Sec. 4.

27. Ibid., Sec. 11.

28. Paul Wallace Gates, *Fifty Million Acres: Conflicts over Kansas Land Policy, 1854–1890* (Ithaca: Cornell University Press, 1954).

29. In 1863, the Kansas Supreme Court declared such an effort to increase a county's share of the state tax by the amount of past uncollected taxes unconstitutional. Such a policy would not result in collection of past taxes but would impose an unequal tax upon present taxpayers. *The State of Kansas v. Leavenworth County Commissioners,* 2 Kans. 56 (1863).

30. James E. Boyle, *The Financial History of Kansas* (Madison: Bulletin of the University of Wisconsin, 247, 1908).

31. Gustave Raymond Gaeddert, *A History of the Establishment of the Kansas State Government* (Ph.D. diss., University of Kansas, Department of History, 1937), 109–11.

32. Ibid.

33. Zornow, *Kansas: A History,* 76–79.

34. Rosa M. Perdue, *The Sources of the Constitution of Kansas,* address delivered before the Kansas State Historical Society, January 15, 1901. *Kansas Constitutional Convention,* reprint of proceedings (Topeka: Kansas State Printing Plant, 1920), 677.

35. Gaeddert, *Establishment of the Kansas State Government,* 159.

36. Ibid., 156.

37. Ibid., 172–77.

38. Perdue, *The Sources of the Constitution,* 690.

39. Ibid., 677.

40. Territory of Kansas, Proceedings of the Territorial Board of Equalization for the Year 1860, *Journal of the House,* 1861, 74–78.

41. Territory of Kansas, Governor's Message, *Journal of the House,* 1861, 45.

6. DEFINING AND VALUING TAXABLE PROPERTY, 1860–1900

1. J. D. Morgan, *Some Controlling Forces in Kansas Population Movements* (Lawrence: University of Kansas, Bureau of Business Research, School of Business, 1953), 85.

2. Territory of Kansas, *Board of Equalization Report* (1860).

3. Gustave Raymond Gaeddert, *A History of the Establishment of the Kansas State Government* (Ph.D. diss., University of Kansas, Department of History, 1937), 10.

4. 2 Kans. 61 (1863).

5. 3 Kans. 186 (1865).

6. The right to impose assessments has its foundation in the taxing power of the government; and yet in practice and as generally understood, there is a distinction between the terms taxes and assessments. Taxes, as the term is generally used, are public burdens imposed generally upon the inhabitants of the whole state, or upon some civil division thereof, for governmental purposes, without reference to peculiar benefits to particular individuals or property. *Black's Law Dictionary* (St. Paul: West Publishing Co., 1968), 1628.

7. *General Laws of the State of Kansas in Force at the Close of the Session of the Legislature Ending March 6th, 1862.* Ch. 197.

8. U.S. Congress, *An Act to Organize the Territories of Nebraska and Kansas,* 33d Cong., 1st sess., approved 30 May 1854, Sec. 24.

9. U.S. Congress, *An Act for the Admission of Kansas into the Union,* 36th Cong., 2d sess., approved 29 January 1861, Secs. 1 and 3.

10. Paul Wallace Gates, *Fifty Million Acres: Conflicts over Kansas Land Policy, 1854–1890* (Ithaca: Cornell University Press, 1954), 3–7.

11. 3 Kans. 299 (1865) [rev. 5 Wall 737, 18 L Ed. 667 (1866)].

12. *The Kansas Indians,* 5 Wall 737, 18 L Ed. 667 (1866).

13. *Laws of Kansas* (1864), Ch. 120.

14. 5 Kans. 362 (1870).

15. In American law, a patent is the instrument by which a government grants public land.

16. *Parker v. Winsor,* 5 Kans. 367–68.

17. 9 Kans. 38 [rev. 16 Wall 603, 21 L Ed. 373] (1872).

18. *Kansas Pac Ry Co. v. Prescot,* 16 Wall 603, 21 L Ed. 373 (1873).

19. Gates, *Fifty Million Acres,* 266–68.

20. *Miami County Commissioners v. Robert Brackenridge,* 12 Kans. 114 (1873).

21. *Oswalt v. Hollowell,* 15 Kans. 124 (1875).

22. *Laws of Kansas* (1866), Ch. 118.

23. *General Statutes of Kansas* (1868), Ch. 107, Secs. 10, 12.

24. Kansas, *Journal of the Senate* (1868), 356–57.

25. Ibid., 357.

26. *General Statutes of Kansas* (1876), Ch. 107, Secs. 12, 15.

27. Irwin Taylor, *Tax Laws of Kansas* (Topeka: George W. Crane Co., 1884), 461.

28. *Washburn College v. Shawnee County Commissioners,* 8 Kans. 344 (1871).

29. *Vail v. Beach,* 10 Kans. 214 (1872).

30. *St. Mary's College v. Crawl, Treasurer,* 10 Kans. 442 (1872).

31. *Board of Regents of Kansas State Agricultural College v. Hamilton,* 28 Kans. 376 (1882).

32. *Durkee v. Greenwood County Commissioners,* 29 Kans. 697 (1883).

33. *Laws of Kansas* (1889), Ch. 249.

34. *Ottawa University v. Commissioners of Franklin County,* 48 Kans. 460, 29 P 599 (1892).

35. *General Statutes of Kansas* (1868), Ch. 107, Art. 1.

36. E. R. A. Seligman, *Essays in Taxation,* 10th ed. rev. (New York: Macmillan Company, 1928, 1st ed. 1895), 103–7.

37. Ibid., 106–7.

38. Theoretically, the proper solution to the problem of taxing the intangibles of corporations is the one adopted by Illinois in 1872. The total value of a corporation as a going concern is determined. From this is subtracted the value of all locally assessed property. The result equals the value of all intangible assets, including such items as goodwill or going concern value. Unfortunately, administrative, jurisdictional, and constitutional problems prevented the capital stock tax from contributing to uniformity. Glenn W. Fisher, *Taxes and Politics: A Study of Illinois Public Finance* (Urbana: University of Illinois Press, 1969), 129–33.

39. Jens Peter Jensen, *Property Taxation in the United States* (Chicago: University of Chicago Press, 1931), 49.

40. Ibid., 50–52.

41. *Laws of Kansas* (1873), Ch. 140.

42. James Ernest Boyle, *The Financial History of Kansas* (Madison: Bulletin of the University of Wisconsin, 247, Economic and Political series, vol. 5, no. 1, 1908), 50.

43. Kansas, *Journal of the House,* "Message of Governor Thomas A. Osborn to the Legislature of Kansas" (1874), 23.

44. *Laws of Kansas* (1874), Ch. 130.

45. Kansas, *Journal of the House,* "Annual Message of Governor Thomas A. Osborn" (13 January 1875), 33.

46. *Lappin v. Nemaha Co.,* 6 Kans. 403 (1870).

47. 9 Kans. 344 (1872).

48. *Mitchell v. Leavenworth County Commissioners,* 91 U.S. 206, 23 L Ed. 302 (1875).

49. The concept of "equity" in English and American law is a rather complicated and varied one. It has its roots in the idea of justice ascertained by natural reason or ethical insight, independent of the formulated body of law. In a more restricted sense, the word denotes equal and impartial justice, as between two persons whose rights are in conflict; justice, that is, as ascertained by natural reason or ethical insight, but independent of the formulated body of law. See *Miller v. Kenniston,* 86 Me. 555, 30 A 114.

50. Equitable relief may be denied on grounds of deceit or impurity of motive, fraud or willful misconduct, unlawful conduct or wrongdoing. *Black's Law Dictionary* (St. Paul, Minn: West Publishing Company, 1968), 318.

51. *People ex rel v. Supervisors of New York,* 7 Wall 26 (1869).

52. Thomas M. Cooley, *A Treatise on the Law of Taxation* (Chicago: Callaghan and Company, 1876), 44.

53. Ibid., 15, 66.

54. Territory of Kansas, *Laws* (1860), Ch. 114, Secs. 7, 12.

55. 8 Kans. 565 (1871).

56. *Laws of Kansas* (1876), Ch. 34, Art. 3, Sec. 4.

57. Ibid., Sec. 7.

58. Ibid., Art. 3, Secs. 8, 12.

59. *General Statutes of Kansas* (1876), Secs. 25–38.

60. *Watterson v. Kirkwood,* 8 Kans. 310 (1871).

61. *Hobson v. Dutton,* 9 Kans. 477 (1872).

62. *General Statutes of Kansas* (1868), Art. 5, Sec. 17.

63. Ibid., Ch. 107, Sec. 18.

64. Ibid., Ch. 107, Secs. 21–22.

65. F. W. Giles, *Review of the Tax System of the State of Kansas* (Topeka: Commonwealth State Printing House, 1872), 17–18.

66. *Laws of Kansas* (1881), Ch. 34.

67. *Graham v. Chautauqua County Commissioners,* 31 Kans. 473, 2 P 549 (1884).

68. *Laws of Kansas* (1881), Ch. 107, Sec. 28.

69. *General Statutes of Kansas* (1876), Ch. 107, Secs. 29, 30.

70. *Laws of Kansas* (1899), Ch. 248.

71. *General Laws of Kansas* (1862), Ch. 197, Sec. 11.

72. *Laws of Kansas* (1866), Ch. 118.

73. Boyle, *Financial History,* 50.

74. *Adams v. Beman,* 10 Kans. 37 (1872).

75. Ibid.

76. 10 Kans. 47 (1872).

7. LOCAL ADMINISTRATION, 1860–1900

1. Alexis De Tocqueville, *Democracy in America,* vol. 1. First Schocken ed. (New York: Schocken Books, 1961), 89.

2. De Tocqueville, *Democracy in America,* 95–96.

3. Frank J. Goodnow, *Politics and Administration* (New York: Macmillan Company, 1900), 51.

4. Kansas State Archives. State Auditor Miscellaneous Files. *Abstract of Assessment Rolls* (1860–1869).

5. Ibid.

6. Kansas, *Fifth Annual Auditor's Report* (1865).

7. Ibid.

8. The Neutral Land League was an organization of settlers organized to protect the rights of settlers in a bitter and violent fight with the Fort Scott Line over land in the Cherokee Neutral Strip. An account of this episode is found in Paul Wallace Gates, *Fifty Million Acres: Conflicts over Kansas Land Policy, 1854–1890* (Ithaca: Cornell University Press, 1954), 153-93.

9. Kansas, *Journal of the House,* "Message of Governor James M. Harvey" (1872).

10. *General Laws of Kansas* (1862), Secs. 42, 121–23.

11. *General Statutes of Kansas* (1868), Art. 5, Secs. 76, 79.

12. *Laws of Kansas* (1869), Ch. 30.

13. *General Statutes of Kansas* (1876), Ch. 110, Sec. 3.

14. Ibid., Ch. 107, Sec. 40; *Laws of Kansas* (1881), Ch. 37, Sec. 79; *Laws of Kansas* (1901), Ch. 112.

15. *General Statutes of Kansas* (1876), Ch. 107, Secs. 9, 10.

16. Ibid., Sec. 14.

17. Ibid., Sec. 61.

18. Ibid., Sec. 65.

19. Ibid., Sec. 43.

20. Ibid., Sec. 51.

21. Ibid., Secs. 52–53, 68.

22. Ibid., Sec. 70.

23. George S. Howard, *An Introduction to the Local Constitutional History of the United States* (Baltimore: Johns Hopkins University Press, 1889), 343.

24. Harley Leist Lutz, *The State Tax Commission: A Study of the Development and Results of State Control over Assessment and Taxation* (Cambridge: Harvard University Press, 1918), 16.

25. *General Statutes of Kansas* (1876), Ch. 107, Sec. 74.

26. *Gillet v. Lyon County Treasurer,* 30 Kans. 166 (1883).

27. 35 Kans. 175, 10 P 459 (1886).

28. *Marion County Commissioners v. Barker,* 25 Kans. 258 (1881).

29. 38 Kans.720, 17 P 476 (1888).

30. *Challiss v. Riggs,* 49 Kans. 119, 30 P 190 (1892).

31. Elbert Jay Benton, *Taxation in Kansas* (Johns Hopkins University Studies in Historical and Political Science 18:3, 1900), 146.

32. Lutz, *State Tax Commission,* 21.

33. *General Statutes of Kansas* (1876), Ch. 107, Sec. 69.

34. *Braden v. Union Trust Company of New York,* 25 Kans. 362 (1881).

35. Benton, *Taxation in Kansas,* 146. Benton cites the attorney general's report of 1883–1884 as authority.

36. Kansas, *State Auditor's Report* (1871).

37. Kansas, *Board of Equalization Report* (various years).

38. Kansas, *Board of Equalization Proceedings* (1897), 128–35.

39. *Laws of Kansas* (1861), Ch. 76, Sec. 5.

40. A constitutional amendment adopted in 1876 amended the provision to state that no appropriation should be for longer than two years. The legislature began to meet biennially, rather than annually, in 1879.

41. *State of Kansas v. William F. Ewing*, 22 Kans. 493 (1879).

42. *Laws of Kansas* (1869), Ch. 80.

43. The school finance act passed in 1992 required that all school districts impose a 32 mill levy for school purposes. Amounts which exceed the districts' needs as calculated by a formula are then remitted to the state for use in other districts. Although legally imposed by the districts rather than the state, the fiscal impact is identical to the impact of a state-levied property tax.

44. *General Laws of Kansas* (1862), Ch. 197, Sec. 27.

45. Ibid., Ch. 163, Secs. 29, 35.

46. Ibid., Ch. 46, Art. 2, Sec. 1.

47. *City of Leavenworth v. Norton,* 1 Kans. 432 (1863).

48. *Smith v. Leavenworth County Commissioners,* 9 Kans. 296 (1871).

49. 10 Kans. 326 (1872).

50. Ibid.

51. 16 Kans. 228 (1876).

52. *State of Kansas v. Marion County Commissioners,* 21 Kans. 308 (1878).

53. *General Statutes of Kansas* (1876), Ch. 107, Art. 13, Sec. 82.

54. Ibid., Secs. 88–90.

55. Ibid., Sec. 92

56. Ibid., Secs. 105–7.

57. Ibid., Secs. 109–14.

58. Ibid., Sec. 118.

59. Ibid., Sec. 127.

60. An analysis by the author shows that twenty-two of the first seventy-six tax cases to be decided by the Kansas Supreme Court dealt with collection.

61. *Bowman v. Cockrill*, 6 Kans. 311 (1870); *Hobson v. Dutton*, 9 Kans. 477 (1872); *Park v. Tinkham*, 9 Kans. 615 (1872); *Haynes v. Heller*, 12 Kans. 381 (1874); *Morrill v. Douglass*, 14 Kans. 228 (1875).

62. Gates reports that interest rates from 36 to 120 percent were commonly paid in land deals in the late 1850s, although 20 percent was the legal rate in Kansas. Gates, *Fifty Million Acres*, 95.

63. James Ernest Boyle, *The Financial History of Kansas* (Madison: Bulletin of the University of Wisconsin 247. Economic and Political Series 5:1, 1908), 34–35.

64. *General Statutes of Kansas* (1901), Ch. 107, Sec. 127.

65. F. W. Giles, *Review of the Tax System of the State of Kansas* (Topeka: Commonwealth State Printing House, 1872), 40.

66. *Adams v. Beman*, 10 Kans. 37 (1872).

67. Giles, *Review of the Tax System*, 9.

68. Ibid., 12.

69. Ibid., 22.

70. Ibid., 38–40.

71. Kansas, *Journal of the House*, "Biennial Message of Governor John A. Martin" (8 January 1889).

72. Kansas, *Journal of the House*, "Biennial Message of Governor L. D. Lewelling" (9 January 1895).

73. Assessment and Taxation Table, *Queen City Herald*, Ottawa, Kansas, 2 February 1888.

74. Boyle, *Financial History*, 122.

75. Ibid., 44–45.

76. *Leavenworth County Commissioners v. Miller*, 7 Kans. 479, 12 Am Rep. 425 (1871); *State of Kansas v. Nemaha County Commissioners*, 7 Kans. 542 (1871).

77. *Laws of Kansas* (1876), Chs. 106, 107.

78. *Commercial National Bank of Cleveland v. the City of Iola*, 9 Kans. 689.

79. Kansas, *State Auditor's Report* (1873), 14–15.

80. Boyle, *Financial History*, 63–65.

81. Kansas, *Journal of the House*, "Message of Governor James M. Harvey" (1872).

82. Kansas, *Journal of the House*, "Annual Message of the Governor, Thomas A. Osborn" (13 January 1875).

83. Kansas, *Journal of the House*, "Annual Message of the Governor, Geo. T. Anthony" (10 January 1877).

84. Boyle, *Financial History*, 170; Kansas Legislative Council Research Department, *Summary History of Kansas Finance: 1861–1937* (Topeka: Publication No. 60., October 1937).

85. These boards and agencies are all mentioned in the Message of Governor John W. Leedy in 1897. Perusal of any state officers' report for this period will show that state government was involved in many aspects of life.

86. James W. Drury, *The Government of Kansas*, rev. ed. (Lawrence: University Press of Kansas, 1970), 223.

87. *Kansas Government Journal* (April 1977), 139.

8. DEFECTIVE IN THEORY OR PRACTICE?

1. Richard T. Ely, *Taxation in American States and Cities* (New York: T. Y. Crowell and Co., 1888).

2. J. H. T. McPherson, "The General Property Tax as a Source of State Revenue," *Conference on State and Local Taxation* (Columbus: National Tax Association, 1908).

3. Charles J. Bullock, "The Taxation of Intangible Property," *State and Local Taxation: Second International Conference* (Columbus: National Tax Association, 1909).

4. Henry Carter Adams, *The Science of Public Finance* (New York: Henry Holt and Company, 1898).

5. For a brief summary of these early works see Glenn W. Fisher, "The Evolution of the General Property Tax in the Nineteenth Century: The Search for Equality," *Property Tax Journal* 6:2 (June 1987): 99–117.

6. E. R. A. Seligman, *Essays on Taxation* (New York: Macmillan Company, 1895), 57.

7. International Tax Association, "State and Local Taxation," Third and Fourth International Conferences, vols. 3 and 4 (Columbus, Ohio: International Tax Association, 1910, 1911).

8. *Laws of Kansas* (1901), Ch. 361.

9. Kansas Tax Commission, *Report and Bill* (November 1901), 4.

10. Ibid.

11. Ibid., 5.

12. Ibid. The statement about the nature of assessors schools was apparently first made in the Bureau of Labor report of 1897 and was repeated many times by critics of the Kansas property tax.

13. Kansas Tax Commission, *Report and Bill* (November 1901), 14–15.

14. Ibid., 44–47.

15. Ibid., 18.

16. Ibid., 19–20.

17. Ibid., 30.

18. Frank J. Goodnow, *Politics and Administration* (New York: Macmillan Company, 1900), 18.

19. James Ernest Boyle, *The Financial History of Kansas* (Madison: Bulletin of the University of Wisconsin 247, Economic and Political series 5:1, 1908), 83.

20. Robert Sherman La Forte, *Leaders of Reform, Progressive Republicans in Kansas, 1900–1916* (Lawrence: University of Kansas Press, 1974), 31–45.

21. Kansas, *Journal of The House,* "Governor E. W. Hoch, Message to the Legislature" (10 January 1905).

22. Kansas, *Journal of the House,* "Message of Governor Hoch" (8 January 1907).

23. *Laws of Kansas* (1907), Ch. 408.

24. Ibid., Sec. 19.

25. Kansas State Archives, "Letter to Governor Hoch" (26 September 1907).

26. Kansas Tax Commission, *First Report* (1908); and International Tax Association, *State and Local Taxation. Second International Conference: Addresses and Proceedings,* vol. 2 (Columbus, Ohio: International Tax Association, 1909).

27. International Tax Association, *State and Local Taxation. Second International Conference: Addresses and Proceedings,* vol. 2 (Columbus, Ohio: International Tax Association, 1909).

28. Kansas, *Journal of the House* (special session), "Message of Governor E. W. Hoch to the 1908 legislature."

29. International Tax Association, *State and Local Taxation. Second International Conference: Addresses and Proceedings,* vol. 2 (Columbus, Ohio: International Tax Association, 1909).

30. Kansas Tax Commission, *First Biennial Report, 1908–9* (Topeka: State Printing Office, 1909).

31. Ibid., 452.

32. Ibid.

33. Kansas State Archives, Kansas Tax Commission Appeal Docket, *S. S. Reynolds, Agt. Chicago Lumber and Coal Company* (1908).

34. Kansas State Archives, Kansas Tax Commission Appeal Docket, *Ludign and Havens Lbr. Co. v. County Board of Equalization of Dickenson County* (1908).

35. Kansas Tax Commission. *Proceedings of the Conference Convention of the Tax Commission and the County Assessors of the State of Kansas, January 28 and 29, 1908* (Topeka: State Printing Office, 1908).

36. Ibid., 8.

37. Ibid., 13–14.

38. Ibid., 47–49.

39. Kansas Tax Commission, *First Report to the Legislature, January 12, 1909* (Topeka: State Printing Office, 1908), 8.

40. Ibid., 37–41.

41. Kansas Tax Commission, *Proceedings of the Second Biennial Conference Convention of the Tax Commission and the County Assessors of the State of Kansas, January 25 and 26, 1910* (Topeka: State Printing Office, 1910), 5–8.

42. Kansas Tax Commission, *First Report to the Legislature, January 12, 1909* (Topeka: State Printing Office, 1908), 8–20.

43. Kansas Tax Commission, *Proceedings of the Fourth Biennial Conference Convention of the Tax Commission and the County Assessors of Kansas held at Topeka, December 8 and 9, 1913* (Topeka: State Printing Office, 1913), 47–50.

44. Harley Leist Lutz, *The State Tax Commission: A Study of the Development and Results of State Control over Assessment of Property for Taxation* (Cambridge: Harvard University Press, 1918), 449.

45. Eric Englund, *Assessment and Equalization of Farm and City Real Estate in Kansas* (Manhattan, Kansas: Agricultural Experiment Station Bulletin, 232, July 1924), 70.

46. See Chapter 9 for more detailed calculations and information about the source of these data.

9. REPLACING THE GENERAL PROPERTY TAX

1. Kansas Legislative Council, Research Department, *Summary History of Kansas Finance, 1861–1937* (Topeka Publication No. 60, October 1937), 25.

2. Eric Englund, *Assessment and Equalization of Farm and City Real Estate in Kansas* (Manhattan, Kansas: Agricultural Experiment Station Bulletin 232, July 1924); Englund, *Tax Revision in Kansas* (Manhattan, Kansas: Agricultural Experiment Station Bulletin 234, December 1924); and Englund, *The Trend of Real Estate Taxation in Kansas From 1910 to*

1923 (Manhattan, Kansas: Agricultural Experiment Station Bulletin 235, September 1925).

3. Englund, *Assessment and Equalization,* 14–27.

4. Englund, *Tax Revision,* 14–17.

5. Kansas Tax Commission, *First Report to the Legislature, January 12, 1909* (Topeka: State Printing Office, 1908).

6. *Laws of Kansas* (1925), Ch. 277.

7. *Voran v. Wright,* 129 Kans. 1, 281 P 939 [aft 129 Kans. 601, 284, p. 807] (1929).

8. Kansas, *Journal of the House,* "Governor's Message" (Special sess., 1928).

9. *Kansas Constitution,* Art. 11, Sec. 9 (1928) [originally Sec. 8].

10. Kansas Tax Code Commission, *Report to the Governor,* (Topeka: Kansas State Printing Office, 1929), 9.

11. Kansas, *Journal of the House* (1929).

12. Kansas Tax Code Commission, *Report to the Governor* (Topeka: Kansas State Printing Office, 1929), 17–36.

13. Ibid., 32.

14. Ibid., 15.

15. Ibid., 37–54.

16. Ibid., 55–75.

17. *Merchants National Bank of Richmond v. City of Richmond,* 256 U.S. 635, 65 L Ed. 1135 (1920).

18. Kansas Tax Code Commission, *Report to the Governor,* (Topeka: Kansas State Printing Office, 1929), 105–18.

19. Ibid., 76–84.

20. William Frank Zornow, *Kansas: A History of the Jayhawk State* (Norman: University of Oklahoma Press, 1957), 246–47.

21. Donald R. McCoy, *Landon of Kansas* (Lincoln: University of Nebraska Press, 1966), 107–8.

22. Kansas, *Journal of the Kansas Senate,* "Governor's Message" (1933).

23. *Laws of Kansas* (1933), Ch. 320.

24. Ibid., Ch. 319.

25. Ibid., Ch. 186.

26. *Kansas Laws* (1933), Ch. 309.

27. Ibid., Ch. 366.

28. Zornow, *Kansas: A History,* 252.

29. *Laws of Kansas* (1936), Ch. 4, SCR no. 3.

30. Ibid., Ch. 5, SCR no. 4.

10. KANSAS TAXATION SINCE 1930

1. Kansas Legislative Research Department, *Kansas Tax Facts* (5th ed., 1983 and 1992 supplements).

2. Parts of the following description of developments in Kansas in the 1950s, 1960s, and 1970s are from the author's report to Kansas, Inc., a Kansas economic development agency. It was issued as *Report on Reappraisal and Classification* by Kansas, Inc. at Topeka on 30 March 1990.

3. Kansas Citizens Commission on Assessment Equalization, *Kansas Assessment-Sales Ratios 1952* (mimeographed, n.d.).

4. Kansas Citizens' Commission on Assessment Equalization, *Report to the Governor and the 1955 Legislature* (Topeka, 15 November 1954).

5. John D. Garwood, "Kansas Citizens Examine Their Property Taxes," *National Tax Journal* 9:3 (September 1956), 258–67.

6. *Laws of Kansas* (1957), Ch. 429.

7. *Laws of Kansas* (1959), Ch. 365.

8. *Kansas Laws* (1961), Ch. 439.

9. *Laws of Kansas* (1963), Ch. 460.

10. *Addington v. Board of County Commissioners,* 191 Kans. 531, (1963).

11. Lawrence A. Leonard, "Property Taxation in Kansas: An Historical Analysis, *National Tax Journal* 9:3 (September 1958), 232–33.

12. Bonnie L. Hickle, *Reappraisal and Equity in Property Taxation* (M.A. thesis, Department of Economics, Wichita State University, August 1968), 64–65.

13. Robert Dan Foster, *An Empirical Investigation of the Kansas Sales Ratio Study* (University of Oregon Ph.D. diss., August 1968), 268.

14. *Laws of Kansas* (1949), Ch. 224.

15. Kansas Department of Revenue, Division of Property Valuation, *Report of Real Estate Assessment Ratio Study, for the Calendar Year, 1962.*

16. Today the coefficient of dispersion is calculated by dividing the average absolute deviation of the individual ratios from the median ratio by the median. Dividing the interquartile range by the median, as in the 1966 study, ignores the highest and lowest one-fourth of the ratios.

17. *Laws of Kansas* (1965), Ch. 516.

18. *Laws of Kansas* (1969), Ch. 435; *Laws of Kansas* (1972), Ch. 363; *Laws of Kansas* (1974), Ch. 428; *Laws of Kansas* (1976), Ch. 423; *Laws of Kansas* (1978), Ch. 396.

19. *Laws of Kansas* (1978), Ch. 396.

20. *Laws of Kansas* (1973), Ch. 292.

21. *Summary and Recommendations for a Report of the Kansas Citizens' Tax Review Commission* (November 1972).

22. Cooperative Extension Service, *Financing State and Local Government in Kansas* (Manhattan, Kansas State University, September 1971).

23. Ibid., 51.

24. Ibid., 45–46.

25. B. L. Flinchbaugh, *Yes or No on Use Value Appraisal of Agricultural Land* (Manhattan: Department of Economics, Cooperative Extension Service, Kansas State University, 1976); Mark A. Edelman and B. L. Flinchbaugh, *Use Value Appraisal Impact Study* (Manhattan: Department of Economics, Cooperative Extension Service, Kansas State University, 1977); B. L. Flinchbaugh and Mark A. Edelman, *Use-Value Assessment: Case Studies* (Manhattan, Kansas State University, Cooperative Extension Service, 1975).

26. Wilfred H. Pine, "100 Years of Farmland Values in Kansas," *Agricultural Experiment Station Bulletin, 611* (Manhattan: Kansas State University, September 1977), 4–5.

27. Kansas Legislature (1977), *House Bill 2732.*

28. Edelman and Flinchbaugh, *Impact Study.*

29. Kansas Legislature, Special Committee on Use Value Appraisal, *Report on Kansas Legislative Interim Studies to the 1978 Legislature* (December 1977).

30. *Laws of Kansas* (1978), Ch. 396.

31. *Topeka Capital Journal,* September 10, 1980.

32. Ibid.

33. *Laws of Kansas* (1978), Ch. 395; *Laws of Kansas* (1979), Ch. 311.

34. *State ex re. Stephen v. Martin,* 227 Kans. 456 (1980).

35. *Kansas Laws* (1981), Ch. 373.

36. *State ex re. Stephen v. Martin,* 230 Kans. 759.

37. Kansas, Board of Tax Appeals, *Order of the Board of Tax Appeals, in the matter of the request for a reappraisal of all real property in Sedgwick, Ford and Rice counties and Statewide equalization of all property. Brittain, Groves, Hornung, and Oakleaf, Docket No. 3278-83-CP and the related complaint of Jack and Dorothy Jannsen, Docket No. 3591-83-CP* (30 January 1985).

38. Elizabeth Owens, "Reappraisal: A Political Disaster? Lessons from the 1960s," *County Connection* (published by the Kansas League of Municipalities, May 1988).

39. Kansas, *Journal of the House,* Message of the Governor (23 January 1979).

40. *Journal of the House of Representatives,* "Message of the Governor" (15 January 1980).

41. Letter to Honorable Paul Burke, *Selected Papers of Governor John Carlin,* Joe P. Pisciotte, ed. (Wichita: Hugo Wall School of Urban and Public Affairs, Wichita State University, 1993), 747.

42. This account is based upon notes of participants in the meetings and personal recollections of the author, who attended several of the meetings.

43. Glenn W. Fisher, *Notes prepared for testimony before Kansas House of Representatives Assessment and Taxation Committee* (21 March 1985).

44. *Laws of Kansas* (1985), Ch. 314.

45. Ibid.

46. George A. Donatello, *Kansas Reappraisal,* (Kansas Department of Revenue, Division of Property Valuation, 14 April 1988), 1.

47. Donatello, *Kansas Reappraisal,* 2–21.

48. *Laws of Kansas* (1992), Ch. 342.

49. *Robert Mock, et al. v. State of Kansas, et al.,* Consolidated Shawnee County Kansas District Court Case No. 91-CV-1009 (October 1991).

50. Kansas has home rule provisions that apply to municipalities and counties, but these do not affect school districts.

51. According to Judge Bullock's decision, the state always had that responsibility, but the financial and political realities were that it was a local responsibility carried out with varying amounts of state financial assistance.

52. *State of Kansas, ex rel., Robert T. Stephen, Attorney General v. Kansas Department of Revenue, et al.,* Shawnee County Kansas District Court Case No. 92-CV-796 (30 June 1992).

53. Judge Terry L. Bullock, *Appraisal Litigation, Remarks from the Bench,* District Court of Shawnee County, Kansas, Division 6 (13 July 1993).

54. *State of Kansas, ex rel., Robert T. Stephen, Attorney General v. Kansas Department of Revenue, et al.,* Shawnee County Kansas District Court Case No. 92-CV-796 (30 June 1993).

11. PROPERTY TAXATION IN THE UNITED STATES TODAY

1. Frederick C. Stocker, *Proposition 13: A Ten Year Retrospective* (Cambridge, Mass.: Lincoln Institute of Land Policy, 1991), 1.

2. John H. Bowman, George E. Hoffer, and Michael D. Pratt, "Current Patterns and Trends in State and Local Intangible Taxation," *National Tax Journal* 63:4, (December 1990), 439–50.

3. Bowman, Hoffer, and Pratt, "Current Patterns and Trends," 439–50.

4. John Mikesell, "Patterns of Exclusion of Personal Property from the American Property Tax Systems," *Public Finance Quarterly* 20:4, (October 1992), 534–35.

5. In some states, the operating property of utility companies is defined as personal property for tax purposes. Such property is not included in these computations.

6. Mikesell, "Patterns of Exclusion," 528–42.

7. Advisory Commission on Intergovernmental Relations, *Significant Features of Fiscal Federalism* vol. 1 (1993), 156–59.

8. John H. Bowman and Michael E. Bell, *Real Property Tax Relief,* mimeo (prepared for the Maryland Commission on State Taxes and Tax Structure, February 1990).

9. Jane H. Malme, "Executive Summary," International Association of Assessing Officers, *Assessment Administration Practices in the U. S. and Canada* (Chicago: 1992), n.p.; Alan S. Dornfest, "Assessment Ratio Study Issues: 1992 Survey Results," *Property Tax Journal* 12:3, (September 1993), 275–302.

10. The description of tax incentives is based on a 778-page manual that lists developmental incentives provided by the states. National Association of State Development Agencies, *Directory of Incentives for Business Investment and Development in the United States,* 3d ed. (Washington, D.C.: Urban Institute Press, 1991).

11. Information about the current circuit breakers and homestead exemptions is for 1991 or 1992 and is taken from Advisory Commission on Intergovernmental Relations, *Significant Features of Fiscal Federalism, 1993,* vol. 1, (Washington, D. C., 1993), 140–55. See also Alan S. Dornfest, "Residential Property Tax Relief: Exemptions and Circuit Breakers," *Assessment Journal* 1:2, (March/April 1994), 44–52.

12. Joseph K. Eckert, ed., *Property Appraisal and Assessment Administration* (Chicago: International Association of Assessing Officers, 1990), 305–8.

13. International Association of Assessing Officers, *Assessment Administration Practices in the U.S. and Canada* (Chicago: 1992), n.p.

14. U.S. Bureau of the Census, *1992 Census of Government* 1:1 (1994), Government Organization, 7.

15. Railroad transportation property is protected by federal law

12. PAST AS PROLOGUE

1. Exceptions would have to be made for the early years of statehood before boundaries had been firmly established.

2. One of the anonymous reviewers of this volume has challenged me to try to prove

this statement. It's an interesting challenge, but one I am reluctant to accept. Because there are so many dimensions of political autonomy, it is hard to develop an empirical test. Clearly the idea is widely accepted. In several empirical studies the authors, with no proof, have used fiscal autonomy as a proxy for political autonomy.

Perhaps the best "proof" is found in the political logic of the situation. Levying taxes is a distasteful process that leads to loss of support, but it can be offset, wholly or in part, by expending the money in ways that will increase support. It follows that no governmental body or level of government will long be comfortable delegating spending to another body or level of government.

A number of political scientists used this line of reasoning to correctly predict that Federal Revenue Sharing would not survive. Categorical grant programs survive because the granting governments maintain control over spending and often are beneficiaries of favorable attention when new grants are announced.

3. Advisory Commission on Intergovernmental Relations, *Significant Features of Fiscal Federalism, 1993* (Washington: D.C., 1993), 76.

4. Paul D. Ballew, Richard Mattoon, and William A. Testa, "School Reform and Tax Reform: A Successful Marriage?" *Government Finance Review* (August 1994), 32.

REFERENCES

BOOKS

Adams, Henry Carter. *Taxation in the United States, 1789–1816.* New York: Burt Franklin, 1970, originally published 1884.
————. *The Science of Public Finance.* New York: Henry Holt and Company, 1898.
Adams, James Ring. *Secrets of the Tax Revolt.* New York: Harcourt Brace Jovanovich, 1984.
Andrews, Wayne, ed. *Concise Dictionary of American History.* New York: Charles Scribner's Sons, 1962.
Baldwin, Leland D. *Whiskey Rebels: The Story of a Frontier Uprising.* Pittsburgh: University of Pittsburgh Press, 1939.
Becker, Robert A. *Revolution, Reform, and the Politics of American Taxation, 1763–1783.* Baton Rouge: Louisiana State University Press, 1980.
Benson, George C. S., Sumner Benson, Harold McClelland, and Procter Thomson. *The American Property Tax: Its History, Administration and Economic Impact.* California: Claremont College Printing Service, 1965.
Benton, Elbert Jay. *Taxation in Kansas.* Johns Hopkins University Studies in Historical and Political Science 18:3, 1900.
Black's Law Dictionary. St. Paul: West Publishing Co., 1968.
Bogart, Ernest Ludlow. *Financial History of Ohio.* Vol. 1, nos. 1 and 2. Urbana: University of Illinois Studies in Social Science, 1912.
Boyle, James Ernest. *The Financial History of Kansas.* Madison: Bulletin of the University of Wisconsin 247, Economic and Political Science series 5:1, 1908.
Burns, James MacGregor. *The Vineyard of Liberty.* New York: Alfred A. Knopf, Inc., 1981.
Cannan, Edwin. *History of Local Rates in England.* 2d ed. London: P. S. King and Son, 1912.
Connelley, William E. *A Standard History of Kansas and Kansans.* New York and Chicago: Lewis Publishing Company, 1918.
Cooley, Thomas M. *A Treatise on the Law of Taxation.* Chicago: Callaghan and Co., 1876.

Dewey, Davis Rich. *Financial History of the United States.* 12th ed. New York: Longmans, Green and Co., 1939.

Dorfman, Joseph. *The Economic Mind in American Civilization, 1606–1865.* Vol. 1. New York: Viking Press, 1946.

Dowell, Stephen. *A History of Taxation and Taxes in England: From the Earliest Times to the Present Day.* 3d ed., 4 vols., reprints of Economic Classics. New York: Augustus M. Kelley, 1965. Originally published by Longmans Green, 1884.

Drury, James W. *The Government of Kansas.* Rev. ed. Lawrence: University Press of Kansas, 1970.

Easton, David. *A Systems Analysis of Political Life.* New York: John Wiley & Sons, 1965.

Eckert, Joseph K., ed. *Property Tax Appraisal and Assessment Administration.* Chicago: International Association of Assessing Officers, 1990.

Ely, Richard T. *Taxation in the American States and Cities.* New York: T. Y. Crowell & Co., 1888.

Englund, Eric. *Assessment and Equalization of Farm and City Real Estate in Kansas.* Manhattan, Kansas: Agricultural Experiment Station Bulletin 232, July 1924.

———. *Tax Revision in Kansas.* Manhattan, Kansas: Agricultural Experiment Station Bulletin 234, December 1924.

———. *The Trend of Real Estate Taxation in Kansas from 1910 to 1923.* Manhattan, Kansas: Agricultural Experiment Station Bulletin 235, September 1925.

Fisher, Glenn W. *Taxes and Politics: A Study of Illinois Public Finance.* Urbana: University of Illinois Press, 1969.

Forsythe, Dall W. *Taxation and Political Change in the Young Nation, 1781–1833.* New York: Columbia University Press, 1977.

Gates, Paul Wallace. *Fifty Million Acres: Conflicts over Kansas Land Policy, 1854–1890.* Ithaca: Cornell University Press, 1954.

Giles, F. W. *Review of the Tax System of the State of Kansas.* Topeka: Commonwealth State Printing House, 1872.

Goodnow, Frank J. *Politics and Administration.* New York: Macmillan Company, 1900.

Greenstone, J. David, and Paul Peterson. *Race and Authority in Urban Politics.* New York: Russell Sage Foundation, 1973.

Haig, Robert Murray. *A History of the General Property Tax in Illinois.* Vol. 3. Urbana: University of Illinois Studies in the Social Sciences, 1914.

Hanna, H. S. *A Financial History of Maryland, 1789–1849.* Baltimore: Johns Hopkins University Press, 1907.

Howard, George S. *An Introduction to the Local Constitutional History of the United States.* Baltimore: Johns Hopkins University Press, 1889.

International Association of Assessing Officers. *Assessment Administrative Practices in the U. S. and Canada.* (Chicago: 1992.)

International Tax Association. *State and Local Taxation, Second International Conference: Addresses and Proceedings.* Vol. 2. Columbus, Ohio: International Tax Association, 1909.

Jarvis, Howard and Robert Peck. *I'm Mad as Hell: The Exclusive Story of the Tax Revolt and Its Leader.* New York: Times Books, 1979.

Jensen, Jens Peter. *Property Taxation in the United States.* Chicago: University of Chicago Press, 1931.

Kohl, Lawrence Frederick. *The Politics of Individualism: Parties and the American Character in the Jacksonian Era.* New York: Oxford University Press, 1989.

La Forte, Robert Sherman. *Leaders of Reform: Progressive Republicans in Kansas, 1900–1916.* Lawrence: The University Press of Kansas, 1974.

Leland, Simeon Elbridge. *The Classified Property Tax in the United States.* Boston and New York: Houghton Mifflin Company, 1928.

Lo, Clarence Y. H. *Small Property versus Big Government: Social Origins of the Property Tax Revolt.* Berkeley: University of California Press, 1990.

Lutz, Harley Leist. *The State Tax Commission: A Study of the Development and Results of State Control over the Assessment of Property for Taxation.* Cambridge: Harvard University Press, 1918.

McCoy, Donald R. *Landon of Kansas.* Lincoln: University of Nebraska Press, 1966.

Morgan, J. D. *Some Controlling Forces in Kansas Population Movements.* Lawrence: University of Kansas, Bureau of Business Research, School of Business, 1953.

National Association of State Development Agencies. *Directory of Incentives for Business Investment and Development in the United States.* 3d ed. Washington, D.C., Urban Institute Press, 1991.

Newhouse, Wade J. *Constitutional Uniformity and Equality In State Taxation.* 2d ed., 2 vols. Buffalo: William S. Hein and Co., 1984.

Pisciotte, Joe P., ed. *Selected Papers of Governor John Carlin.* Wichita: Hugo Wall School of Urban and Public Affairs, 1993.

Poore, B. P. *Federal and State Constitutions.* Washington: Government Printing Office, 1877.

Ratchford, B. U. *American State Debts.* Durham, North Carolina: Duke University Press, 1941.

Richmond, Robert W. *Kansas: A Land of Contrasts.* 2d ed. St. Louis: Forum Press, 1980.

Schlesinger, Arthur W., Jr. *The Age of Jackson.* Boston: Little, Brown and Company, 1945.

Seligman, E. R. A. *Essays in Taxation.* 5th ed. New York: Macmillan Company, 1905. First published 1895.

Sellers, Charles. *The Market Revolution: Jacksonian America, 1815–1846.* New York: Oxford University Press, 1991.

Shearer, Augustus Hunt. *A List of Documentary Material Relating to State Constitutional Conventions 1776–1912.* Chicago: Newberry Library, 1915.

Smith, Adam. *An Inquiry into the Nature and Causes of the Wealth of Nations.* E. Cannan, ed. New York: Modern Library edition, Random House, 1937.

Sowers, Don C. *The Financial History of New York State: From 1789 to 1912.* New York: AMS Press, 1969. First edition published in 1914.

Stocker, Frederick C. *Proposition 13: A Ten Year Retrospective.* Cambridge, Mass: The Lincoln Institute of Land Policy, 1991.

Taussig, F. W. *State Papers and Speeches on the Tariff.* Clifton, N.J.: Augustus M. Kelley, 1972.

Taylor, Irwin. *Tax Laws of Kansas.* Topeka: George W. Crane Co., 1884.

White, Leonard D. *Trends in Public Administration.* New York: McGraw-Hill Book Company, Inc., 1933.

———. *The Jacksonians: A Study in Administrative History, 1829–1861.* New York: Macmillan Company, 1954.

———. *The Federalists: A Study in Administrative History.* New York: Macmillan Company, 1948.

Wood, Gordon S. *The Creation of the American Republic, 1776–1787.* Chapel Hill: published for the Institute of Early American History and Culture at Williamsburg, Va., by the University of North Carolina Press, 1969.

Worthington, Thomas K. *Historical Sketch of the Finances of Pennsylvania.* (Baltimore: publications of the American Economic Association II, 1888.

Zickefoose, Paul W. *Kansas Income Payments, 1900–1953.* Lawrence: University of Kansas School of Business, Bureau of Business Research, 1955.

Zornow, William Frank. *Kansas: A History of the Jayhawk State.* Norman: University of Oklahoma Press, 1957.

ARTICLES

Ballew, Paul D., Richard Mattoon, and William A. Testa. "School Reform and Tax Reform: A Successful Marriage?" *Government Finance Review,* (August 1994): 32–35.

Bowman, John H., George E. Hoffer, and Michael D. Pratt. "Current Patterns and Trends in State and Local Intangible Taxation." *National Tax Journal* 63:4 (December 1990): 439–50.

Dornfest, Alan S. "Assessment Ratio Study Issses: 1992 Survey Results." *Property Tax Journal* 12:3 (September 1993).

Fisher, Glen W. "Property Taxation in the Kansas Territory," *Kansas History: A Journal of the Western Plains,* Vol. 11, No. 3 (Autumn, 1988).

———. "The Evolution of the General Property Tax in the Nineteenth Century: The Search for Equality." *Property Tax Journal* 6:2 (June 1987): 99–117.

Garwood, John D. "Kansas Citizens Examine Their Property Taxes." *National Tax Journal* 9:3 (September 1956): 258–67.

Henderson, H. James. "Taxation and Political Culture." *William and Mary Quarterly* 47:1, Third Series (January 1990), 92, 105.

Leonard, Lawrence A. "Property Taxation in Kansas, An Historical Analysis." *National Tax Journal* 9:3 (September 1958): 230–40.

Marlin, John C. "The Hoogland Examination: The United States v. John Brown, Jr. et al." *Kansas Historical Quarterly* 7 (May 1938): 133–53.

Matthews, William L. "The Function of Constitutional Provisions Requiring Uniformity in Taxation." *Kentucky Law Journal* 38:1 (November 1949): 31–50.

Mikesell, John. "Patterns of Exclusion of Personal Property from the American Property Tax Systems." *Public Finance Quarterly* 20:4 (October 1992): 528–42.

Owens, Elizabeth. "Reappraisal: A Political Disaster? Lessons from the 1960s." *County Connection* (published by the Kansas League of Municipalities, May 1988).

Slaughter, Thomas P. "The Tax Man Cometh: Ideological Opposition to Internal Taxes, 1760–1790." *William and Mary Quarterly* 41:4, Third Series (October 1984), 575.

Wallenstein, Peter. "'More Unequally Taxed than any People in the Civiliized World': The Origins of Georgia's Ad Valorem Tax System." *Georgia Historical Quarterly* 49:4 (Winter, 1985).

DOCUMENTS AND OTHER SOURCES

Advisory Commission on Intergovernmental Relations. *Significant Features of Fiscal Federalism, 1993.* 2 vols. (Washington, D.C., 1993).

Donatello, George A. *Kansas Reappraisal.* (Kansas Department of Revenue, Division of Property Valuation, 14 April 1988.)

Fisher, Glenn W. Notes prepared for testimony before Kansas House of Representatives Assessment and Taxation Committee. 21 March 1985.

Flinchbaugh, B. L. *Yes or No on Use Value Appraisal of Agricultural Land.* Rev. (Manhattan: Kansas State University, Department of Economics, Cooperative Extension Service, May 1976.)

Flinchbaugh, B. L., and Mark A. Edelman. *Use Value Appraisal Impact Study.* (Manhattan: Kansas State University, Department of Economics, Cooperative Extension Service, December 1977.)

Flinchbaugh, B. L., and Mark A. Edelman. *Use-Value Assessment: Case Studies.* (Manhattan: Kansas State University, Department of Economics, Cooperative Extension Service, February 1975.)

Kansas. *Board of Equalization, Proceedings.* 1897.

Kansas. *Board of Equalization, Report.* (Various years).

Kansas. Citizens Commission on Assessment Equalization. *Kansas Assessment-Sales Ratios 1952.* (n.d.)

Kansas. Citizens Commission on Assessment Equalization. *Report to the Governor and the 1955 Legislature.* (Topeka, 15 November 1954.)

Kansas. Citizens' Tax Review Commission. *Summary and Recommendations, from a Report of the Kansas Citizens' Tax Review Commission.* (November 1972.)

Kansas. Constitutional Convention, 1859. *Kansas Constitutional Convention: A Reprint of the Proceedings and Debates of the Convention Which Framed the Constitution on Kansas at Wyandotte in July 1859.* (Topeka: Kansas State Printing Plant, 1920.)

Kansas. Department of Revenue. Division of Property Valuation. *Assessment Manual.* (1958.)

Kansas. Department of Revenue. Division of Property Valuation. *Real Estate Assessment/Sales Ratio Study.* (Various years.)

Kansas. *Journal of the House.* (Various years.)

Kansas. *Journal of the Senate.* (Various years.)

Kansas. Kansas Tax Code Commission. *Report to the Governor.* (Topeka: Kansas State Printing Office, 1929.)

Kansas. Kansas Tax Commission. *Report to the Legislature.* (Topeka: State Printing Office, various years.)

Kansas. Kansas Tax Commission. *Biennial Report.* (Topeka: State Printing Office, various years.)

Kansas. Kansas Tax Commission. *Proceedings of the Conference Convention of the Tax Commission and the County Assessors of the State of Kansas.* (Topeka: State Printing Office, various years.)

Kansas. Kansas State Tax Commission. *Report and Bill.* (November 1901.)

Kansas. Legislature. Special Committee on Use Value Appraisal. *Report on Kansas Legislature Interim Studies to the 1978 Legislature.* (December 1977.)

Kansas. *State Auditor's Report.* (Various years.)

Kansas. *Treasurer's Report.* (Various years.)

Kansas, Inc. *Report on Reappraisal and Classification.* (Topeka, 30 March 1990.)

Kansas Legislative Council. Research Department. *A Summary History of Kansas Finance: 1861–1937.* (Topeka: Publication No. 60, October 1937.)

Kansas Legislative Research Department. *Kansas Tax Facts.* (Fifth Ed., 1983 and 1992 supplements.)

Kansas State Archives. Kansas Tax Commission Appeal Docket. *Ludign and Havens Lbr. Co. v. County Board of Equalization of Dickenson County.* (1908.)

Kansas State Archives. Kansas Tax Commission Appeal Docket. *S. S. Reynolds, Agt. Chicago Lumber and Coal Company.* (1908.)

Kansas State Archives *Letter to Governor Hoch.* (26 September 1907.)

Kansas State Archives. State Auditor Miscellaneous Files. *Abstract of Assessment Rolls.* (1860–1869.)

Malme, Jane H. "Executive Summary." International Association of Assessing Officers. *Assessment Administration Practices in the U. S. and Canada.* (Chicago: 1992, unpaged.)

Pine, Wilfred H. *100 Years of Farm Land Values in Kansas.* (Manhattan: Kansas State University, Agricultural Experiment Station, Bulletin 611, September 1977.)

Territory of Kansas. *Board of Equalization, Report.* (1860.)

Territory of Kansas. *Journal of the Council.* 3 July (1855.)

Territory of Kansas. *Journal of the House.* (Various years.)

U.S. Bureau of the Census. *1992 Census of Government.* Washington, D.C.: U.S. Government Printing Office. (1994.)

U.S. Bureau of the Census. *Government Finances.* Washington, D.C.: U.S. Government Printing Office. (Various years.)

U.S. Bureau of the Census. *Historical Statistics of the United States, 1789–1945.* (Washington, D.C.: U.S. Government Printing Office, 1949.)

U.S. Bureau of the Census. *Wealth, Debt and Taxation, 1913.* (Washington, D.C.: U. S. Government Printing Office, 1915.)

U.S. Congress. *An Act to Organize the Territories of Nebraska and Kansas.* (33d Cong., 1st sess., 1854.)

U.S. Congress. *An Act for the Admission of Kansas into the Union.* (36th Cong., 2d sess., 1861.)

U.S. Congress. House. *Report No. 296.* (27th Cong., 3d sess., 1843.)

DISSERTATIONS AND THESES

Foster, Robert Dan. "An Empirical Investigation of the Kansas Sales Ratio Study." (Ph.D. diss., University of Oregon, 1968.)

Gaeddert, Gustave Raymond. "A History of the Establishment of the Kansas State Government." (Ph.D. diss., University of Kansas, 1937.)

Hickle, Bonnie L. "Reappraisal and Equity in Property Taxation." (Master's thesis, Wichita State University, Department of Economics, August 1968.)

INDEX